8/01

Truancy and Schools

 D0076735

Truancy is currently right at the top of the Government's list of educational issues to be addressed. At present about one million pupils truant from their schools on a daily basis; this book examines the numerous reasons for truanting which include disadvantageous home backgrounds and poor performance in school.

In the long term truancy is closely associated with adult criminal behaviour, disaffection, marital disharmony and unemployment. Many truants go on to spend their adult lives supported by the state and functioning badly within society so evidently truancy is a topic of great concern to anyone involved in education and child welfare.

This book focuses on the social, psychological and educational causes of truancy; recent research is examined and examples of good practice and the latest solutions for tackling this problem are looked at in detail. The text is intended for teachers, heads of year and department heads, form tutors, senior school managers, education welfare officers, social workers, educational psychologists, parents and all those with an interest in or ability to contribute to educational policy and practice.

Professor Ken Reid is Senior Assistant Principal at Swansea Institute of Higher Education. His previous books include *Truancy and School Absenteeism*, *Combating School Absenteeism*, *Disaffection from School*, *Helping Troubled Pupils in Secondary Schools* (2 vols), and *Towards the Effective School*, as well as books on severely handicapped pupils and their families, school organisation, teacher education and professional development.

WITHDRAWN
St. Louis Community College
at Meramec
Library

Truancy and Schools

Ken Reid

London and New York

First published 1999 by Routledge
11 New Fetter Lane, London EC4P 4EE

Simultaneously published in the USA and Canada
by Routledge
29 West 35th Street, New York, NY 10001

Routledge is an imprint of the Taylor & Francis Group

© 1999 Ken Reid

Typeset in Goudy by BC Typesetting, Bristol
Printed and bound in Great Britain by
St Edmundsbury Press, Bury St Edmunds, Suffolk

All rights reserved. No part of this book may be reprinted or reproduced
or utilised in any form or by any electronic, mechanical, or other
means, now known or hereafter invented, including photocopying and
recording, or in any information storage or retrieval system, without
permission in writing from the publishers.

British Library Cataloguing in Publication Data
A catalogue record for this book is available from the British Library

Library of Congress Cataloging in Publication Data
Reid, Ken.
     Truancy and schools/Ken Reid.
         p.   cm.
     Includes bibliographical references (p.) and index.
     ISBN 0–415–20509–3 (pb.: alk. paper)
     1. School attendance – Great Britain.   2. Education and state –
– Great Britain. I. Title.
LB3081.R45   1999
371.2′95′0941–dc21   99-27648
                                                                 CIP

ISBN 0–415–20509–3

Contents

Boxes

Tables

Acknowledgements

I would like to thank several people for all their help during the preparation of this book. First and foremost, I would like to thank Angela Harris not only for typing the manuscript but for all her patience as I edited the text. Second, I would like to thank Professor David Warner for his encouragement to write the book. Third, I am grateful for the support of my wife Pat and three 'children' Becky, Nick and Jo. Fourth, I would like to thank Nina Stibbe for all her professional support and advice. Fifth, I would like to thank several former students, colleagues and professionals for their advice, help and assistance with materials for the book. These include Elaine Reynolds, Stefan James and Professor Carl Parsons. Finally, I would like to thank the following for their consent and permission to reproduce appropriate sections or quotes from LEA documents, reports and school policies within the text of this book. These include Margaret Blenkinson, Director of Education and Arts, Bolton LEA; Richard Mellows, Lindsey School, Humberside; Sue Barr, Springfield School, Grimsby; Ian Price, Principal Education Social Worker, Bolton; Tony Warwick, Area Manager, Midland Bank, Scunthorpe; John Davies, Dwr-y-Felin Comprehensive School, Neath; OHMCI; Crown Copyright Service; and selected teachers who have attended my training courses in the North of England, Midlands, London, South of England, North West England, Scotland and South Wales.

Foreword

This book is intended to be of practical help to serving headteachers, senior staff, middle managers, serving teachers, education welfare officers, education social workers, educational psychologists, teacher educators, student teachers, social workers, child care professionals and educational administrators.

The purpose of this volume is sevenfold. First, it is intended to replace and update my successful book, *Truancy and School Absenteeism*, which was published in 1985. Whereas the aim of that book was to show that truancy and school absenteeism are complex multi-dimensional problems, and that teachers and related professionals need to understand the issues involved in these phenomena if they are to stand any chance of successfully re-integrating non-attenders back into their institutions, this new book, while reinforcing the social, psychological and institutional causes of absenteeism, the various forms of absence, and the incidence and types of truancy, goes very much further. It also focuses upon the Government's latest initiatives, school-based solutions to tackling truancy, and the need for effective school policy documents on absenteeism. It produces the OFSTED guidelines on attendance, considers the role of the education welfare/social work service, and the part played by parents in truancy, and the link between effective schools, good teachers and school-based projects on attendance. Throughout the text are numerous examples of case and project data mostly taken from my own recent research or research carried out by higher degree students on truancy under my supervision. These data focus on case studies of individual truants, schools, parents and other school-based projects such as the one at Mountain Ash Comprehensive School in Mid Glamorgan.

Second, the text primarily focuses on the educational aspects of truancy, paying close attention to the ways in which teachers and other caring professionals can manage truants. The book stresses the need for early intervention; it also reinforces the enlightened position which schools and teachers need to take if the genesis and persistent stages of non-attendance are to be prevented or overcome. The text is eclectic; it does not focus on one method *per se* of overcoming the difficulties. The contents indicate that a whole variety of solutions to truancy are possible. The key thrust is on making pupils aware that their attendance matters.

Third, the book acknowledges that the long-term outlook for truants is not good. In this increasingly technological age, it is probably much worse than many people currently believe. The link between truancy and young offenders, juvenile delinquency, adult criminality and other adult disorders is probably sufficient proof in its own right. However, truants are also closely linked with childhood deprivation and social exclusion. For these reasons, it is hoped that the text, case data and ideas for combating truancy, will provoke teachers and other interested professionals into adopting more innovative and realistic positions which help re-integrate truants rather than merely punishing them for their actions.

Fourth, the title uses the term 'truancy'. This is deliberate; it acknowledges the fact that the book is about pupils who miss school illegally, with or without the consent of their parents. However, at appropriate points in the text, the correct terms utilised in specific research projects (e.g. 'persistent school absentees') are used.

Fifth, the book attempts to show that many truants are not ogres. Rather, they are unfortunate human beings – often emanating from deprived backgrounds – who are worthy of help in much the same way as the elderly, sick or handicapped. In a caring society all people are worth looking after; even those who may cause problems by their non-conformist behaviour.

Sixth, since truancy is a multi-causal phenomenon involving various combinations of home, social, psychological, institutional and educational factors, the book may be viewed as a multi-disciplinary text which has applicability to all fields of education. The text is also concerned with teachers as much as with pupils.

Therefore, the book has three basic aims:

1   to acquaint the reader with much of the latest research in the field of truancy;
2   to focus on schools and school-related policies in order to reduce truancy in schools whenever possible;
3   to promote good and better practice in schools.

It is not concerned with the topic of school phobia or school refusal except on those occasions where it is of considerable relevance to the ensuing discussion.

Seventh, the text is written in such a way as to encourage readability; therefore, the use of references is kept to a minimum. However, a bibliography is presented at the end of the book. This provides the source information for much of the discussion presented in the text.

Finally, and perhaps most importantly, this book could be used alongside my new pack for teachers entitled 'Tackling Truancy in Schools' which is being published at the same time. They have been written as companions. This book provides much more detail and covers a wider range of issues; the pack focuses on practical approaches within schools and professional development topics. Both have been written to help caring professionals in as helpful, empathetic and school-oriented a manner as possible.

Truancy and Schools is divided informally into two parts. Chapters 1 to 6 focus on the background issues which lie behind truancy – most notably on the social, psychological and educational causes – as well as considering the various types of truancy. Chapters 7 to 15 concentrate on finding solutions and approaches to dealing with truancy in schools by teachers and other caring professionals. For those readers who are *only* interested in school-based solutions, it is entirely possible to start reading the book from Chapter 7. For those professionals who require more detailed knowledge and/or evidence on the causes of truancy and other forms of non-attendance at school, it is better to start reading from the beginning in order to fully understand the arguments and rationale outlined in the later chapters. Whichever way you choose to read this book, I hope you enjoy it!

1   The consequences of truancy

'Truancy' is a term which is frequently misused; it can be applied both generically and have local meaning. In different parts of Great Britain, truancy is known amongst other things as 'skipping off', 'mitching', 'dodging', 'skiving', 'bunking-off' and 'going missing'. In popular English literature, truancy is sometimes reported as a natural, impish act of escapism, which is likely to take place at some stage during the normal development of children. Truancy is often, quite rightly, associated with early or later adolescence.

Truancy, as a term, is perversely often associated with fun. That is, it is considered by some to be more fun to be outside a school avoiding formal lessons and in theory doing what you like rather than sitting inside a classroom and 'learning'. This concept is the theme of Webster's famous painting of 'The Truant' in the nineteenth century which depicts two absconders standing, elated, outside their small school-room nervously peering in at the activities inside.

The reality of truancy is very different. Many truants often engage in meaningless activity while away from school. Some are even bored, finding it difficult to while away their time. In fact, if you talk to many truants, they will privately admit that if they had their time over again they would never start truanting. For many persistent cases, the truants have become victims of their own misguided practice. Not only do a lot of truants recognise the error and foolishness of their ways, but they also appreciate that they are long-term victims and losers in life. Many truants – even hardened cases – deep down would like a second opportunity, which is why schools specialising in second chances for disaffected pupils offer one of the best long-term opportunities for eradicating and overcoming the phenomenon and its longer-term consequences. In 1998, the Labour Government began to encourage second opportunities for youngsters who are failing at school or who left school without formal qualifications. Many of these targeted school failures were truants. Hardened by their own experiences when in school, and since leaving school, these young adults are often more receptive to second chance opportunities.

Moreover, there is increasing and worrying evidence that some truants spend their time engaging in fringe activities such as drug taking, prostitution, joyriding, violence, watching video nasties and participating in organised crime. For example, in Liverpool, it has been reported that several truants were embroiled in organised theft from local stores co-ordinated by a 'Mr Big'. In Glasgow, a group of girls were used to create an underage prostitution ring organised and protected by adult minders. In Swansea, a group of truants provided videos, televisions and other electrical items for sale to a second hand shop.

During the 1950s and mid-1960s, it was reported that truancy was 'an isolated activity' undertaken by most children 'on their own'. These days, the evidence is that much more truancy is organised, pre-planned and takes place in groups. One estimate is that group truancy accounts for roughly 70 to 80 per cent of cases; the remainder of truants spending their time on their own. The evidence also shows significant differences between boy and girl truant groups in how they spend their time. Girl groups of truants often focus their activities within a person's home or in town centres. Male truants will also spend time in groups in town. They are however, more often to be found outdoors – perhaps fishing, playing football, or hiding away out of sight in order to smoke and/or drink alcohol. Girl truancy groups, too, also contain a high proportion of smokers.

Boredom, and long bouts of it, is a natural consequence of truancy. This begs the question – Why do they do it? In one of my own studies of truants, I found Paul (see Chapter 2), a 13-year-old boy, spending his time 'skinning mice' in his bedroom. When I asked him whether attending school was worse than skinning mice, he looked nonplussed before adding that he had 'no choice'. Case studies of truants are littered with such sad stories.

Jane is also thirteen. She rarely attends school. When she does, she takes little interest in her lessons. Quite regularly, she leaves home intending to go to school before changing her mind on the way. Her mother is desperate for help. At home, Jane has become impossible to control. She uses the house to eat, sleep and play loud music. Most of the time she spends in the streets; in town during the day, on the estate in the evenings.

Jane's mother feels trapped. She gets little help from the school which she regards as being generally unsympathetic. From time to time she gets a letter or receives a visit from the local 'boardy man'. He leaves her feeling low, reminding her of her own days at school when she herself was a truant. Her social worker is generally more helpful but, in truth, provides little comfort or tangible hope for either change or success. Life for Jane and her mother is tough and the longer-term outlook is even bleaker.

Yet Jane is not alone. In fact, in Britain today, around one million pupils miss school daily. Why?

The specific causes for truancy vary from survey to survey, region to region; but a few facts stand out. The main reason why children truant is that they do not like school. However, findings on the educational causes of truancy vary from school to school. In Jane's case, she began truanting at the age of nine, while at primary school. She found she couldn't get on with her class-mates and didn't like her class teacher. Four years later, Jane finds she is so far behind with her school work that she is completely out of her depth. She is 'hopeless' at maths, 'hates' physical education, 'loathes' RE, 'can't understand French or science' and is 'useless' at history and geography. She says she 'likes' English but can't read aloud in class, is shy and 'finds difficulty putting sentences together' while 'my spelling is worse than hopeless'.

Like so many truants, Jane is trapped within a cycle based on poverty, deprivation, unfulfilled need and ignorance. By truanting, Jane is compounding her own limitations and destroying any possibility for her own upward social mobility.

In other surveys, one of the main reasons for missing school is bullying. However, while bullying can be the most significant cause for truancy in one school, it will not even rate a mention in another, showing that there is no single, universal cause for the truancy phenomenon. For example, in different school surveys, the main reported categories given for truancy have included: 'school is boring'; 'homework not completed'; 'exam avoidance'; 'dislike of a teacher' or 'a subject'; 'being forced to wear school uniform'; 'being shouted at in class'; 'not liking the other kids in my class'; 'feeling generally fed up at school'. These surveys suggest that the curriculum, poor teaching, unsatisfactory teacher–pupil relationships and aspects related to peer group relationships are four of the main reasons for truancy in most schools.

Whatever the precise causes, the consequences of truancy are enormous. Consider a few simple facts. Forty per cent of all street robberies in London, and a third of car thefts, 25 per cent of burglaries and 20 per cent of criminal damage were committed by 10- to 16-year-olds in 1997 and were blamed on truants. Truancy is the greatest single predictor of juvenile and adult crime and of adult psychiatric problems. Two thirds of young offenders begin their criminal activities while truanting. Truancy is also closely linked to a wide range of other difficulties in adult life including: the inability to settle into the routine of work and/or marriage; frequent job changes; isolationism; pathological disorders; poverty; higher separation and divorce rates; living upon income support; illiteracy; depression; temper tantrums; and involvement with social workers and the social services. Truancy is also associated with a significantly higher likelihood of becoming a teenage parent and of being unemployed or homeless in later life. Truancy has immediate and longer-term consequences throughout all stages of adult life. Males who truant are more likely to marry girls who played truant at a similar age at school. 'Truant families' then tend to have sons or daughters who also play truant, thereby perpetuating a truancy syndrome into the next generation, rather like Jane.

The long-term economic consequences for Britain, therefore, are equally large. It has been estimated that a high proportion of truants spend much of their adult lives totally or partially dependent upon the social services in one form or another of state aid. Therefore, in theory, if truancy is either curtailed or eliminated, and potential truants achieve success while at school, millions of pounds could literally be wiped from the long-term cost of the social services' budget, potentially saving billions over the years at a stroke. Yet, achieving this goal is not easy. Why? It is worth remembering research shows that rates of absenteeism and truancy from school have remained constant since 1870. In fact, some more recent pupil-based surveys are beginning to suggest significant increases in the number of recorded truants. This appears to be particularly true since the introduction of the National Curriculum, suggesting that not all subjects have equal meaning and value to less able pupils.

Despite considerable effort, no overwhelming political, social or educational solution has ever been found, which indicates that there is no simple or single panacea for success. In 1998, the Government introduced revised guidelines and targets for schools which now mean that each school has to reduce its own rate of truancy by one third by the year 2002. OFSTED is expected to formally report on any school following an Inspection whose rate of attendance fell below 90 per cent. So, despite all previous endeavours, truancy continues to be a major social, educational and economic problem.

And the economic costs do not only begin in adult life. One school in the Midlands, for example, has built an eight-foot perimeter fence to keep in its truants and specific lesson absentees. Considerable numbers of schools also now use security guards to patrol school gates and adjacent boundaries to keep in potential truants. At one school in Manchester, the cost of this exercise is equivalent to two full-time experienced teachers and the money is taken from the school's budget.

Truancy has other connotations. Legally, truancy is a problem because of the consequences for parents who break their statutory duties by failing to ensure their children receive a suitable full-time education. Educationally, truancy is a source of concern because non-attenders generally tend to fall behind in their work, and their attitude (and behaviour in the case of disruptive truants) affects other pupils and teachers, as well as themselves. In recent OFSTED inspections, school failure is frequently linked to those schools that have large numbers of pupils who truant and behave badly. Psychologically, truancy is symptomatic of pupils who are insecure, have low academic and general levels of self-esteem, and/or have personality disorders. These conditions may foreshadow more serious conditions in later adolescence and adult life. Sociologically, truancy is known to be linked with multiple adverse home conditions, low social class and deprivation. Institutionally, truancy suggests disaffection from school.

Truancy is not a form of behaviour which is generally condoned by the general public. The police recognise the strong link between truancy and juvenile and adult crime. Shopkeepers fear truants because they know that they often lose most of their stolen stock to them. Equally, many teachers have little sympathy with truants. As professionals primarily concerned with imparting knowledge, they tend to feel that good attendance is essential if pupils are to make satisfactory progress. Moreover, teachers are busy people. Their workloads and the organisation of schools ensure that very few of them have the time to know a great deal about those individual pupils who manifest their displeasure with school – and them – by truanting. In turn, this breakdown in communication between teachers and truants makes implementing successful re-integration strategies immensely more difficult. In fact, such is the pressure on today's teachers, that some staff are delighted at the prospect of instructing fewer pupils – especially since those who can be troublesome or backward, require extra attention in class or behave badly.

Yes, teachers can be cynical, but they are also realistic. They tend to feel that their prime duty and responsibility is to regular attenders, higher achievers, those who conform, and who wish to do well at school. Regular attendance is the best barometer of this conformist attitude. Consequently, in some schools, even enlightened schools, innovative policies for dealing with truants have failed. Why?

First, truancy is a multi-causal problem. Second, every truant is unique. Third, many teachers have little understanding or training about truancy. Neither for that matter have many social workers, education welfare officers, educational psychologists or professionals in other forms of childcare or support, including magistrates. Fourth, there are few easy solutions. Increasingly, there are a lot of good ideas about, some having worked better than others. But most of these are local initiatives. There are few national guidelines, and the dissemination of good practice is at best patchy.

It is for all the above reasons that this book for schools and caring professionals has been prepared. It is to be hoped that as professionals gain more insight and understanding into the nature, causes, consequences and solutions, truancy will start to be controlled, and, eventually, defeated. After all, truancy is a phenomenon which is restricted to a few, comparatively successful countries, more especially the United States, Canada, Great Britain, Australasia, and parts of Europe and Scandinavia. It is virtually unknown in other parts of the world, especially those where educational opportunities are limited.

The remainder of this book will focus on the social, psychological and educational causes of truancy. It will go on to consider how schools can prevent, tackle and combat truancy and provide numerous examples of good practice based on empirical and professional evidence undertaken by Government agencies, OFSTED, researchers, teachers, administrators, education welfare officers and education social workers. Specific chapters will focus on the role of whole school policies, LEA guidelines, parents, OFSTED and the education welfare service. Throughout all the remaining 14 chapters, case study exemplars are used at appropriate points, as are good practice guidelines and summaries of findings in traditional text or tabular format. But, first, we will begin by considering the extent and various types of truancy.

2 Types of truants and incidence

Categories of truants

Based on my own previous research (Reid 1985), three categories of truants have been found to emerge, each of which can be easily identified. The usage of these categories can be especially helpful as we develop our knowledge of successful treatment strategies – it is highly likely that in the future we will be able to propose different re-integration strategies for each of them.

This possibility is presently being handicapped by a lack of research. Soon, we will probably discover that there are personality differences between each of the three categories of truant. The result of tightening these constructs will eventually open up numerous possibilities for schools and social workers. We should be able, for example, to be in a position to supply schools with proformas and/or guidelines to enable them to distinguish easily between different kinds of truants alongside appropriate re-integration or other forms of 'treatment'/remedial strategies.

As each truant is unique, a victim of his or her social, psychological, familial and educational circumstances, it is unlikely that we will ever be able to develop re-integration strategies to the point that will satisfy every individual set of circumstances. However, it is extremely probable that the three categories can be sufficiently refined and amended to highlight possible different treatment approaches by group for the different caring professionals who interact with truants. These include teachers, education welfare officers, educational psychologists, social workers and educational social workers, childcare agencies, psychiatrists and, possibly, the police.

The traditional or typical truant

The traditional or typical truant follows the earlier description of the truant offered by Tyerman (1968). Thus, traditional truants tend to be isolates who come from an unsupportive home background, possibly with a tendency to be shy. It is likely that they will have a low self-concept, be introverted, and be the victim of their social circumstances. By nature, traditional truants will be pleasant when spoken to and liable to acquiesce rather than to search for confrontation. They may well be aware of their own social and educational limitations and so seek compensation by insulating themselves from the unrewarding stimuli at school – just like Billy Casper in *Kes*.

The psychological truant

The psychological truant could be the school phobic (school refusal) case but more often than this psychological truants miss school for psychological or psychological-related factors such as illness, psychosomatic complaints, laziness, a fear of attending school for any reason (such as dislike of a teacher, a lesson, an impending confrontation or fear of bullying) or because of other physical or temperamental disadvantages, like handicaps or tantrums. Psychological truants probably need specialist counselling or skilled as well as empathetic pastoral care to help them to overcome their justified or irrational fears or prejudices.

The institutional truant

Institutional truants miss school purely for educational reasons usually related to their school. Unlike traditional truants, they may be extroverts, engage in confrontation and, indeed, may even remain on the school premises although out of lessons. Institutional truants are more likely to indulge in 'on the spur of the moment' absences from lessons and to be selective about days or lessons to miss. They often have a higher self-concept than traditional truants and have quite large numbers of friends. Institutional truants may even be the leaders of groups of absentees, have a complete disregard for authority, and be unconcerned about the outcome of any punitive measures taken against them. Like traditional truants, they are likely to come from deprived and/or unsupportive home backgrounds. It is probable that some institutional truants will have 'matured' on a diet of squabbles at home, in their immediate neighbourhood and in their classrooms.

The generic truant

Technically, there is a fourth category of truant. The generic truant is one who misses school for a variety of reasons at different times. Therefore, at the age of eleven, he or she may be a traditional truant whereas, by the age of fourteen, could have become either a psychological or institutional truant. Some truants manifest symptoms from all three categories because of the make-up of their social, psychological and educational backgrounds. For example, a very high proportion of truants have low academic self-concepts, are in the low to middle ability range, have unfavourable home backgrounds and a host of related personal problems in and out of school.

Case studies: Paul, Claire and Wayne

Paul, Claire and Wayne are three truants from the same form at a comprehensive school in South Wales. Despite being members of the same form group, they have little else in common apart from their socio-economic backgrounds. They all come from deprived socio-economic groups and live on the same council estate approximately two miles from the school. Paul is the son of a single parent. Claire is the only child within her family unit. Wayne comes from a large family; he is the third of four boys and has two younger sisters. Two of his elder brothers previously attended the same school where they were notorious truants.

Before this, Paul, Claire and Wayne had attended the same primary school and been in the same class. Despite this, they had never been friends. Paul and Claire were 'afraid' of Wayne. Paul stated that he 'rarely saw' Wayne and when he did he 'kept out of his way'.

Claire believed Wayne to be one of the ringleaders behind her persecution at school. She said he always called her 'carrot top' or worse and laughed at her when she tried to defend herself. Their only form of communication was through 'arguments'.

Paul

Paul is a traditional truant. He first began to truant in primary school at the age of nine. His class teacher was finding difficulty in forging a relationship with him when she discovered that his abiding interest was watching soccer. She discovered that his pride and joy was a collection of cigarette soccer cards each containing a photograph of a famous footballer. His aim was to collect every card in order to win a prize from a well-known football sponsorship company. Paul's collection was well advanced. He only required a few more cards to have achieved the prize.

After informally discovering this information, his class teacher suggested to Paul that he brought the cards into school to show the rest of the class. A few days later, Paul did so. Immediately after the lesson was over, during morning break, the other pupils got hold of Paul and his cards and ripped them up. Paul was devastated.

The following day, Paul truanted for the first time. Four years later, Paul had become a persistent truant. He rarely attends school. On one occasion, on a visit to his home to meet him, and after entering through the front door, I noticed that there were no carpets, the floorboards were missing and the internal decoration was in a total mess. I found Paul sitting upstairs alone on his bed skinning mice. Above him was a dartboard, without any form of back board. The wall was full of little holes where the darts had missed their target.

When interviewed, Paul told me that his mother was living in a caravan with her 'boyfriend' a few miles away on a local caravan site. He told me that she rarely came home and that he spent most of his time 'bored out of his mind'.

Following a series of 'tests', it emerged that Paul had an exceptionally low academic self-concept, very low levels of general self-esteem, and was unable to read and write properly. When in school, Paul kept to himself; he had no real friends in or out of school. He felt threatened by the other pupils in his form and by some of the teachers. However, he claimed that he quite liked his school and put the blame for his truancy firmly on himself and his individual circumstances. He believed no one liked him or helped him very much in school. He admitted that his problems had stemmed from the incident with the cigarette cards in primary school and he still felt bitter towards his former classmates. Interestingly, he did not blame either his primary school or comprehensive for his present difficulties.

Paul believed that his long-term future was bleak. He wished he could have his time over again as he said he would never have started truanting. Now, however, he felt it was too late. He described his existence and his future job prospects as 'hopeless'.

Claire

Claire is a psychological truant. In appearance, she is short, well-built with a shock of red hair. At fifteen, her truancy has reached the persistent stage. She claims to be deeply unhappy. She first missed school at the age of twelve following a lengthy illness. After returning to school, she found she had fallen behind with her work and her personal assessments began to decline. She then found that the staff in her school began to treat her differently and she started having difficulty with some of her classmates who began to call her 'carrot top'.

At one point, she got into a fight with another girl in her class outside school after a bout of name-calling. After that, she started to truant. Whenever she tried to return to school, she found she was the subject of adverse comments from teachers and classmates alike. She started having temper tantrums in class leading to further confrontation with staff.

Simultaneously, Claire's academic performance continued to decline. She rarely completed her homework and her attendance became totally erratic. She blamed the school and her teachers for not protecting her and for failing to help her to catch up with her schoolwork. When interviewed, Claire indicated that her home life had deteriorated following the decline in her performance at school and the adverse comments being made about her by other pupils and parents outside school.

She stated that her life had become so miserable that she hated school and everything for which it stood. Claire believed she had ability and that she was underachieving through no fault of her own. She admitted that she had made her own problems worse through her own 'hot temper'. Nevertheless, she never meant any harm, nor any of the things she said after being provoked. She accepted that she needed to control her temper better but argued that she had to stand up for herself.

Claire claimed that her form teacher called her a 'truant'. However, she claimed she was not a truant. Rather, she missed school to avoid unpleasant confrontations which spilt over into her home life on the local estate. She believed the school was at fault for her problems. She stated that if the school had helped her to catch up with her work after the initial illness, none of the subsequent problems would have occurred. She hated being called names like 'carrot top', 'tubby' and 'Tyson'.

Wayne

Wayne is fourteen. He started truanting at twelve. He is now an institutional truant. Sometimes he misses school for the day or the week. On other occasions, he turns up for registration, gets his mark and then leaves. More recently however, he has begun to skip particular lessons. He particularly dislikes maths, science and physical education.

At first, Wayne truanted alone. Now, he often truants with a group of friends, normally from the same school, although not all of his gang of truants come from the same form. When truanting, they often visit the local shopping centre or go fishing by the river. Sometimes they plan their truancy in school; on other occasions the night before.

Despite being a truant, Wayne is quite popular among his peers. They find his aggressive attitude towards his teachers to be amusing despite the fact that it often disrupts their lessons. On two separate occasions, Wayne was suspended from school for 'swearing at a teacher' and for 'inciting a riot during a lesson'.

When interviewed, Wayne was blasé about his behaviour in school. Although having a higher general level of self-esteem than either Paul or Jane, his academic self-concept was lower than the average for his form. He described himself as the leader of his truancy circle, whereas both Jane and Paul tended to truant on their own.

Implications

Paul, Claire and Wayne share some common traits. First, they could all remember the first time they had truanted from school. Each agreed that they had truanted in response to a particular situation – a causal point. In each case, they believe the school handled their situation badly. Paul deeply regretted bringing his cigarette cards into school and blamed his teacher (not his classmates) for his cigarette cards being destroyed. Claire blamed her school and the teachers for not helping her to catch up with her schoolwork following her lengthy illness. She claimed that being put in detention for late work was the final straw. Wayne blamed his maths teacher for singling him out for punishment following a class 'prank'. All three agreed however, that they deeply regretted their truancy because they realised they were victimising themselves in the long run.

Second, all three agreed that they might never have become truants if their school had helped them to overcome their initial academic problems. In Paul's case, he claimed his mother was not interested in school and never helped him with schoolwork. Claire felt her parents were keen on school when she had been doing well. They had subsequently lost interest as her attainment declined. Wayne's parents had little interest in his schooling. His mother had been a parental-condoned absentee and his father a truant. Both considered Wayne's behaviour to be quite normal for his age; they would have been surprised if he acted differently.

The major difference between them was in terms of their behaviour in school. Paul was compliant, introspective and liked to be left alone. He neither sought nor enjoyed the attention of his classmates or teachers. Claire wanted to be left alone but became aggressive in response to taunts. Her defence mechanism had become the root cause of her psychological distress. In Wayne's case, he enjoyed attention seeking. He saw engaging in confrontations with teachers as a form of healthy sport. He liked being the leader of a group of truants and despised both Paul and Claire whom he described as 'wimps'.

From experience, research has suggested that while traditional truants frequently reject their schooling, they tend to feel less alienated from their teachers than institutional truants often because their non-attendance has a different causal basis. Whereas, institutional truants are often more outgoing truants who display 'couldn't care less' attitudes towards authority, traditional truants are introverted and often feel inadequate in crowds, in group activities and in their teacher–pupil relationships. Frequently, the general relationship between institutional truants and teachers is not as good as it might be, possibly because it is this category that contains a number of disruptive and aggressive truants who have little fear of punishment. It is the poor behaviour of institutional (disruptive) truants that tends to give all truants a bad name with teachers. It is the institutional truants who teachers do not object to missing their lessons. Traditional truants are much more likely to go unnoticed.

Paradoxically, there is evidence beginning to mount that it is the institutional truants – along with other categories of disruptive pupils – who cause high stress levels among teachers and who, in turn, cause some teachers to miss school more frequently than colleagues. In one school in the Midlands, for example, the school found that specific lesson truancy occurred most frequently from classes where the teachers themselves had a high rate of absenteeism. It is not unknown for the absence patterns of some teachers to be more frequent on, say, a Monday, rather than any other period of the week, when this is the day they are due to teach their most difficult classes. Teacher stress is often relative to daily workloads. Patterns of teacher absence can vary by individual. In one school in a South Wales valley, I discovered that there were twice as many absences on a Monday as a Tuesday, Wednesday or Thursday. However, one female teacher missed six Thursdays out of seven while a male teacher missed every other Monday throughout two terms. In both these individual cases, absences on any other days of the week were rare.

Truancy traits

The three categories of truants have also changed over the last twenty to thirty years. For example, the pioneering work of Tyerman suggested that most truants were 'lonely isolates', a category roughly corresponding to traditional absentees. Research today suggests that traditional truants are now well into a minority. Although the number in the three categories differs survey by survey, my research tends to suggest that traditional truants probably these days comprise up to a quarter of the total; sometimes much less. Psychological truants probably comprise between 2 and 10 per cent; the latter figure being reached in high-confrontation schools. By far and away the largest category in every survey is institutional truancy. This means that most pupils now miss school for school-based reasons. Specific lesson truancy is also much more common among institutional truants than the other two categories. In my own surveys, institutional absenteeism has accounted for between 65 and 80 per cent of all persistent truancy.

These percentages vary by age and gender. For example, girls are twice or three times as likely as boys to be parentally condoned. The younger the pupils, the fewer the reasons for the onset of truancy are given. The older the truants, the more the number of reasons are given to justify their behaviour. Equally, the older the truants, the more school-based reasons are given. Whereas initial truancy can have a specific cause – as in the case of Paul and Claire – once it reaches the persistent stage, there are more reasons given by truants to explain and justify their conduct. Institutional truancy significantly increases by age.

Although specific lesson truancy has always taken place, all the recent evidence now suggests that this phenomenon is the fastest growing brand of truancy; partially explained as a consequence of the development of the National Curriculum and schools' subsequent reorganisations to meet these needs.

Equally, group truancy (rather like individual truancy) has always taken place. Today, however, pupils participating in group truancy significantly outnumber isolated cases.

Much group truancy is premeditated and pre-planned. Some pre-planned group truancy incorporates both male and female membership. Much premeditated group truancy is the result of peer pressure being exerted by a group leader upon his or her friends. The sizes of truancy groups can also vary. Reid found that the size of groups varied between two and six with a mean of approximately three.

The age of onset of truancy is now much younger than hitherto. It is now not unknown for hardened truants to be as young as seven. At least a quarter of all truancy cases begin in primary schools and this percentage appears to be rising fast.

Truancy is undoubtedly related to maturity and adolescence. Thirty or forty years ago, the age of puberty for girls was fifteen and a half. Today, it is twelve. For boys it was sixteen. Now, it is thirteen and a half to fourteen. For both sexes, it is getting younger all the time.

Consequently, the average age of truants in the 1950s and 1960s was fourteen or fifteen. Today, it is thirteen and decreasing. In some comprehensives, 50 per cent of pupils have truanted on at least one occasion by the age of thirteen.

In schools today, there are huge maturational differences between pupils. Although schools group pupils by age, and sometimes by intellectual ability, they often fail to differentiate sufficiently between late and early maturation. Boys at fourteen, for example, are often at different ends of the adolescent scale. Some have voices already broken; others do not. Some are over six-feet; others remain four feet nine inches in height. This partially explains school bullying, as school bullies tend to be early maturers and victims late developers. In truancy terms, institutional truants tend to be early maturers. Traditional and psychological truants often tend to be late developers.

Research shows that in some schools the link with bullying is the greatest single cause of truancy. Yet in other high truancy schools, bullying is unknown. In Cardiff, in one study of two inner-city comprehensives, bullying and extortion were rife in one school and virtually unknown in the other. Yet both schools were located in similarly deprived catchment areas and less than two miles apart. In the high bullying school, truants tended to be the victims, some refusing to pay their 10 pence per day protection money.

Truancy rates vary by school. The reasons for these differences are explored in more detail later. However, it is interesting to note that school rates vary not only by location but by foundation, region and level. For example, in fourteen feeder primary schools for one large comprehensive school in an urban area, two primaries already depicted high rates of truancy, another four low to medium rates, five others low rates, while in another three primaries, truancy was relatively unknown. Such variations in background are bound to have an effect upon the intake and abilities of pupils entering comprehensive schools at the point of secondary transfer.

Equally, schools vary in terms of their policies towards truants and truancy. Some have sound school policy documents on truancy; others do not. Some schools have better prevention strategies than others; some more sophisticated re-integration strategies and better rates of successfully combating truancy than others. Some have better teacher–pupil relationships than others.

Schools differ not only by catchment area, pupils' socio-economic background, and primary school records, but also by their local histories of truancy. Records show that in some parts of the British Isles, truancy has been a problem for 150 years. In other areas, it is a relatively new phenomenon. There are now examples of high truancy regions where the parent(s) of the truants were truants themselves, as were the grandparents, and, it seems, their great grandparents. Yet, the 'truancy syndrome' is a relatively new concept to researchers despite the fact that it has been a well-documented fact in practice, particularly among social workers.

Research is now beginning to discern significant points relating to the introduction and teaching of the National Curriculum. Specific lesson truancy is much more abundant in low achieving schools. Lessons in science, maths (very often), modern languages, religious education (quite often) and physical education (for girls) are often more likely to be targets for specific lesson truancy and this development will be considered in more detail later.

Surveys also show considerable differences between schools in:

(a) the causes of initial and continued absence;
(b) school effects, e.g. most liked and most disliked subjects;
(c) truancy by subject, school year, age and gender.

These differences are frequently commented upon in OFSTED reports, especially since Inspectors have had to report on truancy and behaviour within schools. Schools with clear policy documents and good practice in preventing and combating truancy and indiscipline inevitably do better in these inspections than those which do not.

Individual school surveys often provide significant clues to the causes of truancy within specific schools. Remember each school is unique; so is every truant. From experience, it often surprises me how little some schools understand themselves from the standpoint of their pupils. The use of pupil surveys – undertaken constructively – can facilitate successful school improvement strategies (see Chapter 10).

Finally, the introduction of league tables on pupils' and schools' attainment, attendance and measures of behaviour (e.g. rates of exclusion) is having a significant impact upon national and local rates of truancy and school attendance. It is also having an effect upon research. It is not uncommon for schools to ensure that their rates of unauthorised absence are kept to a minimum by, for example, encouraging parents to write explanatory notes, even in known cases of truancy. Consequently, parental-condoned absence – along with specific lesson truancy – are the two fastest growth areas in recent studies on truancy. It is disappointing that one consequence of league tables has been to 'encourage' schools to lower their own levels of unauthorised absence by whatever means are possible. It is not unknown for some schools to 'mask' their real attendance figures. In one conference on truancy, the Director of Education stated that the two schools in his City Metropolitan area with the best published rates of attendance were, in fact, the worst two truancy schools – and everyone in the city and his department knew it! It only goes to show you can't believe every statistic; not even those on truancy! Today, schools have a vested interest in ensuring that their levels of unauthorised absence are kept as low as possible.

Incidence, school and regional differences

The incidence of truancy

It is extremely difficult to gauge precisely how many children miss school on a daily basis. Of those missing school, it is even more difficult to be precise about how many are truants *per se*. The situation is made more complicated by the significant regional, school, age and gender differences which abound throughout the United Kingdom.

The position is complicated by difficulties associated with the interpretation of figures obtained from registers. For example, absence figures based on school registers often tend to exclude pupils who leave school after having received their mark; these data also often exclude specific lesson truants. The methodological problems in compiling, using and interpreting attendance data taken from registers also complicates the position. When using overall attendance returns, the raw statistics can obscure or mislead researchers. For instance, an 85 per cent overall attendance figure from a school could mean:

(a) that 85 per cent of pupils attend all the time, while 15 per cent never attend; or,
(b) all pupils attend 85 per cent of the time;
(c) variations of (a) and (b).

By 1974, following a national one-day survey on attendance of all pupils in England and Wales, it was reported that approximately 10 per cent of pupils miss school on a daily basis. This statistic has been replicated in other local surveys and continues to be used as the norm by researchers and the media. However, there has been no formal national survey data collected since that time. It is difficult, therefore, to be certain whether levels of truancy and other forms of non-attendance are static, rising or reducing. Local studies seem to suggest that the real levels of truancy have certainly not been reduced. However, national levels of truancy based on rates of unauthorised absence (as marked in school attendance registers) might lead some to this conclusion.

Different local and regional surveys have measured school attendance during a day, a week, a term and a school year. Findings from these studies generally suggest that patterns of attendance show a marked reduction during the day, week, term and school year. Sometimes, however, the spring term can be the worst for attendance, probably due to inclement weather conditions and increased rates of illness. In some parts of Britain, the prospect of part-time work (farming, fruit picking, seaside employment) significantly increases truancy rates during the summer. Rates of non-attendance significantly rise in, for example, Norfolk, Devon and Cornwall during the summer term for these reasons.

In the one-day national survey in 1974, 9.9 per cent of all pupils in secondary and middle schools were absent on the day. Of these, 22.7 per cent (2.2 per cent of all pupils) had no legitimate reason for absence and were classified as truants. Some researchers consider this survey seriously under-estimated the problem. For example, the National Association of Chief Educa-tion Welfare Officers' survey of all secondary pupils in sixteen local education authorities reported that 24 per cent were absent on the day. Of these, it was estimated that between 3.5 and 7 per cent of the pupils were away from school without good cause; in other words truanting.

Researchers for the Pack Report (Scottish Education Department 1977), which involved a six-week study of secondary pupils in Scotland, found 15 per cent of pupils to have been 'unaccountably absent' on at least one occasion.

A study undertaken in Wales in 1996 of twelve comprehensive schools reported that previous research may have seriously underestimated rates of truancy with over half of secondary age pupils admitting to having played truant on at least one or more occasions over the previous twelve months. Findings suggest that when rates of absence are researched, statistics vary depending upon whether schools, parents and/or pupils are asked. A far higher rate of pupils admit to truanting occasionally than in officially pub-lished statistics. Pupil surveys often report higher rates than those for parents or teachers. Again, however, parental surveys often record higher rates of absenteeism than school-based or teacher-based surveys. Even so, parental surveys can mask truancy rates; possibly because they are unaware of their off-spring's truancy; or do not wish to acknowledge it; or they deliberately condoned their child's action.

Official figures show relatively low, and stable levels of truancy, but accord-ing to surveys of young people, the levels are far higher. The twice-daily regis-trations carried out by schools fail to capture the extent to which truancy is the norm for many children.

In 1997, secondary schools reported that 1 per cent of school time was lost to unauthorised absence. For primary schools the figure was 0.5 per cent. About one million children – around 15 per cent of all pupils – took at least one half day off without authority. In primary schools, the average time missed per absent pupil totalled five days over the year. For secondary schools, it was ten days. These numbers have been roughly stable since records began in 1992–93.

However, anonymised surveys of pupils give a very different picture. One major study based on a confidential questionnaire covering 35,000 pupils in Years 10 and 11, showed much higher figures. Thirty per cent of those who responded said they had truanted at least once in the previous half term. Nearly one in ten 15-year-olds truanted at least once a week. Of the truants, all but 10 per cent had engaged in 'post-registration truancy'. The study had an 83 per cent response rate: it is likely that many of those who did not respond were truanting at the time of the survey; therefore the reality was probably much higher.

Other surveys have shown a similar picture:

- in 1992 a Home Office random interview survey showed that 37 per cent of young men and 28 per cent of young women admitted to skipping school for at least one day without permission;
- a 1990 study of 40,000 Year 11 pupils found more than a half had taken unauthorised absence;
- and the latest Youth Cohort Study showed that 2 per cent of children in Year 11 truanted for weeks at a time, a further 2 per cent for several days at a time, and another 34 per cent truanted occasionally.

Truancy and absentee rates vary by age and gender. Research suggests that more boys than girls truant; whether at primary or secondary stages. One study reported that nine times more boys than girls truant. In another, 77 per cent of truants were reported to be boys; more than two thirds were boys over the age of twelve. In this study, the peak age for truancy was fourteen. Yet, at both junior and secondary stages, girls are more frequently absent from school than boys. In studies of infants schools, more boys than girls have been found to be absent.

Truants tend to be older pupils, and from poorer backgrounds. Analysis of Youth Cohort Study data showed that the parents of truants were more likely to be in low skilled than in professional or managerial jobs, and more likely to be in local authority housing than owner occupiers. For boys, living in a single-parent family appears to be a risk factor. Some studies have suggested that truancy is more common in inner-city areas. But there is no particular sex bias.

Some groups are particularly prone to truancy. For example, OFSTED information shows around a fifth of primary school age and a third of secondary age traveller children have attendance levels below 50 per cent. Many others may not even be registered at school. However other groups that show up disproportionately in school exclusions (notably ethnic minorities) are not more likely to be persistent truants.

Some caution is always needed when interpreting the findings of particular studies and, in studies on truancy, this is especially true for several reasons. First, results tend to vary according to researchers' definitions of truancy. Second, research shows that far more girls than boys are parental-condoned absentees. Yet, many researchers do not classify these cases as truancy. Third, in studies based on clinical samples of truants, or on those involving excluded pupils, boys predominate at all ages. It has been established for a long time that delinquent behaviour is more characteristic of boys than girls. Nevertheless, delinquency rates among girls are rising. In fact, in certain schools, and in some classrooms, girls give staff as many, if not more, behavioural problems than boys. While rates of disruptive truants have tended to be higher for boys, girls are beginning to catch up and often depict some of the very worst cases.

Similarly, rates of absenteeism and truancy can vary according to who and what is asked. Why?

In the late 1980s, BBC Wales television undertook a survey of schools across Wales in conjunction with a documentary they were making. The findings showed major differences by school, gender and region. They also suggested that in some schools up to one quarter of pupils occasionally admitted to skipping school; much higher than the national average. The findings suggested that rates of truancy had risen significantly since the introduction of the National Curriculum. Why?

Some of the most important factors behind truancy lie outside school: above all in family relationships and peer pressures. But how schools operate can make a great difference in shaping whether children do in fact truant.

Parents bear the primary responsibility for ensuring that their children attend school regularly and home circumstances exert an important influence over pupils' attendance and punctuality. Poor parental supervision and lack of commitment to education are crucial factors behind truancy. One study found that 44 per cent of truants believed their parents knew they were truanting, while 48 per cent of non-truants said they were held back by fear of their parents finding out. A survey of senior managers, year heads, and form tutors in fourteen local education authorities found that family circumstances or values were consistently cited as causes of non-attendance. Some families condone unauthorised absence, for example, for family shopping trips. Others expect school-age children to look after younger brothers or sisters during the day, or to take on excessive responsibilities for helping out at home.

Surveys of pupils have shown that they see the influence of friends and peers as even more important than family. Home Office research has identified a statistical relationship between truancy and strong attachment to siblings or friends in trouble with the police.

The influence of families and peers on truancy is matched by the effects of problems at school:

- OFSTED has found that in some schools poor attendance is centred among pupils who are weak readers;
- it also found that non-attendance can be a result of anxiety about GCSE coursework deadlines;
- anxiety about bullying is frequently cited as a reason. One research study reports that a third of girls and a quarter of boys described being afraid of going to school at some time because of bullying;
- in a number of surveys, pupils have said that they truant because they dislike particular lessons or teachers, or see school or the National Curriculum as irrelevant.

The importance of what happens in schools in shaping truancy can be gauged by the wide variations in truancy levels between schools that appear to have similar intakes. DfEE research has found that 'there is ample evidence that schools can and do have significant impact in improving attendance and reducing disaffection'. This is borne out by the wide variations between regions and between schools. For example, the level of unauthorised absence in Manchester is four and a half times that in South Tyneside and nearly nine times that in Oxfordshire. And there are many examples of schools with similar intakes and results but very different truancy rates. In some middle-class towns in England (e.g. Beverley, Humberside) rates of truancy are very low. Yet, in other middle-class areas (e.g. Bicester, Banbury, Swindon) rates are much higher.

One worrying recent trend has been the growth of male and female gangs, often composed of truants from school. Some of these street gangs have become associated with violence and intimidation against their own or other schools as well as their regularly attending peers. The tragic death of Philip Lawrence – the head who went to the aid of one of his pupils – and the con-viction of a 16-year-old pupil for murdering a boy from a rival school in a machete attack – are illustrations that a worrying street phenomenon has moved into the playground and the classroom. These gangs are beginning to be associated with intimidation, violence, extortion, victimisation, harassment and drugs. The rise of school-based gangs is presently restricted to a com-paratively small minority of inner-city schools. Research has yet to report on the effects of these gang truants upon rates of attendance and behaviour but, intuitively, one senses a clear link. In one conference on truancy held in Manchester in 1998, some of the staff who attended admitted to being afraid of some of their institutional truants. One school reported that break duties were only conducted in pairs. Delegates stated that the number of verbal and physical attacks upon them were increasing not only within school but during out-of-school activities and in teachers' own leisure time. One teacher stated it was not unusual for her to be abused or intimidated when she went shopping in her local supermarket. Some of these pupils, she claimed, were truants who felt confident that they were 'untouchable'. One female teacher claimed she was sexually harassed by male truants outside school. Another told of how a group of truants descended upon her when she was visiting her local hairdresser.

Attendance rates between schools vary enormously. Some ten years ago, HMI reported that the average daily attendance of pupils in one school in South Wales was 49 per cent. Their report referred to it being the 'worst truancy school in the country' which it almost certainly was not. One school in Walsall was found to have only 45 per cent of pupils attending in 1987. In 1998, ten one-day conferences on truancy were held in Birmingham, London, Manchester and Leeds. According to the participants, attendance rates at their schools varied from 55 to 98 per cent. Rates of unauthorised absence ranged from 1 per cent to 35 per cent. In Wolverhampton, one headteacher reported 90 per cent attendance in Years 7 and 8, but only 50 per cent attendance in Year 11. In one homogeneous, lower middle-class community town in South Wales, with two similarly-sized comprehensives, the average daily attendance rate at one is 79 per cent, while at the other it is 94 per cent.

Most studies find that truancy rates peak in Years 10 and 11, although interestingly, truancy rates in Years 7, 8 and 9 are already much higher in some schools than in others. Rates of attendance also vary considerably between primary schools.

Research also shows huge regional differences in rates of attendance. Parts of South Wales, the North West of England, the North East, Inner and Greater London and Glasgow are among some of the most notable truancy hot spots. However, some schools in rural and suburban areas have disproportionately high levels of truancy. For example, truancy is twice as high in South Wales as in the South West of England. In fact, the truancy rate *per se* in South Wales is almost double that of most of England.

Similarly, reported rates of truancy in Northern Ireland are lower than for both England and Wales; a finding which has been partially attributed to the denominational foundations of schools in the Province.

Similar variations in rates of truancy and attendance are reported in the United States and in other countries. In the United States, for example, major differences have been found in rates of delinquency and truancy by sex, age, racial type and geographical location. In parts of the US, the problem is so bad that some schools in Chicago, New York, Washington, Detroit and the rural south report average daily attendance rates of between 35 and 50 per cent. Recent surveys report that pupil to pupil violence in high truancy schools is rife. So are school-based robberies, vandalism, extortion, insolence to staff, indiscipline and inter-racial conflicts. Some reports indicate that a high proportion of parents, pupils and teachers fear for their safety daily both at school and on their way to and from school. Yet, in other parts of the States, truancy rates are low (e.g. Vermont) and pupil behaviour within schools is exemplary. Some states (e.g. California) have examples of both high and low truancy schools as well as well behaved and poorly behaved schools.

Despite public concern about indiscipline in schools in Britain, the situation is much more under control than in parts of the US. This is true even in inner city areas and in those parts of the UK where rates of absenteeism, vandalism and delinquency are above average. In some parts of Britain, average daily attendance rates hover between 50 and 70 per cent (worse in Years 10 and 11 than in Years 7 and 8) and the related incidence of truancy and vandalism is high. But, generally speaking, most teachers are in control of their classes and certainly do not live in fear of their pupils; unlike some institutions in places like New York and Chicago. There are few ghettos or no-go areas in Britain. They do exist. But, in Britain, the scale of the problems is much lower than in parts of the US.

There is however, one worrying sign on the horizon – drugs. The evidence from research shows that both truancy and rates of violence increase in schools and neighbourhoods with a high incidence of drugs and drug-related crime. Evidence from the United States and Scandinavia suggests that schools in the UK would do well to ensure that drugs and drug-taking (and associated behavioural and criminal activities) do not take hold (or over) our schools and schooling. If this ever occurs, the long-term future for our education system would be bleak.

Historically, it is interesting to note a few points. First, areas of high truancy in the last century have continued to remain high truancy regions up until the present time (e.g. South Wales). This finding may be linked to the generational truancy syndrome. It may also suggest that regional, cultural – social, economic and industrial – factors play a part in the study of truancy.

Second, and despite all the social and educational improvements which have been made in schools since 1870, and despite the introduction of compulsory education in 1918, the national variations in attendance rates in the twentieth century are slight. For example, present reported average rates of attendance in some parts of London of 80 per cent for secondary school children are no higher than they were in 1918. Similar findings have been reported from Scotland and urban and rural areas of England.

By contrast, truancy rates have risen in some other parts of the world over the last 50 to 100 years, most notably in the United States, Scandinavia (especially Sweden), India and Spain. Even emerging African countries are not immune. Yet, in many parts of Europe and the rest of the world, truancy is much less of a problem than in the UK and United States and, in some countries, almost unknown, thereby suggesting both cultural and national characteristics are evident in any global study of the phenomenon.

The nature and extent of absenteeism in Scotland

The Scottish Council for Research in Education Project (1995) undertook research into the nature and extent of absence in selected primary and secondary schools in Scotland. They found that:

Primary schools

- Primary school staff had little experience of truancy;
- pupils' own reports suggest they skipped school more often than teachers knew about;
- when truancy did occur primary staff thought it was usually because parents kept children away from school;
- some primary pupils in both P4 and P7 claimed they had taken time off school without being found out.

Secondary schools

- Secondary school staff had more experience of truancy than primary staff;
- explained absence was greater than unexplained absence in all the secondary schools;
- there were wide variations in absence rates between secondary schools;
- average explained absence rates ranged from 5.1 per cent in school 4 to 13.5 per cent in school 3;
- average unexplained absence rates ranged from 0.7 per cent in school 7 to 11.8 per cent in school 6;
- in general, explained absence rates were higher for girls than for boys, however, unexplained absence rates were similar for both boys and girls;
- in general, explained absence rates were similar in terms 1 and 2, unexplained absence rates were slightly higher in term 2;
- in general, secondary school head teachers felt satisfied with their systems for recording attendance;
- but some secondary staff thought that SCAMP records might not always be accurate;
- time was not always available for the amount of work needed to update the records;
- the records could not show instances of condoned truancy.

Truancy and exclusion

More recently, research has shown a significant and marked increase in rates of exclusion from schools. Far more truants – especially disruptive truants – are excluded from schools than has been the case in the past, possibly due to the introduction of league tables and more regular OFSTED reports. In 1997, 12,500 secondary pupils were excluded; a rise of 13 per cent. Exclusions from primary schools have also risen fast – by 18 per cent in 1997 to 1400 pupils. Some educationalists believe that the number of exclusions is too high with some schools being too ready to get rid of difficult pupils. The growth of permanent exclusions in primary schools and among black children are particular concerns. Black pupils make up a disproportionate number of those expelled. The percentage of all black children expelled is 0.66. This is more than three times the percentage of white children (0.18), and six times that of pupils from the Indian subcontinent (0.11). Boys accounted for 83 per cent of all exclusions. Seventy-eight per cent are aged between 12 and 15. Nearly half are aged 14 or 15. Eighty-three per cent of all excluded pupils emanate from mainstream secondary schools. Special schools account for 5 per cent of exclusions and pupils are four times more likely to be excluded.

In 1998, the Government published its first annual report into Truancy and School Exclusion. It is the first influential study of its kind. Many of the same social and family risk factors apply to exclusion as to truancy. Research findings emphasise the considerable disadvantage excluded pupils generally experience with evidence of high levels of family stress including unemployment, low income and family disruption. OFSTED research highlights poor acquisition of basic skills, particularly literacy; limited aspirations and opportunities; poverty; and poor relationships with pupils, parents or teachers. Since some of these factors have worsened over the last two decades, these factors may explain some of the rise in exclusions. OFSTED notes that:

> what appears to be happening is a degree of polarisation between the great majority of children who appear orderly and a small minority who are becoming increasingly intractable.

Other studies have focused on reasons relating to educational climate and policy, resource constraints and lack of training. For example,

- some feel the problem is that schools have been under such pressure to meet demanding academic standards and compete with each other, that excluding borderline cases could seem more attractive;
- school performance tables have often been blamed for exerting this pressure, particularly since – until recently – raw data only was used, there was no measure of value added, and children moving from grade F to D gained no recognition at all. The Government is currently moving to include value added in the performance tables. The academic achievement of all children will be valued, not just children at the C to D borderline;
- some feel that many behavioural problems are the response of those who have fallen behind and are not being helped to catch up, for whom an academic curriculum seems increasingly difficult, uninteresting, or irrelevant;
- many teachers and LEAs say they need more external support for learning and behavioural needs, and draw attention to the lack of specialist staff, time and expertise within mainstream schools to deal with behavioural difficulties. The need for more training in handling behaviour problems is often mentioned. OFSTED found that many teachers were unsure of the distinction between poor behaviour and behaviour springing from deepseated emotional disturbance, requiring treatment.

Summary of reasons offered by schools for exclusions

A study of exclusions in one large LEA reported the following results, presented in Table 2.1.

These categories are very broad, and some clearly could encompass both serious and more minor incidents. But the broad message concurs with research by others which has found that physical and verbal abuse, particularly to peers, are the most common grounds.

As is the case with truancy, exclusion rates vary widely between schools and LEAs, even after taking account of different local socio-economic conditions:

- in 1997, the exclusions rate in Hammersmith and Fulham was four times that of Newham and more than six times that of Oxfordshire;

Table 2.1 Reasons offered by schools for exclusions

Bullying, fighting and assaults on peers	30.1%
Disruption, misconduct and unacceptable behaviour	17.0%
Verbal abuse to peers	14.9%
Verbal abuse to staff	12.0%
Miscellaneous	8.1%
Theft	5.5%
Defiance and disobedience	5.0%
Drugs (smoking, alcohol, cannabis)	4.0%
Vandalism and arson	2.4%
Physical abuse and assault on staff	1.2%

- the regions with the highest rates are inner and outer London;
- a quarter of secondary schools permanently exclude five or more children a year and are responsible for around two thirds of all permanent exclusions. About a quarter do not permanently exclude any children. If the highest excluding quarter of schools cut their exclusion rate to that of the average, exclusions would be halved.

The number of permanent exclusions is small in relation to the overall school population, but has risen fast in recent years:

- the first survey figures reported 4,000 permanent exclusions in 1991–92, up from 3,000 in 1990–91; by 1995–96, this figure had more than trebled;
- permanent exclusions represent 0.04 per cent of primary school pupils; 0.34 per cent for secondary schools and 0.64 per cent for special schools.

Schools have to report to LEAs fixed-term exclusions totalling more than five days. This information will be collated after September 1999. OFSTED estimates there are around 100,000 a year. Some of these may be repeat exclusions of the same child. All of these figures cover only decisions to exclude in any given year. They do not include children who were excluded in previous years and are still not in school. And obviously, they do not cover children who are excluded 'informally': anecdotal evidence suggests this is not uncommon.

Reasons for exclusion vary greatly from relatively minor incidents to serious criminal offences. The circumstances in which exclusion might be justified are not set out in the law, and the DfEE guidance on the subject does not have statutory force. The guidance says that:

- exclusion should be used 'only in response to serious breaches of a school's policy on behaviour or of the criminal law';
- it should be used as a last resort when all other reasonable steps have been taken and when allowing the child to remain in school would be seriously detrimental to the education or welfare of the pupil or others;

- exclusion is not appropriate for minor misconduct, such as occasional failure to do homework or to bring dinner money;
- pregnancy is not in itself sufficient reason for exclusion.

The draft 'Social Inclusion' guidance speaks of 'mandatory' powers being sought and heads and governors must 'have regard' to it. However, practice varies enormously and in too many schools is at odds with this guidance. There have been press reports of exclusion for relatively minor issues such as wearing trousers not bought from the nominated supplier; a 7-year-old excluded for sticking her tongue out at a teacher; breaking a school rule about using a subway to cross the road; wearing a nose-stud, dreadlocks or having tramlines shaved into hair. Other schools may veer too much in the opposite direction, and are too slow to use exclusion where it is necessary.

To quote OFSTED:

> Some schools are so anxious to avoid exclusions that they incur some danger to themselves as institutions, to staff and pupils. Others are only too ready to exclude. A few are irresponsibly profligate in the use made of exclusion, devaluing it as a sanction.

In one school in South Wales six male teenagers were all excluded because of their truancy. The result was that they formed an excluded group of pupils who terrorised their local estates, shops and the police throughout their period out of school. A police spokesperson indicated that none of the boys would have been a handful on his own. Together, they presented a major problem; not least because while some of the boys were carrying out raids on the estate, others were acting as lookouts and/or 'decoys'. The police spokesman likened their behaviour to a 'pack of dogs', encouraging one another to new depths of depravity.

Despite the Government's lead, and its first influential report into Truancy and Exclusion, there is no definitive study into the link between truancy *per se* and school exclusion. All that can be stated with certainty is that a high proportion of excluded pupils are also truants; normally delinquent or institutional truants – often those that are prepared to engage in confrontation in and out of school. Parsons (1999) has published a book on exclusions from school which shows that the cost of educating excluded pupils is around three to four times more expensive than in the mainstream. He has also reported on the clear link between exclusion and truancy and some of the reasons for it.

Similarly, while there is a clear link between truancy and bullying, no definitive study on the correlation between truancy and bullying exists. While this remains so, it is only conjecture to suggest that some institutional truants may be bullies while traditional and psychological truants are more likely to be those who have been bullied.

3   Types of truancy

Types of truancy

By 1998, the Labour Government had decided that the truancy phenomenon had become so serious that they asked 100 pupils who regularly skip school to join specialist panels to advise the Prime Minister on how to tackle truancy. This initiative was supported by both Unison and the National Association of Social Workers. The panels met in London, Scotland and the North West of England. Their ideas were sent to the Government's Social Exclusion Unit.

The Unison view expressed at the time was:

> It is the first time kids have had a chance to talk about this as a group. They say school is boring and frustrating. There is peer pressure to skip school. Most of them feel they can't go back to school because they will get told off. It doesn't seem to be a very healthy way of dealing with the problem. We have to look at wider things, at schools' attitudes, at parents' attitudes – many parents encourage it – and at the social and economic reasons. Many of these kids want an education but not this one. A lot of them are really bright kids. One million kids daily can't be wrong. There is something wrong with our social and educational system and we need to take a fresh look at it.

Interviews with truants

Interviews with truants themselves suggest they want less pressure at school, more flexibility of choice within the National Curriculum, more fun in school allied to better teaching. Many truants believe 'bunking off' school is cool. That's why Lily and Lucy started. And once they had started, they found they couldn't stop. Lily, who is 16, comes from London. She has not attended school regularly since she was 11.

> 'It's the peer pressure thing. We started bunking off a lesson in the toilets for a laugh. Then you do it for a day, a week, a month. The first time I bunked off for three days no one noticed. School is boring. The excite-

ment of bunking off is that you might get caught. Sometimes you want to be caught.'

She forgot sickness notes from her parents and hung about in friends' houses, burger bars and Oxford Street shops. She isn't anti-education, just anti-school. Now she has a home tutor and is studying for GCSEs and planning to go to college.

Lucy, who attends an all-girls school, did not start truanting until she was 12.

'People kept saying to me why don't you bunk off. So I did. Then I kept missing things and it's hard to go back because in the end you *have* to go back. The others look down on you. They think you've given in.'

Michelle, 15, also feels she is trapped in a pattern she cannot break. 'Teachers should be more understanding. We are doing Macbeth and I keep missing bits so I get confused. The teacher just says, you don't come to school, why should I bother with you?' Sometimes she gets as far as the bus stop in the morning but no further.

For Jack, aged 13, it was not peer pressure but bullying which led to two months' truanting. He told his parents he was going to school each day then hung about in Camden Town. Unlike another panel member, who was beaten up in his first week by sixth-formers, he was not physically attacked, but his classmates made racist comments. A social worker found him roaming the streets and he has now been back at school for a month. He doesn't know why but the racist taunts have stopped.

Most wish someone had tried harder to keep them in school. 'Schools should be harder places to escape from', says Lily.

'There should be more social workers to help people back', says Jack.

'There should be less pressure', says Serra, aged 14. 'It's the pressure of having to get up in the morning. It's the pressure of teachers not letting you go at your own speed and piling on the work. It would be better to do fewer GCSEs'.

Hollie, 12 says: 'Teachers should make lessons more fun and interesting instead of just telling us to copy things down in a book'.

Michael, aged 14, says: 'Teachers should be more friendly. They shout at you about missing lessons and that makes you dislike them more'. He, for one, is not worried about leaving school without qualifications. He intends to be a cab driver like several of his relations.

Truancy

There are several types of truancy. Whereas the general public tends to think of truancy as only having one cause – a desire to bunk off school – in reality there are several different kinds. And even more different causes as we will discover in Chapters 4, 5 and 6.

Teachers and truancy: specific lesson absence

We will now consider every type of truancy because each has its own specific features. 'Specific lesson truancy', sometimes called specific lesson absence, is probably the fastest growth area. Why? Some relate it to the introduction of the National Curriculum. The perception is that some subjects are not as appropriate as others to less able pupils perhaps with multiple special, social and educational needs. Examples of subjects in this category that are often reported in school surveys to be less popular with underachievers like truants are most frequently conceptually sequential subjects like maths, science and modern languages. Paradoxically, truants often list maths along with English (and reading) as two of their highest priority subjects.

It is difficult to consider the innate traits of subjects and pupils likes or dislikes without a related discussion about teaching and teachers' abilities. This is why findings on pupils' preferences for curriculum subjects tend to vary school by school. Some pupils dislike particular subjects for their own idiosyncratic reasons. In some school surveys, for whatever reasons, religious education, girls PE, maths, science (chemistry and physics especially), modern languages (and Welsh in some parts of Wales) often feature prominently among the least popular subjects. However, specific lesson truancy is undoubtedly related to the quality of teaching and teachers' attitudes and abilities. Why is it that some pupils attend most classes yet regularly miss others?

Some pupils dislike particular teachers. Research suggests that pupils dislike four particular traits in teachers or 'types' of teacher:

1   Teachers who are 'inhuman' and interpret their role too literally. These types of teachers are perceived by pupils as being 'faceless', 'robots', 'a load of rubbish', and 'time servers'. This finding suggests that 'stand-offish' approaches are unlikely to work with pupils.
2   Teachers who treat pupils as anonymous beings. Despite existing low teacher–pupil ratios, it is vital that pupils are treated as individuals. Pupils like teachers to know something about them – e.g. which football team do they support? Which pop/girl/boy band do they like? What are they good at outside school?
3   Teachers who are soft and/or inconsistent.
4   Teachers who are 'unfair', 'biased', and make unreasonable demands on pupils. Pupils particularly dislike two extremes; teachers who are 'weak' and those who are regarded as 'bullies'. A lot of pupils who feel they have been 'picked upon' by teachers or a teacher often seek 'revenge' by staying away from their classes.

Research indicates that successful schools are characterised by:

1 Teachers who are able to keep control at all times.
2 Teachers who are able to 'have a laugh' with pupils.
3 Teachers who foster warm, empathetic relationships with pupils.
4 Teachers who like and understand children.
5 Teachers who teach their subjects well, with enthusiasm and in interesting ways.
6 Teachers who teach all the time rather than indulging in aimless activities.
7 Teachers who are consistent and fair.
8 Teachers who treat children with respect and as equals.
9 Teachers who allow pupils a sense of freedom in class.

Positive individual relationships between staff and pupils are perhaps the key determinant of successful progress at school. Parents will understand the impact made by good and bad teaching and witness the effects on their children's attitudes and progress. Even for able pupils, student choices about which subjects to take for GCSE or A level can be significantly influenced by the choice of the teacher who is likely to be taking the subject. Pupils, for example, often choose to study their degree subjects in higher education based on the calibre of the person who taught them at school rather than their love of the subject *per se*.

For low to moderate ability pupils, the category in which the vast majority of truants are to be found, the same is equally true. The impact of teachers' attitudes, allied to the school's ethos, may be the two most important two variables which explain the differences between high and low truancy schools. These, of course, are closely linked to school leadership and managerial policies and strategies.

Take, for example, two neighbouring comprehensives, located in a reasonably-sized town. The town is well known for its rugby team, for its local traditions and 'sport', and for being at the cutting edge of new techno-logical development following the decline of its traditional industry. The socio-economic backgrounds of the pupils in the two schools are almost identical. Yet, one is a high truancy school; the other is not. One has a great deal of specific lesson truancy; the other has very little. In one, there is an intimidating atmosphere in which bullying is not uncommon. The other is characterised by warm, friendly teacher–pupil relationships. The key difference between the two schools appears to be that in one the pupils are content and happy; in the other they are not. Truancy breeds and develops in climates of hostility, fear, negativity and low expectations. Senior staff within schools would do well to remember this maxim. After all, it is the head, the manage-ment team and the staff themselves who set the standards which are expected from the pupils. It is the pupils who respond to this lead. Too often, this simple fact is forgotten by those in authority.

It equally follows, therefore, that pupils will attend classes which they consider to be well taught, relevant and interesting. They are more likely to miss classes which are dull, irrelevant and 'boring'. If a school finds that significant numbers of its pupils are missing specific lessons it has a problem. It usually means that there is:

(a) poor teaching taking place;
(b) a breakdown in teacher–pupil relationships;
(c) differential standards being applied.

The latter category is perhaps the most complex to explain. Why?

Research shows that most teachers prefer teaching able to less able pupils. They also prefer teaching the sixth form to, for example, 10Q or 11Q. It is not unknown for some teachers to set themselves very high standards with high ability teaching groups and to lower these standards (consciously or otherwise) when they are teaching lower ability groups.

Pupils are very astute at discerning changes in teachers' attitudes, whether these signs are more or less overt. For instance, they soon realise that they can wear their shirts outside their trousers/skirts with one teacher and not with another. They can eat sweets in one class and not in another. Equally, they have to work hard in one class and not in another. They are given significant amounts of help and homework in one class and not in another. If they ask a question within one class, they will receive a polite answer. If they ask a question in another class, they will be shouted at, abused or ridiculed. Guess from which kinds of classes the majority of specific lesson absence takes place?

Equally, specific lesson absence gives schools a clue about its subject profile. If pupils attend physics and biology and skip chemistry, it is a sure sign there is something amiss with the teaching of chemistry within the school. Equally, with history or geography. Yet, these traits do occur and often continue unchecked year upon year. In one school in South Wales, it is the norm for parents in the area to pay privately for tuition in chemistry if they wish their children to be successful. Obviously, among the parental and pupil network, pupils know there is a problem. But, do the school? If so, what are they doing about it? Not very much it seems. If able pupils are struggling with chemistry, what chance for the less able?

Too often, schools condone specific lesson truancy. Let me give you an example. In one school in a South Wales valley it is possible to see the specific lesson truants as you approach in your car. They stand (some smoking) below a high wall at the far end of the school yard in the certain knowledge that they cannot be observed from the school corridors. But, do the staff *really* not know where their specific lesson truants are 'hiding'? Throughout my visits to this school over the years, I have never observed any teacher walk in the direction of the wall and ensure the pupils return to their classes. It is almost as if there is another form of absence – teacher-condoned specific lesson absence!

Post registration truancy

Specific lesson absence is also known as post-registration truancy although there is a subtle difference. Specific lesson absence means pupils missing particular lessons (week on week). Post-registration truancy occurs when pupils register as being present at school (usually in form periods) and then subsequently skip school. Whereas specific lesson truants miss particular lessons (often taught by teachers they do not 'respect'), post-registration truants will miss whole clusters of classes, on different days, for different reasons, sometimes on a whim.

Post-registration truancy is often not reflected in published figures of unauthorised absence. Some recent research now suggests that post-registration truancy probably accounts for much or most of the actual truancy that takes place in some schools. This is why official statistics based on attendance registers tend to underestimate the scale of the problem. A significantly large number of individual schools also tend to underestimate the extent of their own post-registration truancy rates; perhaps deliberately. Some would probably be surprised if they realised its true extent.

Human nature being what it is, there can be little doubt that some teachers may be secretly quite pleased when certain disruptive, difficult, less able or disinterested pupils fail to attend their lessons. This is understandable. However, there is a down side. Condoning post-registration truancy can place the teacher in a very invidious position. It may, for example, place the teacher concerned in a very difficult position should anything happen to that pupil either when out of school or out of lessons but on the school premises. Condoning post-registration truancy also sends very mixed messages both to the pupil(s) who are not in the lesson as well as to those who attend regularly.

Post-registration truancy is often not only related to teachers' attitudes but also to teachers' personal conduct. For example, regular lateness to lessons provides an indication to pupils that there is something wrong with a teacher's attitude towards his or her job or towards them. It also has a more serious side.

Based on a true story, Jeff had his career ruined by being inadvertently late for a class. In his case, as a conscientious teacher and head of Year 10, he was investigating the discovery of a female colleague's handbag which had had the purse and her money removed from it. Subsequently, they were found stuffed down the loo during morning break. Consequently, Jeff arrived at his English class ten minutes late. In the meantime, a boy in the class had started flicking pellets around the room using elastic bands. One of these pellets caught another boy in the eye. The injured boy subsequently went blind in this eye. The local authority and the school lost the ensuing legal case and had to pay substantial damages. The ruling of the court was based on the premise that *in loco parentis* meant the caring teacher should have been in class on time. The class had been due to start at eleven o'clock. Arriving at eleven ten, while there were mitigating circumstances, did not excuse the school or the teacher from its responsibilities. If a class is due to start at eleven o'clock, it should begin at eleven o'clock.

Following the court case, Jeff had a nervous breakdown. Not long afterwards, he took early retirement. He never forgave himself, although, strictly, it was not his fault. Many teachers in managerial positions are often put into these kinds of invidious position on a daily basis. However, as courts interpret the in loco parentis concept very strictly, and as The Children's Act of 1989 embodies the principle that 'the welfare of the child is paramount', schools and teachers should be well advised to follow their statutory obligations.

Conversely, in cases of repeated pupil lateness, schools should remember that repeated absences at the beginning of a school session can amount to failure to attend regularly for the purposes of Section 199 of the 1993 Education Act. Evidence is mounting that both specific lesson absence and post-registration truancy have increased since the introduction of the National Curriculum. Some studies are now beginning to suggest that taken together, specific lesson absence and post-registration truancy form the largest single category of truants in school-based surveys. O'Keefe (1993) reported that post-registration truancy was the major form of non-attendance in some schools and that there were indications that this form of truancy was increasing.

Parental-condoned truancy

A considerable debate exists in the literature as to whether parental-condoned absence is in fact truancy. By definition, one or more of the parents has agreed to the child missing school. Often, parents will ask their offspring to stay home for a variety of reasons. These reasons include – at the lowest level – for company. But, at the highest level, they include protection, especially in families where violence or abuse is the norm.

Sometimes, parents can believe that by allowing their children to stay home they are helping them. This is a totally false and misguided belief. Regular attendance at school matters and is critically important for a child's schooling and personal, social and academic development. Occasionally, a short break from school, perhaps to help a neurotic or very intense child to overcome irrational fears, pressures or worries, can be justified especially when parents are keeping their children at home to prevent physical (and, sometimes mental) bullying at school.

Technically, parental-condoned truancy occurs when the parent is aware of the child's absence from school, but is unwilling or unable to do anything about it. Even this however, is not as simple as it sounds. For example, in a case which happened in West Glamorgan, a 15-year-old boy physically beat up his father because he did not want to go to school and his father insisted he did so. The father required 133 stitches to his face and hospitalisation. The boy was over six feet tall; his father a mere five feet six. The boy weighed almost fourteen stone; his father about ten stone.

It can too easily be forgotten that while parents have strict legal require-ments to send their children to school, it is never easy when adolescent-age pupils refuse.

In one project in Mid Glamorgan, it was found that some parents of truants were at their 'wits end' with their own children. They had done everything reasonable to get them to attend school. This even involved informing their local school and the social services. And still the children continued to truant. Sometimes therefore, it is the parents who need the help as much as their offspring.

Parental-condoned truancy is a category which shows significant differences between groups in statistical returns in research projects. For example, parent-condoned absence is frequently the highest category of truancy among girls, especially teenage girls. In some studies, up to two thirds of girl truants have been found to be parental-condoned. By contrast, twice as many boys as girls truant.

Among ethnic minority households, rates of parental-condoned absence are often significantly higher. There are differing reasons for this. These include:

- using children to undertake familial tasks or needs (e.g. visit social services departments, complete Inland Revenue forms) often because of language difficulties among the parents;
- sending children on short or longer visits to their countries of origin (e.g. India or Pakistan);
- parents not wishing their children (especially, in some cases, their daughters) to become too educated because of the cultural challenges this may pose (e.g. rebellion against arranged marriages);
- avoiding extortion or racial victimisation at school.

Studies, too, show differing parental attitudes towards schooling between families of, for example, West Indian origin when compared with those from Asia. Too often, schools are inclined to forget that inherent cultural differ-ences between races not only exist, but can be exacerbated by tensions between pupils within schools.

Some parents simply encourage pupils to stay home in order, for example, to perform household chores, help in the family business, to care for an invalid relative or to help with younger sick or handicapped siblings, etc. In such cases, the parent may send a note to school citing 'sickness' or some other reason as the reason for absence – irrespective of the real cause.

For this reason, parental-condoned truancy is extremely difficult to detect. It also masks and tends to reduce the truancy rates both locally and nationally. After all, are parents going to tell schools or education welfare officers the real reasons why their child is missing school?

Whether deliberately or otherwise, since the introduction of league tables for schools, official published rates of non-attendance – unauthorised absence –

have decreased. This is surprising as all the evidence from research projects, the Government's own initiatives and increased media attention, suggest that national rates are rising or, at the very least, remaining unchanged. One reason for this is that many schools go to considerable pains to ensure that the category 'unauthorised absence' (e.g. truancy) is kept to a minimum. Could it be that some schools are inadvertently turning a blind eye (or even encouraging) the use of parental notes to justify unauthorised absence? If so, then the real rates of parental-condoned truancy will be found to have increased considerably in any meaningful national survey.

Undoubtedly, the introduction of league tables, and OFSTED inspections, have brought pressure upon schools to minimise their published rates of unauthorised absence. On more than one recent occasion, one has wondered why a school has needed a consultant, or staff to spend time in a training event on truancy, when its own published rates on attendance are so high. It is quite clear that there are untenable differences between official published rates of unauthorised absence and the true figures. Of these published statistics, the category of parental-condoned absence is the most difficult to quantify accurately.

Case studies of parental-condoned absence

Defining practical examples of parental-condoned absence is never easy as the following case studies indicate.

Barry

Barry's father was an unemployed shipyard worker who, at the time of the interview, was attending a further education college in the evening to study GCSE German. He had previously taken history, and names this as his favourite subject at school – though school in general had not been of much use: 'You learn more later on'. However, on the importance of education for his son, he stated: 'It's everything isn't it – it's the basis of life, that's what I try and tell him'. Barry, it was acknowledged, disliked school and attended poorly. His whereabouts when absent were unknown – 'I wish I did know', his father stated. (The absence had been assigned to the 'other reasons' category by the EWO.)

Barry's father had strong opinions about the headteacher of the school, describing him as unreasonable and dictatorial. He preferred the previous head, and had no wish to maintain contact with the school under the present staff. He strongly resented the way the staff in the school spoke to him at parents' evenings and on other occasions.

Barry subsequently described his activities when absent as playing snooker and pool at the local estate working men's club. About school he stated: 'I couldn't care less about it' – but when asked why he didn't want to go, added: 'It doesn't annoy me. You get thrown out anyway'. He had no wish to change schools. 'When my parents get a visit, they cover for me. They say I'm off sick. They don't like me missing school but they don't like me getting into trouble either – nor do they want to be in trouble themselves'.

Maureen

Maureen's absence of 29 days was described by her teacher (this school had no EWO) at the time of the survey as a combination of illness and 'condonement'. Maureen's mother claimed that she herself had always liked school, had attended regularly and given the chance would like to 'do it over again'. Maureen, she said, would like to become a mechanic, but she discouraged this, as she did not feel it was a suitable occupation for a girl; a better option would be to go on to the local college of further education.

Her daughter's attendance was unsatisfactory but this had come about as a result of 'back trouble' resulting from gymnastics. Maureen was spoken of as being depressed, but her mother quickly added: 'We've never had any bother with Maureen – this is a happy home'.

The school was described as satisfactory, the only reservation being that the parents were asked to meet members of staff for trivial reasons (i.e. about minor misdemeanours or smoking). Maureen gave her motives for missing school as 'IT and cookery', but she described the school as being 'all right – it keeps you occupied'. She had stayed off when she wasn't sick, and yes, her parents knew about it. 'They keep saying you'll have to go back – but I keep on and then they give in'. When she was at home, Maureen generally cleaned the house or went shopping. There was no one in school to whom she felt she could talk about the reasons for her absence.

Marie

Marie's absence of 39 days was described as occurring with parental knowledge and for no apparent reason, with the added comment by the school that she 'has been suspended several times for misdemeanours'.

On being interviewed, Marie's mother immediately drew attention to the school's practice of suspension as a punishment. She was unhappy with the school – suspension was too frequent, the head was described as an 'outsider' (i.e. a nun from a different order from that traditionally associated with the school) and residents of the area where Marie lived were discriminated against – 'This school wasn't meant for working class people'.

Marie's attendance, it was acknowledged, had been poor, but only 'because of the school'. If she stayed at home, Marie would do housework. Marie herself found going to school unimportant: 'It doesn't teach you much'; she added 'they should explain it more'. Her reasons for staying off were related to a dislike of one particular teacher; another senior member of staff had removed her from these classes and she had felt happier since then. If absent, she helped at home, or else 'wandered around'. Her mother would tell her off if she was 'mitching', but otherwise she would say nothing.

Raymond

Raymond had 26 days absence, designated by the EWO as 'for no apparent reason and with parent's knowledge'. His mother, a widow, claimed that she insisted on her son's attendance but that he repeatedly came home during the day. His activities at home were listed as 'playing records, sleeping and working on his motorbike'. Raymond, she said, had 'interests which didn't fit in with school – he started to smoke three months ago and wants to be more grown-up'. Of her five children, he was the only one who had been 'in trouble'. He is now on probation. 'You can do so much', she said, 'and then it's up to the child'.

A subsequent and highly emotional interview with Raymond confirmed a number of these points and produced some additional information. School had 'no point – it doesn't help – it doesn't teach you anything'. There was no one in school he could talk to, or if he did talk to anyone, it would be about his girlfriend whom he had been forbidden to see. Raymond's plans for the future centred on leaving school, getting a flat and becoming engaged. His activities at home were described as 'drinking tea', 'sitting in the house', 'working on my bike' – the last of these he claimed, helped him to stop thinking about his girlfriend. His mother, he said would 'shout at me a lot saying she'll be prosecuted'.

Kim

Kim's attendance was, her mother acknowledged, 'not as good as it should be'. (She had missed 26 days in the previous term.) She had hated school from the age of 11 onwards, and while 'bright' had 'no interest' in schoolwork. On the question of insisting upon attendance, the mother laughingly admitted that sometimes she suspected her daughter of faking illness but could not really be sure. When Kim stayed at home, her activities were described as 'sleeping' or 'visiting her grandmother'. 'No, she doesn't help me, dear'.

At a later point in the interview, when asked if she would like more contact with the school, the mother indicated that this was simply not feasible: she had had a hip replacement operation and was also looking after her mother-in-law, who was blind. Her husband was unemployed and they had no transport.

Kim's own version of her absence was somewhat different. While admitting that she disliked school, finding it 'important for some but not for others', she claimed that her own absence was due entirely to her mother's illness – 'and I stayed off once when my sister got married'. Her mother, she said, would tell her to go to school, 'but I wouldn't like to, so I'd stay home anyway. How would my mother manage on her own?'

Charles

Charles' absence of 31 days was categorised by the EWO as mainly 'other reasons' with some element of illness. His mother readily acknowledged that her son's attendance was 'not as good as it should be' but quickly pointed out that this was her fault, not that of her son. She related how in the early years of the 'troubles' she had been merely threatened, but later, she had to leave her job in the bakery and had never worked since. Since her matrimonial troubles had started, her health had deteriorated significantly.

She claimed to initially suffer from 'bad nerves'. But some years later, she had a stroke which left her completely incapacitated. Her son had, often with her permission, performed many of the household chores and looked after his mother. Charles, she insisted, liked school and would always want to go; she herself was 'very happy with school – oh, they're very fair, they have time for you'.

Charles subsequently confirmed this account of his absence: he always attended except in the case of his own illness or that of his mother – this was distinct from 'mitching' which he had never done. There were some minor reservations about school – some days were 'okay' others weren't, particularly those where he had to stay in the same room for long periods. When asked 'What is the main reason why you wouldn't want to come to school?' he promptly replied 'lessons', though he claimed that he had never absented himself for such a reason. Charles certainly viewed his own non-attendance as necessary and legitimate, and given the 'other reasons' classification perhaps the EWO also took this view.

Issues arising

These brief case studies reflect the diversity of experience even among pupils in the same non-attendance category – in this case parental-condoned absence. They indicate that the activities involved in by the pupils when not at school could be divided into two: those to do with caring and the home; and those with a leisure or recreational orientation. The differences between boys and girls can be significant – girls being more involved in the home and boys in some form of leisure activity. However, there is no norm here as the case of Charles indicates.

It is not always clear from the case studies whether the motivation for staying away from school is based on specific features of schools, the home, or both. For example, Charles did not like 'lessons', nor sitting in the same room for long periods, but his mother's incapacity provided him, in both their perceptions, with a legitimate excuse for not going to school. Likewise, Kim perceived her mother's problems as being sufficient reason to absent herself from school, although her mother did not see this as being helpful. Marie, on the other hand, saw the reason for her non-attendance as being 'because of the school' and, in particular, one teacher. Her mother also perceived the school as unsympathetic and responsible for her daughter's attitude. The reasons for Marie's non-attendance were specifically related to certain aspects of the school itself and not to any rejection of the need for education. It is clear that a number of parental-condoned absentees miss school because of their dislike of a specific teacher, or implicitly, for the same reason, but expressed as a dislike of a particular subject. Where suspension is incurred, as in Marie's case, the degree of frustration and bitterness expressed is considerable. Parents, like Maureen's and Barry's, appear to find school personally threatening and on the whole tended to reject the value of education. It is interesting to note that some parents of working-class pupils place the highest possible value on education and see schooling as a real opportunity for upward social mobility. By contrast, others reject schooling and are openly hostile to education.

Whether the main motivation for staying away from school lies within the school, or in the greater importance or attraction of the alternative activities, there are several aspects of non-attendance which have implications for schools.

First, the pupil may dislike school because of his or her perceptions of a particular teacher, a subject or even (but very rarely) the overall curriculum in general. The parent, although not liking the non-attendance at school, may feel helpless in the face of an intransigent teenager who does not want to go to school and could, after some protest, allow the absence to continue. Raymond's mother expressed the apparent helplessness of such a situation: 'You can do so much – then it's up to the child'. And Maureen described how she wore down the opposition of her parents. 'They keep saying you'll have to go back – but I keep on and then they give in'. In these situations it is understandable that schools feel that the time and effort expended in order to get a 15- or 16-year-old back to school is often excessive and unproductive.

Second, while boredom, dislike of a subject or a teacher, is often given as an important feature of not going to school, this is often associated with failure and consequent low self-esteem in the school environment. Barry and Raymond believed that the school could do nothing for them so there was no point in going.

Third, both parents and pupils emphasised the importance of outcomes in terms of competencies or the ability to 'get a job' but appeared unable to articulate the value of education for them. This seems to suggest that some parents' perceptions of 'relevance' and 'value' may be different from those of some teachers and some schools. This divergence of view might help to explain some parents' reluctance to make or sustain contact with schools. When required to do so, as in cases of suspension, they feel embarrassed and threatened. It is important that this feeling be set in the context of parents' and pupils' apparent acceptance of the individual's responsibility for his or her own success or failure. For this reason they did not appear to desire a change of school. Like Barry they felt: 'It wouldn't make any difference, they're all the same'. It would also appear that the incompatibility of the pupil, the home and the school is often accepted by pupils. Although some parents protest sincerely about their children's poor attendance they also tend to accept it.

In situations where pupils express a dislike of individual teachers or subjects, it is often a reflection of how the individual pupil is treated. A pupil may dislike the lack of control of his or her own behaviour *and* the authority of the school to dictate what he or she should do, when to do it and how it is to be done. These case study pupils demonstrate in their lives outside school an ability to take decisions for themselves and sometimes for others; and cope in stressful situations which are unfamiliar to many teachers. Often, such absentees are labelled and stigmatised as failures because they reject a regime which is alien to them as individuals and to their lifestyles. A radical response to this might be to contract with each pupil an agreed amount of work over the course of an academic term. This contract would specify an amount of work, a required number of days attendance and the sanctions to be imposed for non-completion of the contract. It would be agreed and signed by pupils, parents and teachers. The contract could be reviewed at set intervals by pupils, parents and teachers and satisfactory progress recorded or appropriate sanctions applied. It would allow the pupil to take responsibility and be involved in the process of his or her own learning. There would be clear academic and social behaviour goals; an agreement about order and discipline, a higher expectation of success and a closer monitoring of progress to provide feedback on difficulties; and variety in both teaching and learning strategies. In certain cases, it may be better to allow regular absentees to attend school and follow a restricted curriculum rather than expect them to return and study every subject. Sometimes, the recognition that there is a problem can, in itself, be a help. Perhaps some pupils would be better following a combination of school subjects allied to appropriate study at a local further education college.

Such a response from schools to their pupils would, of necessity, have implications for the current National Curriculum. However, the quest for relevance, motivation and interest would be mutual and real. The ability to read and write might well be linked with the development of self-citizenship, social awareness, preparation for adulthood, and aspects of work and leisure, rather than with the traditional study of a collection of accepted disciplines some of which might be irrelevant to less able pupils. The boredom, which is often suggested by pupils as an explanation of their continuing absence, would be offset by a curriculum that reflects the contemporary world of the young adult. Such a curriculum could be developed within the context of the individually-negotiated learning programme contract, with objectives set by the learner and agreed by the parent(s) and teaching staff.

The learning would be self-programmed and incorporate individual and active learning assessed by procedures agreed by learner and teacher which would form part of the individual's record of achievement profile, as would the self-evaluation sheets completed by both teachers and learners.

Attendance would only be compulsory on agreed days and at set times. The pupils would decide on any additional attendance for themselves. There would have to be a highly developed counselling service which would be seen as confidential, useful and above all easily accessed by vulnerable young adults in a complex and difficult world. Sometimes, the curriculum and attendance agreement could be shared between the local school and neighbouring further education college. After all, studies on the curriculum show that relevance is a key factor in both achievement *and* attendance.

Finally, this section has shown that the diverse causes of parental condoned truancy involve the interaction between the pupil, the school and the home. The process of non-attendance is always highly complex and individual. It may be necessary, therefore, for any school response to parental-condoned truancy to incorporate the development of meaningful ways of involving parents in the education of their children. The barriers which some parents currently feel exist between them and the school must be broken down and a new partnership defined. This may demand a fundamental change in attitude by both some parents and some teachers. The parents need to really believe that schools matter. In return, the schools must show they care. This is why 'second chance' learning opportunities for dropouts and truants (including those who have already left school) could prove extremely successful in the long run. These schemes have the potential not only of giving former school failures a fresh start, but also of taking advantage of latent learning potential; after youngsters have faced what it means to be a failure in the real world.

Blanket truancy

Teachers and schools need to note an additional point as well. Blanket truancy exists when the child fails to attend school and lacks authorisation for failing to do so. Technically, it is only the school's headteacher who has the authority to grant such authorisation. A note from a parent can only be authorised by the head who, usually, in practice, delegates this duty to a school's form tutors. A parental note, by itself, does not automatically make an absence authorised. It is the school's acceptance of the explanation offered by that note which authorises the absence. Quite often, schools expect notes from parents when pupils miss half or whole days from school, or make a visit to, for example, the dentist. They do not always ask for similar notes when pupils miss specific lessons or disappear after registration. They should!

Psychological absence

Psychological absence (sometimes referred to as 'near truancy') occurs when a child physically attends school yet fails to participate in any other meaningful way. For example, a pupil may 'switch off' in lessons allowing his or her mind to wander. As the rest of the class is taught, a pupil may mentally be thinking of his or her weekend activities, forthcoming pop concert or next date.

Consequently, simply accepting that attendance means participation (or interest in a lesson) can be misguided.

Some researchers have argued that physical truancy is only part of the problem. Quiet children who are present in the classroom but who do not take part in the lessons, are sometimes regarded as being just as absent as those who fail to attend school.

Research suggests that there are four categories of psychological absence all related to withdrawn behaviour. These are:

1 those who try to make themselves invisible by avoiding all contact with the teacher;
2 those who refuse to acknowledge what the teacher asks them to do;
3 those pupils who appear to be on task but on closer inspection would appear to be doing something else. Some do this by remaining on the periphery of an activity; others through an inappropriate focus. In the latter case this means a pupil would be involved in an activity which would bear little or no relation to what the class had been asked to do;
4 those pupils who appear to be paying attention but whose minds, in reality, are focused on 'external' events (e.g. a forthcoming pop concert, football match).

Research indicates that there are common threads between physical truancy and psychological absence. This link includes low academic self-concepts, a general lack of self-confidence and higher than average levels of anxiety about schoolwork. A high proportion of psychological absence involves pupils who are very shy.

Research also suggests that psychological absence can be reduced by:

(a) dividing classes into smaller groups to enable withdrawn pupils to participate more comfortably;
(b) providing empathetic help and support for their emotional and behavioural needs aimed at restoring and raising self-concepts.

The need for active participation by *all* pupils in classes should be recognised and made explicit to all teachers and pupils and be seen to be part of normal practice. Pupils need to develop their oral as well as their written skills.

Occasionally, psychological absence can be related to disruptive behaviour as some disinterested or disaffected pupils may enjoy creating confrontations between teachers and their classmates almost as a form of sport. This is often part of an attention-seeking pattern. The solution lies in the teacher not falling into the pupil's trap and overreacting.

Psychological absence is rarely an overt problem within schools, except when it is related to disruptive pupils. Most pupils who are prone to psychological absence are excellent attendees in every other way.

Post-registration truancy, parental-condoned truancy and blanket truancy are the primary causes of concern to schools. They are also inter-related. None of these three conditions is exclusive of the others. The boundaries can frequently blur, particularly in the case of parental-condoned truancy.

It is the term 'truancy' which links the three. The prime characteristic of truancy is that the child (individually or collectively) makes the decision not to attend. The nature of this decision-making is central to the concept of truancy. Truancy is unjustified absence and as such is illegal and runs contrary to the 1944 Education Act as amended by more recent legislation.

And this brings us to another crucial distinction. There is a subtle difference between parental-condoned absence and parental-condoned truancy. Parental-condoned truancy is illegal. Technically, and it is a fine point, parental-condoned absence is not truancy. When a child is actually kept away from school by a parent it is not truancy. In reality, it is almost impossible to distinguish between parental-condoned truancy and parental-condoned absence – unless you actually know the precise nature of the absence, the reasons for it, and have interviewed the child and parent(s); preferably separately.

School refusal or school phobia

School refusal, often called school phobia, is normally considered to be at the opposite end of the continuum from truancy. The incidence of school refusal or school phobia cases is comparatively rare. Some experts however, believe that it is more common than generally accepted because so many cases lie undetected, especially amongst families from lower socio-economic backgrounds.

The treatment of school refusal requires specialist counselling help from a qualified practitioner. School refusal is closely linked to anxiety (including test or examination anxiety). It is also highly related to intelligence, paternal and maternal pressure and is often compounded by a heightened sense of failure. It is particularly found among high achievers from very favourable social backgrounds, often with parents in well-paid, professional occupations.

The incidence of school refusal varies study by study and the literature includes research conducted in the UK and United States. Official estimates tend to vary in terms of the precise number of school refusal cases between one in a thousand to one in ten thousand absentees from school. Some school refusers are successfully reintegrated back into schools, others are not. Some are given specialist tuition outside school (where they often cope better) while others readjust well and are successfully reintegrated after a short period of time outside school.

Genuine cases of school refusal can justifiably be included within the medical category in official statistics although not going to school is the main symptom of the illness. This principle has long been accepted by local education authorities. In some cases, illness may itself be one of the precipitating factors leading to school refusal.

Truancy and school refusal are easily distinguished. Truancy depicts socio-educational problems. School refusal is a psychological and medical condition. Although school refusal is certainly a form of unauthorised absence – in the technical sense – it is not strictly speaking truancy. More recently, there is a body of opinion which suggests that school refusal cases have been under-estimated. The reason for this is simple. Parents from upper or middle-class backgrounds prefer to have their stressed and/or non-attending offspring diagnosed as school refusal cases. No such pressure is exerted from parents from working-class backgrounds. The suggestion, therefore, is that some pupils from working-class backgrounds who are labelled as truants are in fact school refusal cases. Their real condition has never been detected.

Finally, some pupils are classified as school refusal cases because they have been threatened or bullied in school and are afraid to return. Rather than face the consequences of naming the bullies in school, the pupils prefer to give other reasons for their absence to their parents and/or the school. Consequently, they become labelled as school refusal cases even though their non-attendance has a legitimate basis.

4 Causes of truancy: social perspectives

Causes of truancy

There is no single cause of truancy. If there was, finding a solution would be easy.

Every truant is unique. So is every school and every family unit. The decision to start truanting is an extremely significant one. Usually, pupils decide to start 'mitching' school because they are:

(a) avoiding a potentially difficult situation (e.g. bullying);
(b) sending out a signal that they need help or are, in some other way, at risk;
(c) overwhelmed by their home or social circumstances;
(d) psychologically distressed;
(e) at a point of no return, perhaps at the end of their tether;
(f) seriously disenchanted with school, a teacher or fellow pupils;
(g) struggling with their schoolwork;
(h) unwell;
(i) under peer pressure to miss school.

Some of these reasons are social, some psychological, and some educational. To a greater or lesser extent, every truant has some social, psychological and educational reasons for missing school. However, the initial 'trigger-point' for truancy is normally a single incident which may be social, psychological or educational. Later, in Chapter 6, evidence is presented which shows that the majority of initial 'trigger-points' for truancy are educational.

As truants graduate from the occasional to the persistent stage, the number of reasons given to justify the truancy are likely to increase significantly. Whereas there may be one specific trigger-point for the onset of the truancy behaviour, truants will give all kinds of extra reasons to justify their actions by the time it has reached the persistent stage. The increase in reasons between initial and persistent truancy is partly born of personal experience and partly a result of cognitive dissonance; a psychological process whereby the brain rationalises and justifies our behaviour and actions.

Pupils at risk

The following far from exhaustive list identifies those pupils who may potentially be poor attenders. Many of the categories clearly overlap and are interconnected. It is not inferred that such pupils are automatically prone to poor attendance, nor does the list seek to stigmatise such pupils in any way. But such a checklist can be a useful tool for schools in helping to identify at an early stage those pupils who might be beginning to experience difficulties. They include pupils:

- whose parents have recently separated;
- who have recently moved to the district;
- who join a school midway through the school year;
- who have recently missed a lot of school time through illness;
- whose siblings (and/or parents) have been poor school attenders;
- whose performance/attainment level in school tends to be poor;
- who tend to be teased or bullied;
- who have difficulty accessing the curriculum yet do not have a statement of SEN;
- who are persistently disruptive;
- who have previously been excluded;
- whose parents are experiencing severe financial hardship (and cannot afford bus fare, uniform, etc.);
- under pressure from examinations;
- are experiencing difficulty forming relationships with their peers and/or are unpopular in school;
- are shy or highly introverted;
- who fail to undertake their homework on a regular basis;
- arrived at school (and/or lessons) late without good reason;
- who get into trouble a lot outside school.

Social indices of truancy

The clear link between social disadvantages and truancy has long been established in the literature. The majority of truants emanate from the lowest social class groupings. However, as only a minority of pupils from the lower social class groupings become truants, the home, social and socio-economic factors are only one part of a complex phenomenon.

Boxes 4.1 and 4.2 provide a summary of research findings into those home background and socio-economic factors which are related to truancy. These data confirm that most truants endure a considerable degree of social deprivation in their everyday lives, which is often compounded by their educational disadvantages at school. Many truants endure a regular diet of failure at school and a fight for survival at home and find themselves having to cope in

Box 4.1 The home backgrounds of truants

Truants are most likely to come from:

- broken homes (in which divorce, separation, cohabiting, 'mixed' siblings are often the norm);
- families where the father or father-figure is away from home for long periods, either for reasons of work (merchant seamen, long-distance lorry drivers) or for other reasons;
- families with an above average number of children;
- families living in overcrowded conditions;
- families living in council-owned housing;
- families living in poor quality and/or old housing (often rented) in a dilapidated state both internally and externally;
- families involved with the social services, either for reasons overcoming or experiencing marital disharmony (divorce, separation, violence, abuse);
- one-parent families;
- poor material conditions within the home;
- families where the parent/s are unable to cope with a single or variety of social pathologies which threaten their lifestyles and lead to abnormal conditions within the home: these factors include alcoholism, physical illness, violence, abuse, familial conflicts, and associated stress factors;
- families in which the parents are uncooperative and/or hostile to authority in general; frequently being hostile to external professional support, including teachers, headteachers and education social work interventions;
- families where the parent(s) are not interested in their children's progress at school;
- families where the parent(s) do not insist their children attend school: or take no notice of their absence and often condone it;
- families which do not insist on their offspring's prompt attendance at school as manifested by their children oversleeping, being late and failing to turn up for school buses;
- families where the parents are passive victims of a dreadful environment and unsure of their constitutional rights;
- families where the children are left unattended for long periods of time or where the children have minimal contact with adults;
- families with criminal records and/or convictions.

Box 4.2 The socio-economic backgrounds of truants

Truants are likely to emanate from:

- families at the lower end of the social scale – the father and/or mother are employed in unskilled (labouring, cleaning) or semi-skilled work;
- families where paternal unemployment or irregular employment is the norm;
- families on low incomes;
- families where maternal unemployment, inability to find work, or full or part-time employment in low income occupations is rife;
- families where the children are supplied with free school meals;
- families on income support;
- families with severe financial (and/or financial management) difficulties;
- homes caught in a poverty trap in which the culture of social exclusion is the norm;
- homes where the children are poorly clothed and eat cheap, low quality food;
- families with transport difficulties (especially in rural areas).

---

situations where the 'laws of the jungle' apply. This is not being unkind; it is a hard fact of life – ask social workers.

It is often difficult for teachers who have been raised with middle-class social values to appreciate the full extent and meaning of the deprivation of some of the pupils they teach. The daily lifestyle for many truants is one in which they receive little or no parental encouragement and support at home (especially for schooling), have few materials with which to undertake their schoolwork, have little space at home to call their own (in order, for example, to be able to do their homework), have few, if any, books, and live in an atmosphere where reading literature is unusual. They also participate in a social environment dominated by television and, not infrequently, alcohol.

Many studies on attendance have reported that the parents of truants tend to display anti-education values. As many truants live in families in which the father or mother or both were themselves truants (the truancy syndrome), this is hardly surprising. For example, charts of the number of visits made by parents to school have been devised. Invariably, these show that the parents of truants tend to make fewer visits to schools than the parents of good attenders.

There is however, another side to the equation. Recent studies are beginning to show that some parents are desperate to ensure that their children attend school regularly but are unable to do so. In some cases, parents are at their wits end and desperate for help. Family values and parenting skills are often much poorer than many of us sometimes appreciate. As children are maturing younger and younger these days, some parents find it very difficult to ensure that their twelve stone, six feet tall son leaves home on time for school regularly. This physical and emotional confrontation which can occur within some households over truancy and related school issues can be the cause of heated arguments between parent(s) and child.

The truth is that while a significantly high proportion of parents of truants condone the absence and collude in the falsification of absence notes to schools, a lot of the parents of truants are themselves desperate that their children do better in later life than they have managed themselves. This fact provides schools and the caring professions with hope. It shows that in the right set of circumstances, the parents of truants will co-operate with schools in attempting to improve the educational abilities and achievement of their offspring, and we will consider these possibilities further in Chapter 14.

Family life and truancy

Home factors which influence pupils in schools include:

1 Circumstances which force children to acquire adult status too early – either because of their domestic situation or for other reasons. Thereafter, school life can seem boring, irrelevant, petty and restrictive. Such attitudes often lead to withdrawal and conflict.
2 Well-integrated families who are notably anti-school, anti-authoritarian and anti-establishment. Sometimes these negative familial attitudes are supported by a prevailing neighbourhood culture which devalues schooling and overvalues alternative ideals like work, or fosters anti-social tendencies – sometimes through group identities.
3 Families which suffer from too much intra-familial friction such as unstable parental relationships (constant arguing), violence in the home, difficult sibling relationships and very poor parent–child relationships which can be hurtful, derisive, neglectful, punitive, harsh, overdemanding or characterised by minimal contact or affection. Signs of these difficulties include:

   (a) lax or inconsistent paternal discipline;
   (b) maternal inadequacy in the supervision of the offspring;
   (c) poor parent–child relationships, including indifference and hostility;
   (d) a dis-unified family in terms of corporate spirit and social and household relationships;
   (e) disagreements between parents about child rearing;
   (f) poor husband–wife relationships;
   (g) parents who disapprove of many traits (e.g. friends, hobbies, nightclubs) in their children;
   (h) mothers who feel unhappy in the community in which they live;

(i)   parents who are unable to control their tempers and who have a tendency to resort to angry, physical punishment when their children misbehave;

(j)   parents who belittle their own influence upon their children and who think that other children exerted bad influences upon their children;

(k)   parents whose leisure time is devoid of purposeful activity or includes few cultural or intellectual engagements;

(l)   parents who are not members of a church or only attend spasmodically;

(m) parents who are less well educated than the average population and, if employed, are in lower-level occupations of a semi-skilled or unskilled type.

Life-styles of persistent absentees

Relationships between home and school

Reid undertook a study of persistent school absenteeism, using Kelly's Repertory Grid technique with a one in three sample of 128 non-attenders in order to uncover original data on the individual 'lives' and 'problems' of a group of persistent absentees.

To illustrate the overall findings, potted social and educational histories of Alan and Diane are presented. These summaries indicate the types of data that were collected.

Alan

Alan's parents were divorced when he was eleven. Since that time, his home circumstances have deteriorated. Following the divorce Alan, his mother and sister were forced to sell their home in order to go and live on a nearby council estate. Despite all the efforts of Alan's mother, she has subsequently never been able to obtain regular employment. Consequently, her only means of support are provided by way of maintenance order, child benefit and income support.

During one of his interviews, Alan admitted that he had never been able to accept the finality of his parents' divorce. At one point, he made the following revealing statement: 'I get nasty if I see my father around town. When I get home, I seem to shout at everything and everyone'. In fact, Alan rarely sees or visits his father for a variety of reasons, including lack of paternal interest.

Alan's records show that since the divorce, his behaviour in school has drastically deteriorated. He was excluded from school for the first time after creating havoc in a lesson. On another occasion, a social worker found him 'mitching' at home with a 'few marks on his legs'. Her confidential report spoke of 'victimisation for unknown reasons by an unknown source – a case to be watched'.

The education welfare officer believes that Alan's mother wants her son to attend school regularly. He feels, however, that she is 'too weak to really do anything about it'. Privately, he considers that Alan's mother is grateful for the company of her son as she leads a very quiet existence. After one of the education welfare officer's visits to the home, Alan claimed that his mother had shaken him continually and told him that he mustn't miss school again. Apart from this, there is no evidence of any further action ever having been taken.

Throughout his interviews, Alan was convivial but pale and badly dressed. In appearance, he is tall and 'gangly' with a mass of pimples and uncombed hair. Mentally, Alan often appeared to be preoccupied and distressed. Sometimes it was difficult to communicate with him.

There can be little doubt that Alan's home circumstances have had and are having an adverse effect upon his progress in school both socially and academically. Prior to the divorce, Alan's performance in school was officially described as 'slow but consistent' by his form teacher. Two years after the divorce, Alan was reported as being 'sullen, deceitful, lazy and a dreadful attender' by a different form teacher. On the same report, the headmaster commented that 'he is unlikely to achieve anything until he starts to attend school regularly. His attendance this year has been shocking and I must say that I think he is being very foolish'.

An examination of Alan's grid shows the very high esteem in which he still holds his father, despite the divorce. The subsequent trauma of life at home without his father has proved a stumbling block which he has been unable to face or overcome either at home or at school. It is also clear that he sees his teachers as being 'dominating', 'strict' and 'showing off' while at the same time, paradoxically, he considers them to be 'helpful'.

Diane

Diane's childhood was enormously complicated. She was born illegitimately, one of seven children including stepbrothers and stepsisters. By the age of fifteen, she had had two stepfathers, both of whom had subsequently divorced her mother. In addition, throughout her childhood, Diane experienced a number of unfortunate traumas. On one occasion in her early teens, for example, she was 'placed with her grandmother for safety' on the advice of a social worker. On another, Diane's general practitioner expressed his serious concern about her 'psychological welfare' after she had voluntarily been to see him because she claimed she was having a 'nervous breakdown'. After the visit, the doctor reported Diane's circumstances to the social services. This eventually led to a multi-disciplinary conference being called to discuss her plight. The confidential report written at the time referred to Diane as a 'mental cruelty case'.

At various points during the fieldwork, Diane gave a succession of reasons for her non-attendance at school. These included: 'Mainly because my parents didn't care whether I went to school or not'; 'Because my elder sister didn't go to school'; Because I was frightened of the teachers'. In fact, Diane's history of absenteeism began in her primary school. Despite having a reasonable IQ, she received a number of adverse reports on her behaviour during her earliest school-days. For example, a succession of comments on her primary school report referred to her as having frequent bouts of unruly conduct and being a poor attender. Diane claimed that she missed school the first time because of the jibes of some of the other children in her form. She said that they made detrimental remarks about her personal circumstances at home which offended and upset her. Diane's childhood was punctuated by deprivation and uncertainty at home and by hostility and confrontation at school.

The really significant point about Diane's case (like so many others in the study) is that she makes allowances for her home circumstances but not for her teachers. This trend is highlighted by the following statements, which she made at various points during the fieldwork.

> *First statement* 'All the teachers are very distant from me. They've got to share their feelings with so many other pupils that they haven't got any time for one person . . . I dislike most of the teachers. They're all the same. They're all mad on the use of the word "good". Be "good" in class. Be a "good" attender. Be a "good" girl. They don't believe you're a real person . . . that you can have real problems. They fail to understand your feelings. They don't care. All they think about is themselves and their work. Nothing else matters . . . it's always your fault – never theirs. When I was away from school and missed my exams they all blamed me – none of them even bothered to ask me why I had been away [a note showed she was supposed to have had flu]. They all assumed I had done it on purpose . . .'

> *Second statement* 'I hate school. Even when I come to school I hate it. There's nothing about it which can make me like it . . . The teachers don't speak to you unless they're shouting at you . . . If you explain something to them they just get angry . . . What they say goes. Some teachers remind me of what Hitler must have been like . . . Nothing you say or do matters . . . It's only them . . .'

> *Third statement* 'Teachers should be more like social workers and try to help you. What more can I say? They just don't know how to treat children as people. Schools should change. There should be more facilities at break and lunch-times . . . There should be less favouritism . . . Teachers only speak to the high fliers, not the less able . . . the way they treat the less able children is terrible.'

The most revealing feature of Diane's grid is the dichotomy between the constructs chosen to describe her mother and her teachers. For example, the key constructs chosen to describe the teachers were: 'strangers', 'poor communicators', 'outsiders', 'unable to take a joke', 'uncaring', 'remote', and 'untrustworthy'. By contrast, her mother was described as 'kind', 'lovely', 'beautiful' and 'caring'.

Alan and Diane provide fairly typical examples of the various social, educational and psychological circumstances of absentees and truants. In no way do they represent the worst cases. What their profiles aptly highlight is the link between some of the social, psychological and institutional factors in the lives of individual absentees about which we currently have too little information. The general picture which emerges is one of a struggle for identification, survival and affection both at home and at school.

The findings are in some ways less important than their implications for teachers, social workers and educational psychologists. If it could be proved that raising absentees' and truants' self-concepts (as and when necessary) would lead to an improvement in their attendance, or forestall certain at-risk pupils from starting to miss school, then a considerable step forward would have been taken. One way to change and overcome the attitudes of certain absentees towards their schools and schooling is to raise their self-concepts. But how can this be achieved?

The simple and pessimistic answer is with difficulty, given the present organisation and ethos of schools. Many schools are simply not in the business of helping those who have rejected the aims and objectives which they are offering. It is a paradoxical situation. The responsibility for raising the self-concepts of pupils involved in illegal actions rests with agents of an institution which the truants have already rejected. So the prognosis for such intervention, unless sensitively handled, is that conflict is likely, especially as potential and hardened truants require understanding not coercion.

Let us consider briefly a statement made by Jason, a notorious 14-year-old truant from a large comprehensive school in South Wales.

'I guess I just gave up in the end. Every time I came to school, I got told off about my appearance, behaviour and work . . . Someone would send for me and tell me off again, usually threaten me if I didn't improve I'd be suspended. Then I'd go back to class and be told off for the same things again . . . Then it was my work. I'd got so far behind in everything, but nobody said let me help you catch up. It was just "carry on" all the time. When I stayed at home, I was in trouble with my mother. In the end, I gave up. Nobody seemed to understand me or care. I decided the best thing I could do was to go to the park and meet my mates – regular like. At least they were having the same problems. I wanted to learn – but couldn't. Finally, we all said we'd never go back to school but keep one another company instead. Life seemed less of a problem after that . . . at least for a while . . . Then the Boardy-man called at our house and told my mother that if I didn't go back to school, she'd have to go to court. That night my father shouted at me like never before.

After that, I tried to go back to school, but I kept being told off and getting Ds and Es. Well, that's how it is all the time. I try to come so as not to have to go back to court. But when I do, it's a waste of time. I'm in a kind of trap . . . No one ever helps me.'

Jason's case is not unusual. Empirical evidence suggests that many persistent absentees feel extremely sad about their plight, almost as if they are trapped in some kind of truancy syndrome. Once they start to stay away, they get further and further behind in their school work and it becomes progressively more difficult for them to return to school – even after the original 'thrill' of deliberately skipping school has vanished. When teachers are unsympathetic to the needs of truants, it is likely that they will inadvertently reinforce the initial deviant conduct which they are trying to overcome. Better teacher–pupil relationships are absolutely essential if the self-esteem of truants is to be raised.

Schools and teachers need to develop new enlightened policies if they are going to combat successfully truancy in their institutions and many will have to change their overt negative attitudes towards truants. They have to be prepared to devise more individual treatment programmes for truants. These schemes should be practical, sympathetic and therapeutic. Such programmes should make it much easier for truants to return to their schools on a regular basis without the risk of further conflict as soon as they enter the school building.

Some of these measures could be quite simple – personal tutor schemes (the choice of person is critical), mentoring, additional help with reading and writing, sympathetic exclusion from certain lessons, bonus schemes for good attendance and general encouragement and praise whenever an opportunity arises. All of these and other schemes can be successful, especially on a short-term basis. Unfortunately, these suggestions are not welcomed in every quarter as they place the onus firmly on to the shoulders of the staff in schools.

The ideas are not new. Their value has already been recognised in previous studies on deviant groups. The Home Office Research Unit for example, proposed courses on 'Self-concept Therapy' to give girls in trouble more self-respect and confidence.

Likewise, Hamblin has argued that if schools are to begin to combat and eradicate persistent school absenteeism, then they need to start to understand and eliminate those processes which build and foster negative identities in pupils and which reinforce avoidance behaviour. This means that different types of illegitimate absence require different strategies. School policies need to be flexible, finding the right solution for each individual pupil.

There is no doubt that many absentees make clear-cut distinctions between their parents and their teachers, usually unfavourable to the latter. This seems to happen even when confidential social reports show that individual absentees have been ill or badly treated at home. The absentees' responses suggest that they see their teachers as being very different from their parents. While it is possible that some absentees make favourable responses about their parents because of the natural loyalties, which are commonly associated with family ties, it is interesting that the teachers do not receive the same benefit of the doubt. Teachers, social workers and educational psychologists are out-siders; parents are insiders. This shows the great skill which professionals have to employ if successful outcomes are to be achieved. If teachers want to gain credibility with truants, then they may have to be prepared to take con-siderable interest in an individual truant over a fairly long period. Truants must feel confident that they can trust the professional to deal with their 'problems' in as empathetic a manner as possible. It is not easy to acquire this skill without a great deal of thought and hard work.

Unfortunately, the findings obtained from the repertory grids show another equally important dimension. There was a tendency for all teachers in the school to be tarred by the same brush. The absentees did not appear to make any allowances, even when it was known that individual teachers (frequently a form teacher) had bent over backwards to help or be kind to them. Most teachers were seen, therefore, as representatives of unfavoured and rejected institutions whose job was to promote learning and good attendance, two processes which the absentees had already disregarded. Hence, teachers (and other professionals) have to be prepared for the possibility that their most skilful attempts at intervention will be rejected by absentees without good reason, perhaps even when some 'progress' has been made. Teachers should not be too disappointed if and when this does happen and certainly they should not take it personally. From the opposite perspective, and despite all the mitigating circumstances, the findings obtained from the grids are a condemnation of the pastoral work of teachers. Clearly, very few teachers enamoured themselves to the absentees, or eased their problems in school.

There can be little wonder, therefore, that a high proportion of absentees associate teachers with failure and conflict. In their eyes, this is justified.

Finally, the evidence from the study showed:

(a) many teachers seem only to punish poor attenders rather than attempt to re-integrate them;
(b) few schools have appropriate re-integration strategies for non-attenders or other 'at risk' pupils (e.g. those who have been off school for a while, sick);
(c) a high proportion of the absentees in the sample associated their teachers with failure and conflict. In turn, this probably helps to increase their alienation towards school, lower their academic self-concepts and general levels of self-esteem and worsen their behaviour when they do return to school. It is all part of a vicious circle.

This research suggests that some pupils from deprived home backgrounds who are already socially excluded because of their social class and environ-mental origins are having their educational disadvantages compounded by action taken by schools. Most truants from deprived social backgrounds are fed on a regular diet of failure in school. To prevent and overcome truancy, pupils need to be made to feel wanted and to be successful. This is the nub of the problem. How to make social and educationally disadvantaged pupils feel wanted and needed – made to realise that their attendance matters – and if they attend and try hard they, in turn, can make a success of their lives.

5 Causes of truancy: psychological indices

We have very little understanding of the psychological impact events in school can make on the emotional, intellectual and behavioural state of our pupils; or why these effects are disproportionately worse for some pupils than others. All we know is that some pupils who manifest certain traits (e.g. low self-concepts) tend to miss school rather more than others who do not. For this reason, Tables 5.1 to 5.3 provide a possible check list, neither exhaustive or all-embracing, of certain warning or tell-tale signs for which teachers and other caring professionals need to be on the look out. Any one of these comparatively minor warning signs could be masking much more serious problems or indeed, be a 'hidden' plea for help. Research to date indicates that persistent absentees and/or truants are more likely to be delinquent, 'maladjusted', have lower general levels of self-esteem and academic self-concepts, be more anxious, and have lower career aspirations than the normal school-age population.

Delinquency and truancy

The link between delinquency and truancy has long been established; the first published study took place in 1915. Since then, numerous researchers have reported that like truants, delinquents often come from an unfavourable and deprived home background, characterised by multiple adversities, and tend to have well known anti-social and deviant lifestyles in and out of school. Future research may be able to show that delinquent truants are more likely to come from the category of institutional truants rather than from the traditional or psychological groups. Research suggests that the interaction which often takes place in adverse home backgrounds can produce anti-social, anti-educational and anti-establishment people.

Research conducted in the USA has found that delinquent behaviour within school can be a major reason for truancy. In Philadelphia, for example, one study reported that a large percentage of youngsters felt unsafe during the time spent both in travelling to school and on the return journey. In fact, a majority of parents in the study were fearful that their children could be injured or robbed while at school.

In New York and Chicago, studies have reported that many teachers feel unsafe in their schools. Cases of teacher assault, even rape, are not unusual. There are scores of cases of teachers being assaulted on their way to school, on playground duty, and while teaching in classes during the day and in the evenings. There are reported cases of teachers being knifed or shot by delinquent pupils. Even in Britain, the number of cases of teachers being assaulted in some conurbations has increased in the last twenty years, as has the amount of publicity which has been given to this topic by the media.

Wayne

Wayne, 15, a pupil with a long history of absenteeism and disruptive behaviour in school, has been 'suspended' on four separate occasions including once for striking a teacher and once for 'repeated verbal abuse and foul language in class without provocation'. In addition, he has appeared in court for truancy, theft and trespassing on private property.

Wayne's father has a long history of unemployment following a serious accident at work which left him partially disabled. Except for a small disability pension, child benefit and income support, the family has few means of support, although Wayne's mother has a cleaning job for two hours a day.

A report from a social worker described Wayne as being 'out of control at home. He is constantly in trouble with his neighbours because of his aggressive nature and language. He is widely suspected on the estate of being responsible for more than a little of the considerable vandalism in the neighbourhood'.

At the end of the Children's Behaviour Questionnaire, Wayne's form teacher wrote 'it is better for the entire form as well as the staff when he is away. He is a born troublemaker'.

The following extract is indicative of the way Wayne spoke about his school and the staff during several interviews:

Wayne: If I had one wish it would be that someone would do Mr X in or I could get my revenge. He's always had it in for me, ever since I first came here. One day he walked into our class and took me down to his office and punished me because he said I started a riot in Miss Y's lesson. He and everyone else knew there were lots of other people involved but it was only me he punished. Always me. Every time he sees me, I know I'm in trouble. I hate him.

Researcher: Wouldn't you say that with your school record he needs to give you special attention?

Wayne: Maybe. But he's not fair. None of the teachers here are. Once they've got you down as a villain that's the end of it.

Researcher: Then why don't you try and change and improve your conduct in school?

Wayne: I've tried. Several times. You've no idea what it's like being me. Every day is a problem – at home with my parents, out on the estate and here. Especially here.

Researcher: Surely then you really need to change for your own sake?

Wayne: I can't.

Researcher: Why not?

Wayne: I don't know. Maybe it's too late. Anyway I loathe this place. All it's ever got me is trouble. Mr X in particular is always out to get me. He taunts me when I come back to school. He tries to make me say I was away with a cold and produce a sick note. He knows I can't. Can you imagine what it's like in our class? What would be the use of sitting quietly all the time like most of the girls? We never do anything decent. All we ever do is copy from the blackboard or fill in stupid work sheets. And what do we copy? Rubbish. It's just filling in time. I'm better off when I'm not here. At least I don't get punished for that and I don't have to put up with the like of him [Mr X].

Most commentators agree that very few children are disruptive all the time and that most have a good relationship with at least one teacher. Chronic absentees and disruptive pupils, however, generally have poorer teacher–pupil relationships than most.

Research shows that pupils prefer teachers who are relatively strict but fair and approachable and who show an interest in them. Teachers who are regarded as 'soft', ineffective, rigid, harsh, uncaring and remote, and who incite physical confrontations, can provoke deep resentment which may lead to indiscipline and disruption.

Attempting to re-integrate non-conforming and disruptive pupils into the norms of school life can be a hazardous exercise. Persuading disruptive absentees to return to school, for example, can lead to stormy scenes of confrontation. Similarly, pupils who absent themselves from lessons, but remain on the school premises, do not always welcome being forced to return to their classrooms.

One trap to avoid is giving disruptive pupils 'special' privileges in school (official or otherwise) in order to achieve some degree of success in controlling them. If this happens, some conforming pupils may well be unable to comprehend the differences in standards expected between them and their disenchanted peers and this in turn can lead to a lowering of morale throughout the school. In schools where pupil–teacher confrontation is the norm, constant disputes can lead to a lowering of staff as well as pupil morale.

Teachers need to be able to distinguish between genuine pleas for help from those truants and absentees whose home backgrounds, social and educational circumstances require understanding and positive remedial assistance and those

whose non-attendance is but one manifestation of aggressive, anti-social conduct which often lies outside the scope of many of them to counteract. Above
all, teachers need to attempt to maintain control in class through empathetic
and positive rather than harsh and provocative means. The worst thing
teachers can do is to be too weak because this plays into the hands of the
'agents provocateurs' who will thrive on their ineptitude.

Formal sanctions and disruptive behaviour

When exceptional outbursts of disruptive behaviour occur in schools, headteachers have two major 'weapons' at their disposal. The first of these is
exclusion which is the ultimate sanction and is used very sparingly indeed.
Although exclusion is legally permissible, some local education authorities
attempt to 'dissuade' headteachers from using this option. Exclusion means
expelling pupils and removing their names from the official school roll which
can create an administrative headache for LEAs in making alternative, often
short-term, educational provision.

Exclusion remains the ultimate sanction of fee-paying public schools with
which it is more commonly associated. Expelling pupils from private schools
is a much easier process and sometimes invoked for comparatively minor
offences such as smoking or drinking because of its deterrent effect upon the
conforming majority.

Suspension, or fixed-term exclusion, is a procedure which operates closely to
exclusion and has a similar effect upon recipients. Suspending pupils means
that they are forbidden to return to school or enter the school premises until
the sanction has been lifted. Moreover, there is little possibility of a pupil
being readmitted in the short term until the headteacher and LEA are satisfied
that readmission will not interfere with or endanger staff or other pupils or
normal school life.

Headteachers are obliged to notify parents, the chief education officer and
school governors that suspension proceedings against a pupil have been implemented. The formal act of suspension is incorporated in Schools' Articles of
Government, subject to safeguards contained in the 1959 School Regulations
that pupils can only be excluded or refused admission on reasonable grounds.
Appeal procedures against suspension are available. The kind of situation
which warrants suspension is shown in the following extract.

Jane

> Jane was participating in a fourth year French conversation class being
> taken by Miss D. When the teacher turned to write a few words on the
> blackboard, Jane sneaked forward and emptied the contents of Miss D's
> handbag on to the floor. The teacher turned round and ordered Jane to
> pick them up. She refused and repeatedly used foul language to Miss D.
> After the teacher had retrieved her own handbag, she was suddenly and

unexpectedly attacked by Jane and knocked to the floor. In the ensuing struggle, Miss D had her arm broken. Jane was pulled off the teacher by other members of the form and subsequently suspended; a long drawn-out process to remedy the immediate situation and redress the harm done to Miss D was started.

Suspension or fixed-term exclusion is normally used to provide a cooling-off period. It also gives schools time to plan new strategies for dealing with particularly difficult pupils.

Headteachers are empowered to use suspensions under conditions laid down by the 1986 Education Act and the 1936 Public Health Act. The average length of time for which suspensions operate vary by authority and school ranging from, say, one day to several weeks, although the latter is rare. Three days is an average amount of time.

Ronald

Ronald rarely attends school. When he does, he often remains on the premises but out of the classroom. At morning break and lunchtime, he persistently picks on younger pupils in the playground. This has led to a number of confrontations with staff on duty, a deputy head and other pupils. During one of the deliberations, he repeatedly swore at a female teacher. After she had returned to her own classroom to take a lesson on technology (home economics), Ronald appeared outside the room on the grass verge and threw a stone through the window. He was immediately suspended. A letter was then sent to his parents inviting them to see the headteacher to discuss his behaviour and the conditions for his readmittance to the school.

A few pupils graduate from periods of suspension to longer-term exclusion. Frequently, however, a bout of exclusion is sufficient warning, especially in cases where the parents co-operate with the school. In extreme cases, exclusion has little effect upon pupils and/or parents as, for instance, in Ronald's case. He returned to school a week after being suspended, remained for four days before his absenteeism re-commenced.

Exclusions and suspensions are not merely penalties against pupils and warnings to parents. They can be used by some headteachers as ploys to obtain renewed interest in a case as these measures indicate to LEAs, parents and outside agencies the seriousness with which the school regards the pupils' conduct.

Reasons for suspension often include assault on teachers and pupils and serious acts of vandalism against school property. Reasons for exclusion can include verbal abuse and insolence, persistent disobedience or breaches of the peace in school, perpetual or isolated instances of disruptive behaviour, refusal to accept and/or obey school rules and major breaches of school discipline.

According to headteachers, their reasons for suspending pupils often include the safety of staff and pupils, the deterrent effect on other pupils, and in order to make the LEA provide an alternative form of education for the pupil. Some headteachers have been accused of being too willing to suspend children living in care in the belief that the social services will make alternative provision for them.

During periods of suspension, pupils are in a state of limbo and are often liable to get into further trouble or seek employment illegally. One study reported that 70 per cent of excluded or suspended pupils receive alternative educational provision or return to their original schools within an eight-week period. By contrast, periods of suspension may operate for much longer. In one London borough the average delay before any kind of part- or full-time provision was made for suspended pupils amounted to three to four months and for nearly a quarter of the cases took six months or longer. Delaying tactics are often a useful weapon in the armoury of local education authorities.

Home tuition can be given to excluded pupils or fixed-term exclusions of more than 15 days after September 1999 under conditions laid down in the 1944 Education Act but is to be used very sparingly. About half of suspended pupils receive home tuition either alone or in groups. However, this applied to only 12 per cent in another study of suspended and excluded pupils.

Statistics on outcomes for suspended and excluded pupils are fairly revealing. Half of one LEA's suspended pupils did not receive any further full-time educational provision again before they were legally entitled to leave school. This was partly due to their age at the time of suspension and suggests that some headteachers are more liable to use this sanction as pupils enter their mid-teens. It is probably also attributable to the fact that some pupils become bolder in their disruptive behaviour at school as they mature. Research into suspended pupils has shown that a quarter are eventually readmitted to their original school while a fifth never receive any formal education again. The remainder tend to be transferred to other schools including special schools, centres for disruptive pupils, or other forms of alternative education. Permanently excluded pupils normally do not return to their original school.

Early explanations for disruptive conduct centred on family and personal factors, although the search for school aspects has gained momentum. One early study investigated 41 children excluded from school in Edinburgh. The researchers examined the personal characteristics of the children, their family backgrounds, IQs and behaviour as measured by standardised tests. They found that excluded children tend to come from lower-class origins; live in homes which experience or have experienced marital discord; manifest personality disorders and are less able intellectually. The researchers suggested that exclusion is the culmination of a series of aggressive acts by seriously disturbed children from stressful and socially deprived familial backgrounds.

Another study examined 58 pupils suspended from schools in Sheffield and found that both the pupils and their parents had histories of illness. The children were likely to have been in care at one time or another, to have low IQs and to be seriously backward in reading. Contrary to the study in Edinburgh, and cases of absenteeism, the Sheffield research team concluded that social class and socio-economic disadvantage were not reliable predictors of suspension rates.

A third study compared the personality and behaviour of children excluded from school with their peers who were not. This study reported that there were no significant personality differences between the groups as measured by standardised tests. Excluded children, however, did score higher on certain tests which measured maladjusted behaviour. The researcher suggested that some disruptive pupils' behaviour in schools is more influenced by their desire to maintain their position in their local sub-culture rather than by anything else.

A fourth study reported that a third of the sample of suspended pupils had longstanding differences with particular teachers. The study noted the tendency for minor acts of disruption to escalate in schools leading to suspension. Several investigations have reported that the behaviour of some suspended pupils improves following school transfers.

Some schools frequently use their own internal measures rather than formal sanctions for coping and/or dealing with their potential suspended or excluded pupils. One such practice is personal tutor schemes. This often operates by technically removing or suspending disruptive pupils from all or certain lessons and giving them a special or separate timetable, room and member/s of staff to look after them. These schemes can sometimes last for days, weeks or a whole term. Very little is known about these measures and their effectiveness.

When teaching, the author once had a pupil attached to him for the entire day for a period of several weeks. He attended every lesson I taught acting as a kind of co-helper. He was given his own special assignments which, naturally, were different from those undertaken in my regular classes. We stuck so close together during this period that he even wore my cricket cap in school matches and followed me around when on duty at breaks. Unfortunately, within two days of the practice ceasing, he was suspended for threatening behaviour towards another member of staff.

Like so many innovative schemes, it is hard to know when to return a deviant to the fold. Sometimes schools have no option but to try their own measures with difficult pupils as the demand for placement in special units, both off and on site, generally greatly exceeds the supply.

Comparisons between non-attenders and disrupters

A number of comparisons between formal sanctions used with non-attenders and disruptive pupils can be made.

1   Formal sanctions for dealing with both absentees and disrupters are marked by conflicts of interest between caring and punitive actions. This is why

such pupils so often find it hard to relate to their teachers and social workers as professionals have to castigate and help non-conformers at differing times. Some pupils must become very confused by these two extremes.

2   Sanctions aimed at overcoming severe disruptive conduct normally seek to remove offenders from classrooms and/or schools in order to give teachers and other pupils some respite. By contrast, legal proceedings for truancy have the reverse object.

3   Fixed-term exclusion and permanent exclusions for disruptive behaviour are carried out at the discretion and instigation of the school. Conversely, the outcome for truancy is entirely in the hands of the courts.

4   Decision-making processes in formal proceedings used against both truants and disrupters are characterised by their variance, an idiosyncrasy which often borders on arbitrariness to the eyes of untrained observers.

5   Non-attendance cases usually rely heavily on school and home background reports. Generally speaking, adverse familial backgrounds, social deprivation and poor educational attainment are three features which stand out in truancy cases. The evidence in instances of fixed-term exclusion and permanent exclusion, however, is mixed. Some research suggests that excluded pupils have similar social and home backgrounds to absentees and truants. By contrast, other research reports that pupils' chances of exclusion are related as much, if not more, to the schools they attend, as any familial, stress or constitutional factors within the pupils themselves.

The end of the line: young offenders

The two cases of Craig and Jason are fairly extreme. They depict pupils whom teachers and schools find difficult to contain, who require skilled specialist help from external agencies, and who have graduated from the disruptive truant stage to delinquency and young offender status. Craig is atypical. He comes from an affluent family background, attended a private fee-paying day school and only really started displaying disaffected and disruptive behaviour at home and at school at the age of fifteen, partially in response to a specific discovery.

Jason is more typical of cases described in the literature. He is the eldest son of a chronically disabled father. He comes from a poor and deprived home and social background; a member of a disadvantaged working-class family with its inevitable bickering and arguments and usual crop of misunderstandings born of strife and struggle for human survival. The family live in a small council home dependent upon income support and a war disablement pension. Unlike Craig, Jason has openly shown his hostility towards schooling from the age of eleven onwards. Both Craig and Jason were part of a study of young offenders undertaken by the author.

Craig

Craig is nineteen. He is a young offender. He is a tall, well spoken boy with a faint moustache. Before entering prison, his main interests were cars and rugby. Since starting his sentence, he has taken up bodybuilding. At the time of writing, he has served seven months of a 2-year sentence after being caught in possession of a stolen motor bike. Originally, Craig was stopped on suspicion by a police officer for displaying false number-plates. After being cautioned, Craig reacted so badly and violently that he attacked the officer causing him actual grievous bodily harm. In fact, the officer was taken by ambulance to hospital where he was detained for a considerable period while his injuries healed and he overcame the shock caused by the ferocity of the attack.

This is Craig's story told in his own words in response to a series of questions.

Craig: I suppose I first got into trouble, real bother at the age of 15. One night when I was at home my mother called me into the kitchen to have a chat with me. For some reason, I can't understand why, she told me that I was adopted, that my brothers and sisters were really foster brothers and sisters and I was a foster child. I don't know why but I couldn't take it. I was really angry. Fancy being told at fifteen that you haven't got any real parents and no one knows who your real parents are. It blew my mind. I couldn't grasp the situation.

         After that everything changed. I couldn't speak or look at my father. Well, sort of father. I decided to get my own back on them. They should have told me the truth from the very beginning, when I was 5 or something. How would you feel if you discovered that your two younger brothers and sisters belonged to your parents and you didn't like?

Researcher: What happened then?

Craig: For a while I couldn't believe the news. It left me cold. It numbed my mind. I didn't know what to do. At first, I didn't do anything too stupid apart from starting to truant. I couldn't face school any longer. Then when I went back, I began cheeking the teachers and disrupting their classes. One day the deputy head called me into his office and told me off for my lack of enthusiasm. Things went from bad to worse from there. I got suspended from school for truanting and being disruptive in class. The school couldn't understand it. I was due to sit nine mock GCSEs that term and there I was being suspended. My father was furious. We had some terrible rows at home – really unpleasant. One day I decided I'd had enough. I told my parents I was going to run away. My father said that if I ran away I shouldn't ever come back. So that's what happened.

Researcher: How long did this phase last?

Craig: About three or four weeks. Later, I got in touch with my grand-parents to see if they could help me. I was fed up of living rough. They put me in touch with a social worker. She managed to get my parents to agree to a trial reconciliation so I went back home. This only lasted for three days. I couldn't stand it. The atmosphere was awful. My father ignored me. He pretended not to hear when I spoke to him. So I left home again. Then I went into care.

Researcher: What happened then?

Craig: After that my social worker arranged for me to be transferred to a state school. I didn't mind this. I went there to take my exams but never did. When I left school I went on to the dole.

Researcher: How did you find your new school?

Craig: The school was all right, I suppose. I knew most of the boys there from playing rugby. I used to get on with all the lads from my first school because of sport, rugby like. I was a good wing forward and in the school first fifteen by the fourth year. But I had other problems at the time.

Researcher: What were these?

Craig: I kept getting transferred from one home to another.

Researcher: Why?

Craig: Mainly because I couldn't settle and I kept on getting into trouble. This carried on until I was aged eighteen. Then I left care. Dr Barnardo's agreed to help me out and set me up in a bedsit where I stayed for one year.

Researcher: Is this when you started getting into a lot of trouble?

Craig: No. It began before this. When I was in care I got prosecuted for trespassing. Honestly, I really didn't know I was trespassing at the time.

Researcher: So what happened when you were in your bedsit?

Craig: Well I had to make a living. I wanted to take my GCSEs and 'A' levels and join either the Air Force or the Army but no one would take a criminal, would they? So I began to look after myself.

Researcher: What did you do?

Craig: I stole and handled stolen goods.

Researcher: Such as?

Craig: Crates of beer, cassettes – you name it.

Researcher: Is this what led you to being here?

Craig: Yes. I saw the bike. I liked it and wanted it for my own. Then I decided I had to have it, so I stole it.

Researcher: Did you ever try contacting your parents for advice or help?

Craig: One day I rang my parents from a coin box. My father answered the phone. I spoke to him but he never answered once. He knew it was me. I kept trying to speak to him for five minutes but it was no use so eventually I put the phone down again.

Researcher: Did your schools try to help you?

Craig: Neither of them cared. They were only worried about how I affected the other boys. After the deputy head at my first school found out that I began running a protection racket he gave up on me. The other school didn't really know me, did they? They were only helping my social worker out.

Researcher: Looking back, how do you think your circumstances could have been improved for you?

Craig: What do you mean?

Researcher: If you started life all over again, what would you like to be different?

Craig: I'd have liked a better relationship with my father. He isolated himself from me. He never took me out anywhere. He always left me behind when the family visited my grandparents. I wasn't like a son to him. When I was eleven and twelve my mother and I had a lot of problems with my father. They nearly got divorced because of it. She took me away with her, leaving my two younger brothers and two younger sisters behind. We went and stayed in a hotel for a while. Then we went back. But it was never the same for me after that.

Researcher: Is there anything else you would change?

Craig: I wish my father could say 'sorry' to me and I had it in me to say 'sorry' to him. But neither of us have. The social worker says it's a classic breakdown of a family situation. She says it happens all the time.

Researcher: What do you think the future holds for you?

Craig: Not much, I suppose. I'm hoping to start work on a new project soon with motor bikes. My probation officer said he'll try and fix it for me when I get out. I also hope to pass my test so I can get a licence.

Researcher: Will you go back and see your parents or continue your education?

Craig: I won't go and see my parents. You have to understand. It was my father who put the clamps on me. He wanted me to grow up to help him in his business. When I worked for him he didn't pay me much. I suppose I could go back as an employee provided he didn't want me as a son and I lived away. If I don't get parole I'll ask to be transferred from here and take my City and Guilds in Mechanics. That should come in handy.

Researcher: Do you miss your brothers and sisters?

Craig:	No, they're mostly too young. My eldest brother is very different from me. I like sport and cars. He hates sport and cars. He likes sitting around doing nothing except watching television.
Researcher:	Who do you blame for what has happened to you – yourself, your parents or your school?
Craig:	In a way everybody. Mostly me I suppose. I couldn't handle finding out that I was illegitimate. But my father is also to blame. He should have told me the truth from the very beginning instead of acting differently to me from the rest all the time.
Researcher:	What about your school?
Craig:	I just took it out on them. It wasn't their fault. I wanted revenge on my parents, especially my father. It was easier to take it out on people at school than anywhere else.
Researcher:	Do you regret this now?
Craig:	I suppose so. But you'd have to be me to understand. Everything could have been so different.
Researcher:	Do you think it's too late now?
Craig:	Maybe. Who knows? I expect so.

Jason

Jason is eighteen. He is also a young offender. He is currently on remand awaiting sentence for shoplifting. He is asking the magistrate for community work but fears he may get another six months as he has already served one sentence of twelve months in prison for burglary.

Jason is one of life's born losers, repeatedly in trouble, weak and with little chance of breaking the trend. His pimpled face and soft spoken voice belie his well-developed criminal brain. This is his story. It is a tale of disaffection eventually turning sour.

Jason has three younger sisters and one younger brother. The family live in a council house on a notorious housing estate somewhere in South Wales. Jason's father is disabled following a serious war wound which severely affects his mobility. His father has never worked since his injury and the family rely on a war disablement pension and income support for their means of support. His mother has never worked.

At the age of ten, Jason was referred to the social services for the first time because he was unable to get on with the rest of his family, especially his father. For him, domestic life was nothing but a series of quarrels and bickering.

Between the age of ten and fifteen, he had a succession of some seven or eight social workers. Some left his case after a short while to take up new posts but others asked to be taken off his case because of his repeated insults towards them. 'I was too much for them. Anyway, they weren't a lot of help', he stated proudly.

For the last three years, he has had the same male social worker. 'He's much better. He doesn't do much for me really, except find out about things'.

Jason began truanting at the age of eleven. He never adjusted to life at his local comprehensive.

> 'Things didn't seem to work out for me. The school put me in the wrong class straight away. I was made to go into a class with a lot of dumbos – kids who were much duller than me. That didn't give me a chance, did it?'

At first, Jason enjoyed the thrill of missing school. Then boredom crept in and he returned to school occasionally, sometimes for the odd lesson, day or week. But these instances became increasingly rare.

When present at school, he was always in trouble for not wearing school uniform or having the requisite sports kit but mainly for disrupting nearly every class he attended.

> 'I didn't like the teachers, the lessons, going to school – anything. I never got on with any of the teachers. I got punished a few times but it had no effect. What did I care. One day I told the deputy head to — off.'

This was the cause of his first suspension but not his last. In five short years of secondary education, Jason was excluded for twelve months and sent to three other schools, none of which could handle him. Eventually, he always returned to his first school.

> 'I had one decent form teacher who taught me about maths. I still love maths today. Maths is much better than English. One year I turned up for my maths exam at school but none of the rest. The other teachers taught me what I learnt in junior school – kids stuff. It used to make me sick. So I decided to pay them back. I used to walk into a lesson, sit down and then walk out again. Sometimes I'd walk into the middle of a lesson, shout out and then leave.
>
> Some of the teachers, I really hated. I told one woman to piss off and mind her . . . business. I remember that because she never gave me any cheek again.
>
> I used to go and sit at the back of the class and talk to my mates. If any teachers said anything to me I'd give them hell. If they called out "shut up" or "be quiet", I'd tell them where to go. It was great. Some of them got fed up and ignored me. Then I'd talk louder and fool around even more. I was never quiet.'

Not surprisingly, Jason's turbulent school history was a succession of truancy and suspension. Ironically, however, it was not his truancy which first brought him to the attention of the courts.

'I started shoplifting on my own. Then a group of us started pinching things together. It began as something to do, a kind of dare. Later, I found I couldn't stop it and it has become a way of life.'

Jason left school at sixteen. Since then, he has had two short periods of employment.

'I got my first job through a Government Scheme. It didn't last long. I got sacked. My next full-time job was as a sales assistant for — (a well-known double glazing firm). I got sacked after I robbed the manager's house of his video.'

Jason himself believes it will be difficult to change his life-style and sees little prospect of betterment in the years which lie ahead.

'I went to the juvenile court about forty or fifty times for shoplifting. Since leaving school, I've been to the magistrate's court for shoplifting and burglary twice. It's become my way of life. You have to survive, don't you?'

In fact, when out of prison Jason does not fare very well. He mainly lives rough in bed and breakfast establishments, flats, empty houses or with his 'mates' whenever he can.

'I never go home. I might do one day. I'm too much trouble for my parents. After my brother was sent to Borstal for shoplifting, it was the end. They never want to see me again. I think my parents got fed up of the police calling back and forth to the house all the time.'

Jason has adjusted well to prison life. In his first term of imprisonment he obtained a distinction in his maths City and Guilds 1 examination. He is very proud of his achievement.

'It's just as good as any GCSE or "A" level. I might take my City and Guilds 2 in maths if the magistrate sends me down again.'

Inside prison, Jason mainly watches television in his leisure time. He plays the odd game of 'pool' or table tennis to occupy his mind. He has strong views about education and his parents.

'I didn't get on with people at school – teachers, that is. And I couldn't stand my parents. So I decided for spite to get them back, to get them fined. That's why I started truanting. My best friend felt the same. He got his parents much bigger fines than me. I could never get taken to court for truancy but he did.

Education is a waste of time. In the prison all we do is rubbish. There's nothing formally organised. We don't have any normal lessons like maths and English. I wish I could do more maths. One hour a week is not enough. We need more relief from our cells. We don't learn enough.'

In fact, under the terms of their sentences, Craig and Jason receive a minimum of one hour a day of compulsory education. Young offenders on remand are not obliged to take education classes but in practice most elect to do so. This helps to break up their daily routines which are normally comprised of physical education and education in the mornings, workshops in the afternoons (sewing mailbags, etc.) followed by a period in the cells. In the evening there is supper and association (recreation with inmates within the prison wings) followed by return to cells at 8.30 pm. The educational programme for young offenders at Jason's prison has three objectives: to improve cognitive clarity and communication skills and achieve better personal relationships. A varied curriculum includes modules on such options as life skills and remedial education. The education officer attempts to make the curriculum as enjoyable and meaningful as possible and as different from the school environment as common sense allows. He acknowledges that young offenders in prison can be as bloody-minded as pupils in schools. Hence, his staff use attitudinal, verbal and material rewards whenever possible. One such reward for good motivation and achievement is the showing of the latest videos on Friday evenings.

Jason's education officer accepted some of his criticisms about the curriculum. However, he pointed out that his hands were tied because of an acute shortage of resources, difficulties arising out of coping with untrained part and full-time staff, differences between the perceptions and demands of educational programmes on the part of prison and educational staff, as well as the individual needs of constantly changing inmates. In reality, being a prison education officer is not easy as the intellectual levels of young offenders cover people with several GCSEs and 'A' levels as well as those who are innumerate and illiterate.

Jason gets on well with his peers in prison.

'Most of them I knew at school or from my first term in jail. They're a good lot – understanding the ropes. Some of us used to work together flogging our stolen goods. It was easy money.'

Nevertheless, he is far from optimistic about his future.

'Last time when I was out I had five interviews for a job. I never got anywhere. They always gave them to someone else. They're not prepared to give people second chances. I'll never go for another interview again. I'd rather just sign on the dole.'

Jason was quite forthcoming in his views about why pupils truant from school and disrupt lessons.

'Kids miss school either because they want to spite their parents, or because they hate their teachers, or because they get bored. Some kids truant because they're afraid of getting bullied. You should know what school is like. A lot of teachers don't teach and what they teach is rubbish. Most teachers are stuck up and don't understand their pupils. That's why we truant and misbehave. Honestly, I never did anything wrong in my maths lessons when I had a decent teacher.

No school could keep me for long. Any teacher who spoke to me I ignored. It went in one ear and out the other. I couldn't be bothered with teachers. Now I can't be bothered with work. Why should I when obtaining money is so easy . . .'

Implications

These two detailed extracts from Craig and Jason's case histories warrant further discussion. Craig is an example of a complete over-reaction following the receipt of ill-timed and badly handled news on the part of his parents; crucial information which was always likely to have a devastating impact on the rest of his life. How much thought had his parents really given to the likely effect upon Craig of discovering that he was an adopted, probably illegitimate child? Why tell him at fifteen prior to taking his mock GCSEs? Why not have left the information until after the exams were over or even until he was much older? After all, if they had left the news until later, perhaps delaying the announcement to around his eighteenth or twenty-first birthday, surely, his increased emotional maturity might have enabled him to cope far better with the shock. Who knows, by then Craig might even have been grateful to his parents for their care and concern throughout his childhood.

But perhaps the cracks had begun to take place much earlier, before or after Craig and his mother left home for a while when he was twelve. Perhaps the father wanted to get back at his successful adopted son – nine possible GCSEs and already a place in the first fifteen. Perhaps Craig was achieving too much and making his father jealous, especially as his own offspring showed less natural talent.

Alternatively, had Craig's father ever loved him? Or, had the father rejected Craig in favour of his own offspring many years earlier? Was Craig really born to his mother before she had married Craig's father? Unfortunately, the case files do not answer any of these possibilities. What they do show is an over-concentration on the outcome of Craig's actions rather than on the real motives or reasons for his misbehaviour. Therefore, educationalists and social workers alike had been treating the consequences of the distress rather than the root cause. The files also show that Craig had crammed eighteen years' misery into three since the discovery that he was an adopted child. And these three short years had probably ruined his future career and in the process ensured that he carried a scar for life.

Jason's case is less complex. He was born into a disadvantaged home; a home in which his father's physical and mental state, as well as poverty, were all-consuming.

Alas, Jason's case is typical of many of his generation – pupils from deprived home and social backgrounds who underachieve and whose life-styles magnify their own disadvantage through the folly of missing school and, later, indulging in criminal activities. Retrospectively, there is little doubt that Jason's intellectual ability was greater than his achievements at school indicate. There can also be no doubt that his downward spiral will continue unless chance or good fortune intervene. He is probably destined to spend much of his life in prison as a compulsive shoplifter and burglar.

Few teachers will probably have much sympathy for Jason when they read his history of teacher-baiting and disruption at school. Nevertheless, staff at his schools can take little credit for their work with him. They failed to control him at any time, understand his genuine difficulties or really tried to get to know him. It seems that only one teacher really got through to him. The fact that this one maths teacher made such an impression on Jason in a comparatively short period is indicative of what might have been achieved. In some ways, Jason is an unwitting victim of an educational system which ensures minimal individual treatment for many lower- and middle-band pupils from disadvantaged backgrounds.

It is ludicrous that so much credence is given to pastoral care in schools and social work when so little is sometimes achieved. If we truly live in a caring society, surely much more should be done for pupils like Jason before it is too late: hard though this work might be. Surely it was elementary for staff to spot that much of his attention-seeking behaviour was really a plea for help. A plea to ensure that he had the opportunity for upward social mobility in later life, rather than a stark recognition that he faced a struggle in life similar to that of his own parents. Surely this is really why being placed in an unfavourable group of less able and similarly disadvantaged pupils concerned him so much. What would have happened if staff had taken the trouble to relocate him in another and more demanding form in that crucial first year of secondary education? Might he have made normal or better progress? Of this, no one can be sure. What both he and his records do indicate, however, is that his attendance and achievement up to the age of eleven were both quite satisfactory, despite his home difficulties.

Craig and Jason's cases also suggest that some disaffected truants and disrupters deliberately and wilfully plan their own self-destruction in the mistaken belief that they are really hurting others; in these cases parents and teachers. Unless teachers and social workers are trained to spot these tell-tale signs and learn how to handle such difficult cases, the opportunity for society to prevent such wanton self-destruction is strictly limited.

Craig and Jason represent aspects of some of the worst features of disruptive absentees. It is a tragic fact that some of the traits they show are far from uncommon which is an indictment of much pastoral care and social work. Many truants and disrupters absent themselves from school or misbehave because they have anxieties and concerns which remain unsolved. For all these pupils, the end of the line is never far away unless wise, properly trained professionals intervene and respond correctly. Craig and Jason received no such wise counselling, only a great deal of corrective work designed to smooth away the rough edges rather than tackling the major problems. In Jason's case the real cause for his misbehaviour either lay undetected or was misunderstood even though he was prepared to tell all and sundry of the real reason for his aggressive behaviour; his fear of following in his parent's footsteps. In Craig's case, the receipt of crucial information that he was an adopted child was bungled by parents and teachers alike. Indeed, the school was only concerned about Craig's behaviour affecting the other pupils, thereby passing the buck on to the social services. There is often a lack of cohesion and agreement between educationalists and social workers on following unified schemes to tackle serious cases of need. Partly because of these faults Craig and Jason both reached the end of the line before some of their less able, disadvantaged and unfortunate peers. No doubt they will be endlessly punished for their misfortunes for the rest of their lives – if only psychologically.

Despite complex legal, school and local authority policies for dealing with cases of truancy and disruption, the evidence suggests that there is widespread variation in the implementation, use and outcomes of formal sanctions. Whatever measures are used, they all too rarely achieve their objectives – ensuring that non-attenders return to school regularly or that disrupters cease their misdemeanours. For this reason, Tables 5.1 to 5.3 could provide useful checklists for schools.

Less able pupils and behaviour

Research has shown that a high proportion of truants are also less able. The tolerance thresholds of individual truants vary enormously dependent on such factors as health, physical appearance and defects, parental interest in education, family size and everyday 'security' within the home environment. One study has reported that six times as many truants as non-truants are less able. Interestingly however, the same study showed that the social backgrounds of good attenders living in the same neighbourhoods as the truants often varied little – suggesting an environmental factor in pupils' behaviour within and outside school.

In one of Reid's studies, 77 persistent absentees and two matching control groups were given the Rutter Children's Behaviour Questionnaire (Scale B). All the pupils came from Years 9, 10 and 11 and attended a deprived social priority school in Cardiff. Control group 1 came from the same forms as the persistent absentees and were matched for nearest birth date and gender. The control group 2 pupils came from the academic bands and were also matched for nearest birth date and gender. The findings showed that the persistent absentees displayed significantly worse behavioural traits than the pupils in the two control groups as well as manifesting higher levels of neurotic and anti-social conduct. Some interesting group and gender differences occurred within these data. For example, the behaviour of the institutional absentees was much poorer than those in the psychological and traditional categories.

It is important to discuss the implications of the findings further both for their own sake and in the light of previous research. A closer inspection of the results revealed that the absentees had some behavioural problems, which were not wholly confined to their erratic attendance at school. It may be, therefore, that further research is needed into the personalities of school absentees as some of the conduct disorders ('is often disobedient', 'often appears miserable, unhappy, tearful or distressed') are not explainable purely in terms of the non-attendance.

These contentions are supported by the facts. For example, while there was some minority support for Tyerman's (1968) assertion that truants (note: not

Table 5.1 Warning signs

Has the pupil:

- been severely punished recently;
- been excluded;
- been unduly moody or tearful;
- been changed form or set;
- gone up or down a year;
- joined a school midway through a year;
- parents who have just separated or been divorced;
- been fostered;
- a sibling (brother or sister) who has started truanting;
- quarrelled seriously with a teacher;
- attainment in school suddenly dipped;
- become withdrawn;
- fallen out with peers;
- started to look dishevelled;
- become a loner;
- overreacted to teasing or to other classroom situations;
- been statemented for SEN;
- spent a long period of time overseas (especially children of Asian parents);
- been under pressure from examinations;
- been bullied;
- had parents in the local news (criminal convictions, bankruptcy cases, etc.)

Table 5.2 Truants compared with the normal school-age population

---

Research shows that a higher proportion of truants than the normal school-age population:

- prefer fewer and different subjects to high ability pupils;
- prefer fewer and different subjects to pupils from similar socio-economic backgrounds who are good attenders;
- prefer a curriculum based on core subjects (English, maths);
- tend to dislike learning a language, science (and, often girls PE and religious education);
- are underachieving or performed badly in a range of school subjects;
- have contrasting views to other pupils on school rules, regulations and internal processes (e.g. attendance regulations, school uniform);
- enjoy school life less;
- experience more problems when in school;
- require more pastoral care help;
- vary on the personnel in school they would visit if and when they had problems in school;
- are given homework less;
- fail to undertake their homework when it is given;
- prefer fewer teachers in their schools;
- have a poorer relationship with form tutors;
- tend to have fewer friends in school;
- also tend to have fewer friends with their form groups;
- less parental interest in academic school progress;
- fewer parental visits to school (e.g. parents' evenings);
- make allowances for problems at home but not those which occur within schools;
- have lower long-term career aspirations;
- higher levels of anxiety when in school and over school work;
- suffer from psychosomatic illnesses;
- are prone to periods of time off school due to ill health.

---

absentees) are frequently 'lonely' and 'unhappy' people with few friends, over three fifths of the absentees in this study did not display any neurotic symptoms in the estimations of their form teachers. Furthermore, the evidence shows that even among hardened school absentees, anti-social conduct is a minority tendency. In this enquiry, disruptive behaviour in school was attributable to only 35 per cent of the absentees.

Interestingly, the findings that the control group 1 pupils claimed to have more friends in school and in their own forms than the persistent absentees and control group 2 pupils suggest that some less able and potentially disruptive lower ability students attend school for compensatory social rather than educational reasons. If so, this suggests that the temperamental and personality characteristics of pupils like truants and absentees are even more important than some people have hitherto realised. If not, why should so many pupils from low social class and deprived home backgrounds attend school when others do not? This could also partially explain why male and female absentees appear to have so much in common – as it may be their personality types rather than their gender *per se* which lead them to withdraw from school.

Throughout most of these data, male pupils tended to score higher on the main scale than their female counterparts, suggesting that more male than female absentees behave badly when in school. Illustratively, the overall means for the male pupils in all three groups were higher than those for the females on both the Rutter Scale and its anti-social subscale. By contrast, the means for the two genders on the neuroticism subscale were almost identical, although interestingly, the females in control group 2 scored higher than the males on this measure.

Hence, the means for the male and female absentees were approximately three times as high as for the good attenders in both control groups on the main scale and on most of the comparisons of the two subscales. This is an important result as it confirms that the behaviour of male and female absentees has more in common with one another than with good attenders.

Nevertheless, another fact should not be overlooked. The male absentees tended to score more frequently on those items which related to either mal-adjusted or delinquent conduct than the girls. Once again, these findings accord well with previous studies. Hence, although the total scores for the male and female absentees were similar, there were considerable item-differences between them. This is only to be expected in view of well-known maturational differences between adolescent male and female pupils aged 13 to 15-plus.

What the evidence seems to suggest is that some pupils are better able to cope with all forms of negative reinforcement – social, psychological, and institutional – than their peers, irrespective of whether they are male or female. If so, the importance of the pupils' self-concepts is again apparent. Furthermore, the precise correlation between the low self-concepts of persistent absentees and their behaviour in school is another area which requires further research.

Self-concepts

The same three groups were tested for measures of self-concept using the Coopersmith Self-Esteem Inventory and academic self-concepts using the Brookover *et al.* Self-Concept of Academic Ability Scale.

The findings show the persistent absentees had significant lower self-concepts than the pupils in the two control groups as measured by these instruments. There were no major gender differences between the male and female absentees although there were highly significant inter-group differences to be found between the male absentees when compared with the male pupils in each of the two control groups and between the female absentees and the females in the two control groups. These findings suggest that, like behaviour, taken collectively, absentees have more in common with one another (whether male or female) than with good attenders.

A closer inspection of the findings obtained when using the Brookover Scale revealed that the absentees rated themselves as having much less ability than their peers in the two control groups. They also thought they had less chance of entering a professional occupation when they left school. They rated their own work lower than the pupils in the two control groups, irrespective of how the teachers marked their work.

The Coopersmith Scale showed that the greatest differences between the persistent absentees and the two control groups were found on six items. The absentees had a tendency to say things like: 'There are lots of things about myself I'd change if I could'; 'It's pretty tough to be me'; 'Things are all mixed up in my life'; 'I often feel upset in school'; 'I often get discouraged in school'; 'I can't be depended on'. All these key findings are summarised in Table 5.3.

The implications of these findings are that the absentees recorded lower scores than the two control groups because they had become more accustomed to patterns of failure at home and at school than their regularly attending peers. It is possible that consistent patterns of failure in school might lead some pupils to withdraw from the offending stimuli. For example, when pupils perpetually receive low grades in school, their academic self-concepts may be reduced to such a point that to absent themselves from school becomes

Table 5.3 Main differences between truants and the normal school-age population

Research suggests that a higher proportion of truants than the normal school-age population have:

- LOWER ACADEMIC SELF-CONCEPTS
- LOW GENERAL LEVELS OF SELF-ESTEEM
- GREATER PATTERNS OF ALIENATION FROM SCHOOL OVER CERTAIN ISSUES
  (they feel more 'confused';
  less part of the school community;
  unable to influence decision-making;
  that some schools are too large;
  tend to feel generally helpless at school)
- HIGHER LEVELS OF NEUROTICISM
- HIGHER LEVELS OF ANTI-SOCIAL BEHAVIOUR
  (they tend to be absent from school for trivial reasons;
  not liked much by other children;
  often appear miserable, unhappy, tearful or distressed;
  have poor concentration or short attention span;
  often tell lies;
  often disobedient;
  have stolen things on one or more occasions)

a source of relief. These findings suggest that teachers need to give more thought to the way in which they mark their pupils' work in schools. This could be particularly important for potentially at-risk pupils who are known to come from deprived and unsupportive backgrounds.

To some extent, the findings reinforce the fact that schools are a more rewarding place for academic pupils than for those in the lower ability forms. This conclusion is supported by the fact that both the absentees and their matching controls from the same forms had lower self-concepts than the academic pupils in control group 2.

It is not easy to suggest why there were statistically significant differences between the academic self-concepts and general levels of self-esteem of the absentees and control group 1 pupils who came from identical forms. It seems that the self-concepts of the control group 1 pupils were also adversely affected by regular patterns of failure in school – even if not to the same extent as those of the absentees.

Nevertheless, these findings can be explained. Presumably, as the control group 1 pupils were attending school regularly, they were receiving positive reinforcement from their schools and homes alike, despite the fact that the occupational status of their parents and their housing and general home circumstances were lower and less favourable than the control group 2 pupils. It is probably significant, for example, that the control group 1 pupils had more friends in their particular form and the school as a whole than the absentees.

What these results mean is that the self-esteem of the persistent absentees appears to be more adversely affected by negative reinforcement than by positive reinforcement than that of pupils in both control groups – good attenders. Self-esteem, however, is always relative: some persistent absentees scored higher than some controls on both scales, although this trend was far more marked on the Coopersmith Scale. As a result, these data suggest that it is not just the social and educational backgrounds of absentees which make them miss school but also something from within – presumably temperamental and personality factors.

Longer-term career aspirations

Previously unpublished data collated from Reid's work suggests that pupils' long-term career aspirations may affect their attitudes towards their schools and teachers. The persistent absentees and two control groups were asked what careers and/or jobs they hoped to go into after leaving school. Analysis of these data showed that significantly more of the absentees and their controls from the same forms hoped to obtain employment in unskilled or semi-skilled work, in occupations where career openings are decreasing and likely to diminish further in the future. By contrast, the academic controls generally aspired to enter higher or further education, the professions or prestigious technical occupations. Consequently, both the absentees and matching controls placed considerable emphasis upon the vocational importance of such subjects as mathematics and English which, they recognised, could influence their opportunities to find suitable employment when they left school at 16.

Evidence obtained from their interviews suggested that when the absentees and matching controls perceived they were doing badly in these key subjects, or were dissatisfied with either the teaching or their teachers, then this proved a considerable source of bitterness to them, often exacerbating their disaffection and alienation from school. Unlike their academic peers, these pupils were unable or unwilling to bring parental pressure to bear upon the school. Undoubtedly, this was partially because they knew or feared that such parental intervention would inevitably be used to discuss other matters like their classroom behaviour or non-attendance. In fact, any action which they took of their own volition in terms of groups or individual complaints usually only got them into further trouble.

Andrew, 15, for example, claimed that he was being victimised by a teacher at his school because he complained about her inability to teach or help him with his reading in class. He claimed that he was desperate to learn to read and his inability to do so lay behind much of his frustration in school, culminating in his disruptive conduct in certain classes and, eventually, his persistent absenteeism and long-term withdrawal from school.

Anxiety

The relationship between school refusal and anxiety has long been established. A related problem, a general fear of going to school without this ever reaching the phobic stage, has also been the subject of a great deal of research at the nursery, primary and secondary stages. Children are particularly reluctant when they first begin voluntary or compulsory education in nursery or infant sections – ask most mothers. Sympathetic support from parents and teachers has been found to be a key variable in helping children to overcome their worries. Starting school is bound to seem strange to young children used to being at home every day.

Likewise, it is only natural that a large percentage of children should prefer to be at home or out playing than at school. If there is any doubt on this score, just listen to the tone of conversation or look at the facial expressions on many pupils at the end of any school term. Despite these preferences, most children and teachers turn up at school willingly and inwardly accept the social and educational advantages of regular attendance. Indeed, some children and teachers appear to prefer being at school to being at home (without ever being considered 'workaholics') as a number of people will willingly testify during the summer holidays.

From time to time, many children from a variety of social and educational backgrounds develop a fear of either attending school or failing once there. This is only normal. Factors contributing to this syndrome can include: the type of work being undertaken, school transfers, demotions, promotions, new or different teachers, teaching styles and subjects, changes in the curriculum, dislike or fear of a particular member of staff or punishment of some kind, bullying, extortion, speaking out aloud in class and many others. Sometimes irrational fears about going to school can be reinforced by illness, falling behind in schoolwork, the failure to complete homework or do it well, unpopularity with peers, inability to participate in or do well at an activity (such as games, swimming, art, drama, music), as well as the failure to wear or have a school uniform. Much depends on the age, sex, ability and temperament of the child but such fears are usually short-lived and overcome by teachers and parents alike without too much difficulty.

Truants' feelings when away from school

The psychology of being away from school illegally is in itself an interesting phenomenon. Irrespective of the reason for non-attendance, missing school is a profoundly unsatisfactory experience for the vast majority of absentees and truants. Of those interviewed, only a minority stated that they were 'pleased' or 'did not care'. Indeed, a small proportion indicated that they wished circumstances could be found whereby they could start again in school with a clean sheet. This poses an interesting psychological question. Why do so many absentees elect to miss school when their behaviour causes them considerable short-term anxiety, worry, fear and guilt and longer-term disadvantages? Although this concern is self-imposed, there can be little doubt that the resultant worry is at least equal to any pressure exerted on the pupils by staff in schools. Seen in this light, the plight of regular non-attenders is even more pitiful.

The following verbatim statements indicate the sort of mental pressure to which the persistent absentees feel subjected:

'I just know I've got to go back sometime to face them. The longer I carry on the worse I make it for myself'. (Year 11 boy)

'I worry all the time in case a teacher or someone else sees me in town and I get caught'. (Year 11 girl)

'I feel guilty about coming back to school . . . you have to make up some stupid lies about why you've been away . . . I keep telling them I've had the flu . . . They know it's not true . . . This makes walking around the school worse'. (Year 11 boy)

A disconcerting picture of the persistent absentees' daily lives was obtained by enquiring into what they did when they were away from school. The findings suggest that boredom is a major problem. In a number of cases these data were almost pathetic, illustrating the desperate search for activities which while time away as satisfactorily as possible.

The activities referred to by the absentees for how they spend their time when away from school included doing domestic chores, watching television, going to 'Bingo', staying in bed, lazing around the house, looking after siblings, visiting relatives, wandering around streets, walking around the city centre, sitting by the river, playing with pets, fishing, 'hiding' in another school, catching rabbits in woods, smoking, helping travelling people with their horses, playing football, training, swimming, visiting cafes, listening to records, visiting girlfriends, playing cards, helping a building contractor and attending drama rehearsals.

These activities were subsequently divided into broad categories: domestic, wandering and social. It is somewhat ironic that in this technological age, the kinds of activities undertaken by school absentees have not changed much in over 100 years. The general picture which emerges is:

(a) most truants are bored while out of school;
(b) whiling away time can lead to criminal activity;
(c) there is a significant difference between occasional 'mitching' for fun and persistent non-attendance;
(d) few absentees are psychologically at ease with their decision not to attend school;
(e) the longer the absence, the worse the problems get.

Therefore, truancy is a sign of educational failure. Teachers know it; parents know it; and, most of all, the truants themselves know it. Yet, despite recognising their own failure, and, despite being bored while truanting, they continue to miss school. This is why truancy is regarded as such a 'sad' phenomenon.

Future research may be able to show that certain personality types are more likely than others to become truants. If so, this may provide significant clues not only towards possible treatment strategies but also on early identification techniques. We may then begin to utilise group-based solutions in preventing and combating truancy. At present, part of the difficulty in dealing with truants is that each case is unique.

This chapter however, reminds us all that the 'mind-set' and 'mind games' which take place in the cognitive thinking and decision-making processes of young people (and adults) are a critical part of the process in understanding the origins and causes of truancy.

6   Educational causes of truancy

The educational causes of truancy

This chapter focuses upon the educational and institutional causes of truancy. These data have been collected from a variety of sources. Table 6.1 presents evidence collected from persistent absentees in selected schools in South Wales. This table shows the very wide range of educational reasons which truants and persistent absentees can give for missing school.

Table 6.2 shows the list of pupil-related factors which cause truants to miss school. These data highlight the importance of pupils' own relationships with their classmates and other pupils in schools as well as peer pressure. The importance of peer pressure should never be underestimated as any parent will tell you – especially among teenagers!

Table 6.3 presents a list of teacher-related factors which can cause pupils to miss school. There is a world of difference between pupils being taught by competent, caring and task-orientated staff and those who are poor, weak and relatively uninterested in the pupils they teach as people in their own right.

Table 6.4 provides a summary of the reasons given by 128 persistent absentees for missing school. Table 6.5 shows how regularly attending pupils believe their schools can be improved. By contrast, Table 6.6 presents data on how truants think school can be improved. It is an interesting exercise to compare Table 6.5 with Table 6.6. Why not try it? What are the similarities and differences between the two?

Table 6.7 describes the qualities which truants and good attenders from Years 9, 10 and 11 look for in good teachers. Note the similarities between the regular attenders and the non-attenders in this table. Only on two variables was there much difference between these two groups. It seems, therefore, that most pupils intuitively agree upon what makes a good teacher.

Table 6.8 provides data taken from a BBC television survey undertaken in the late 1990s from a cross section of pupils in Years 9, 10 and 11 from twelve different comprehensive schools in South Wales. These data show that:

(a) a majority of pupils admit to having 'mitched' from school at one time or another. These data are much higher than in most other published statistics;

(b) 15 per cent of pupils admit 'mitching' more than twenty times; 5 per cent higher than national norms;

(c) 64 per cent of pupils 'mitched' because they did not like some classes;

(d) 83 per cent of pupils 'mitched' for curriculum or other school-based reasons;

(e) a minority of parents were aware (43 per cent) of their children's truancy;

(f) 86 per cent of the pupils knew other pupils who 'mitched';

(g) the overwhelming majority (85 per cent) 'mitched' in groups;

(h) 97 per cent of pupils thought gaining qualifications was important. This includes a high proportion of truants and provides a clue to treatment strategies;

(i) 11 per cent of pupils had got into trouble when mitching;

(j) 34 per cent of pupils who 'mitch' have been bullied (see later). Of these, being bullied was the cause of the truancy for 5 per cent of the pupils.

Finally, Tables 6.9 and 6.10 provide data on why 128 persistent absentees first decided to miss school and then continued not to attend. Once again, it is interesting to compare and contrast Table 6.8 with Tables 6.9 and 6.10. Why?

First, the studies were both undertaken by Reid in the same geographical location using similar schools but with a considerable time lapse in between the two. Second, the studies both suggest that school-related reasons are the prime cause for the absence. Third, the reasons given for the curriculum being the prime cause of truancy have risen since the introduction of the National Curriculum. Why not discover what reasons the good and poor attenders in your school give to the same issues?

Schools and truancy

Table 6.1 not only shows the very wide range of potential 'causes' of truancy and other forms of non-attendance within schools, but also gives a clue to the very wide ranging strategies which need to be in place to prevent and combat these forms of behaviour. Issues can range from differences between schools in terms of structures, policies, ethos, teacher–pupil relationships and curriculum issues to gender and ethnic differences, rates of bullying and exclusion, literacy and numeracy levels, pupils' social origins, geographical location and, of course, individual schools' policies to combat truancy. This is why overcoming non-attendance within schools is never an easy topic. And, once again, there is no magic formula which will enable schools to achieve this aim. Combating school absenteeism requires appropriate school-based structures and policies as well as a great deal of sustained hard work. Even schools which successfully reduce their levels of absence for a while can inadvertently see them rise again once they take their foot off the accelerator.

Table 6.2 provides a checklist of pupil-related factors which cause truants to miss school. This table suggests that these issues can be broken down into around fourteen different aspects. Notice in Table 6.2 how some of these issues are psychological while others are related to social and/or educational reasons.

Table 6.3 is important. The data provided here are often those which schools are inclined to sweep under the carpet and, even, deny exist. No fewer than sixteen different teacher-related aspects are identified. It is a fortunate school indeed which manifests none of these syndromes.

Table 6.4 shows the types of educational excuse used by persistent absentees for missing school. Again, these can be grouped into thirteen different categories.

Table 6.5 provides data on how Year 9, 10 and 11 pupils think their comprehensive schools can be improved. It is interesting to compare these data with Table 6.6 which shows how truants from the same forms and schools think their schools can be improved. A comparison between these two tables shows how regular attenders can emphasise different issues from truants. Both tables, however, do have one thing in common. They show the importance of the social and facilities side of schools in pupils' minds. Perhaps in the year 2000 and beyond, we should begin to realise that most pupils in Years 9, 10 and 11 are no longer children but mature young adults. How many schools reflect this change in maturity within their policies and systems? Pupils aged fifteen and sixteen today are far more mature than their peers of fifty or sixty years ago.

Table 6.7 provides data on the qualities which truants and regularly attending pupils in Years 9, 10 and 11 look for in good teachers. On these issues, both groups have largely similar ideas.

Reasons why persistent absentees first miss and continue to miss school

This section presents and discusses data based on the perceptions of 128 persistent school absentees on their initial and continued reasons for missing school. The findings suggest that despite the absentees' generally unfavourable social and educational backgrounds, a greater proportion of pupils are inclined to blame their institutions rather than social or psychological factors for their behaviour. The results are discussed in the light of the circumstances under which the survey was undertaken, and areas for further research are suggested.

Few previous studies, if any, have explored either the onset or the continuation of the absenteeism from the perceptions of the absentees themselves. The theoretical basis for the study was derived from the fundamental postulate of George Kelly that if one could not understand a problem it was best to ask all the people concerned.

The sample

One hundred and twenty-eight persistent school absentees were selected from two large inner-city comprehensive schools in a deprived area in industrial South Wales. The location of the research may be important especially as it has been established that South Wales in particular has special problems over the non-attendance of pupils at school. All the absentees were drawn from Years 9 ($n = 44$), 10 ($n = 40$) and 11 ($n = 44$) in the schools and mainly from the lower bands. Sixty-seven of the absentees were male and sixty-one female. The absentees were selected after close consultation with the senior teachers and education welfare officers in the schools. Every absentee had missed a minimum of 65 per cent of school time in the year preceding the enquiry for illegal reasons, many hardly attending school at all.

The social and educational backgrounds of the absentees are worthy of further description. Forty-four per cent of the absentees had made less than 65 per cent of possible attendances in the last two years prior to their transfer to secondary school. The IQs of the absentees were significantly lower than for the 'normal' population at the age of 11. The absentees' school reports showed that the vast majority (almost 70 per cent) of them had been given an average overall grade of 'C' or lower in their last two years of primary education. Moreover, this pattern of failure had continued and increased in the two secondary schools, with 65 per cent of the absentees receiving an average 'D' grade or lower in the year preceding the study. Obviously, these low average grades were usually influenced by the pupils' records of persistent non-attendance. Comments about the absentees' poor attendance histories were littered throughout their school files, indicating the diligence of the staff in attempting to remedy their behaviour.

Over two-fifths of the absentees (43.8 per cent) came from a domestic background which had known disruption of one sort or another such as a parental divorce, separation, death or a single-parent household. Two thirds of the absentees (almost 70 per cent) had fathers or father figures who were either deceased, divorced, separated, redundant, unemployed, retired or 'never seen'. Almost one-fifth (18 per cent) of the absentees had a 'father' who was liable to periods away from the home owing to the demands of his employment. The vast majority of the absentees came from working-class backgrounds, with the largest group originating in social class V. Over two-thirds of the absentees (71 per cent) were part of large families of four or more children. A majority of the absentees (42 per cent) were either born last or had a low birth order position. Only 43 per cent of the absentees lived in privately owned houses. A high proportion of the absentees were delinquents (38 per cent), in receipt of free school meals (36 per cent) or had a known involvement with the local social services department (42 per cent). Thus the composition of the sample accorded well with previous investigations and suggested that the social and educational backgrounds of the pupils were major contributory factors in their absenteeism.

Table 6.1 Educational reasons: a checklist of school-related factors that cause pupils to miss school

---

Factors:

- issues associated with school differences
- primary school experiences
- school climate
- the implementation of a school's behaviour policy and practice
- self-fulfilling prophecies
- aspects related to the National Curriculum
- literacy and numeracy levels
- school failure
- attainment targets
- poor assessment and examination performance
- bullying and teasing
- aspects relating to school rules and punishment
- issues related to school organisation
- school management and leadership
- progression issues
- relationships between home and school communication
- role of education welfare officer
- homework policies
- underachievement
- gender and ethnic differences
- special educational needs policies
- primary school liaison
- proportion of pupils requiring free school meals
- local transport policies
- financial hardship cases
- lack of re-integration strategies
- truancy syndromes
- school governance
- league tables
- school histories/reputations
- exclusion policies
- pastoral care policy and practice
- school transfers – all kinds, internal and external

Table 6.2 A checklist of pupil-related factors that cause truants to miss school

Factors:

- issues associated with adolescence and maturation
- low self-concepts (shyness, introversion)
- maladjusted behaviour
- neurotic and anti-social conduct
- pupils' perceptions of their schools and teachers
- peer group relationships, including peer pressure
- pupil–pupil bullying
- pupils' likes and dislikes (subject and teacher choice)
- illness
- personality issues
- appearance difficulties (e.g. obesity, red hair)
- organised group truancy
- part-time underage employment (e.g. fruit picking)
- participating in external activities (e.g. local pantomime, taking part in a sponsored sail around Britain, going to the local gym)

Table 6.3 A checklist of teacher-related factors that cause pupils to miss school

Factors:

- schools that are failing and have a long history of pupils underachieving and/or failing
- all kinds of internal and external school transfers
- teacher absences
- unsuitable teaching styles
- poor teacher–pupil relationships
- teachers' negative attitudes towards pupils
- teachers' victimisation of pupils
- teachers' language towards pupils
- bullying and victimisation of pupils
- poor teaching
- teacher disaffection
- school disaffection
- negative budgets
- redeployment among staff
- falling school rolls
- pupil failure

Table 6.4 Reasons given by persistent absentees for missing school

Issues associated with:

- the form group (e.g. 'not being with my friends')
- the curriculum (e.g. 'not being given homework', 'forced to do French and RE', 'disliking science')
- school rules and regulations ('being forced to wear uniform')
- bullying ('I need better protection in school')
- parent–school relationships ('my father loathes Mr B', 'my parents hated school and never come here')
- specific teachers ('I used to like maths, but now I hate it because of Miss W'; 'Mr G calls me "tich"')
- teachers and their teaching styles ('not giving us homework', 'favouring brighter pupils')
- school punishments ('being forced to do detention after school')
- pastoral care ('no one helps me or my mother with our problems', 'who can I tell about my sister?')
- primary/secondary transfer ('I used to like the other school (primary) but hate this one – it is too big')
- literacy and numeracy ('why do I have to do French and science when I can't read or write?')
- early problems starting in primary schools ('one of the kids ripped up my football cards that's how it started')
- school transfers (both internal and external)

Notes
The reasons are taken from a survey of selected comprehensive schools in South Wales. The responses from the truants have been grouped together to form the categories shown.

Table 6.5 How regularly attending Year 9, 10 and 11 pupils think school can be improved

Replies:

- clean and tidy up the school more
- stop the problems on the way to school more
- have a common-room for all pupils over 14
- provide us with a covered area for wet days
- make all games lessons optional
- more choice in choosing our GCSEs (why can't I take both history and geography?)
- stop assemblies
- have a shorter registration period
- give me different teachers in some subjects and pay pupils attendance money by age
- have a Wednesday afternoon free
- let the lower stream have more success in their books instead of always getting low marks

- suspend teachers who don't teach us
- put disruptive pupils into special units away from the school
- stop calling pupils names (e.g. 'tich')
- more revision periods before exams
- stop the bullying
- more pupil responsibility once you're in Year 11
- more young teachers
- give us chairs to sit on in assembly
- allow us a school union
- more functions in school in the evening (e.g. school dances, concerts)

Notes
Taken from a survey of selected comprehensive schools in South Wales. The replies are presented verbatim.

Table 6.6 How truants think school can be improved

Replies:

- more help with reading and writing
- more of your own friends in your forms
- more facilities at breaks and lunch-times
- more prevention of bullying
- more careers help
- allow us to attend smaller schools
- let us leave at fifteen with our parents' consent
- allow the pupils to choose their own timetables
- free school meals for everyone
- stop compulsory swimming
- more school trips
- better discipline in the school
- more social workers in the school
- allow everyone to take the GCSEs they would like to study
- allow me to come and go from school as I like

Notes
Taken from a survey of selected comprehensive schools in South Wales. The replies are presented verbatim.

Table 6.7 The qualities that truants and their regularly attending peers in Years 9, 10 and 11 look for in good teachers (not in order)

Qualities:

- the ability to be strict but fair
- the ability to give individual attention to pupils while teaching
- the ability to assist pupils with their personal problems
- a good personality (e.g. 'able to be patient and understanding', 'to have a sense of humour')
- the ability to give remedial attention to pupils with special needs*
- someone who likes and can talk to his or her pupils
- a person who is really enthusiastic about their subject**

Notes
* ranked more highly by less able pupils and by persistent absentees than by able pupils.
** ranked much higher by able pupils than by less able pupils and by persistent absentees.

Table 6.8 Findings from a BBC survey of a cross section of Year 9, 10 and 11 pupils from 12 comprehensive schools in South Wales

Question	Answer	Number	Total	%	Total %
1 Do you ever mitch off school?	YES	716		57	
	NO	534	1250	43	100
2 How many times have you mitched off?	1–10 times	535		73	
	11–20 times	88		12	
	Over 20 times	107	730	15	100
3 Do you mitch because:	You do not like school?	136		19	
	You do not like some classes?	466		64	
	Other reasons?	126	728	17	100
4 Do your parents know?	YES	312		43	
	NO	418	730	57	100
5 Do your friends mitch?	YES	1078		86	
	NO	171	1249	14	100
6 Do you mitch . . .	Alone?	109		15	
	With friends?	618	727	85	100
7 Do you think gaining qualifications is important?	YES	1226		97	
	NO	33	1259	3	100
8 Have you ever got into trouble while mitching?	YES	91		11	
	NO	710	801	89	100
9 Have you ever been bullied?	YES	429		34	
	NO	820	1249	66	100
10 Was being bullied the reason for mitching?	YES	57		5	
	NO	1191	1248	95	100

Results

Table 6.9 presents the reasons given by the absentees for first missing school. This table has been subdivided into three parts and reveals that a majority of the absentees claimed to first skip school for institutional (56 per cent) rather than social and psychological reasons. Furthermore, Table 6.9 also shows that it was possible to formulate 13 categories for the absentees' initial actions, with school transfers (all types), domestic reasons, bullying, peer group influences and curriculum and examinations being the five most important aspects. These categories will now be described further using verbatim data from the pupils' responses.

- *Domestic reasons*   'My cousin had food poisoning and my mother asked me to stay home to look after him . . . that's how it all began'. (Year 9 girl)
- *Peer group influences*   'I was "dared" by a friend to miss school and go to his house'. (Year 9 boy)
- *Entertainment*   'because I was in a Christmas Pantomime in the West Country'. (Year 10 girl)
- *Employment*   'because I preferred to work in a market stall than come to school anymore'. (Year 11 boy)
- *Illness*   'I got behind in my work following an illness . . . it was too hard to catch up so then I thought it would be clever to stay away'. (Year 10 boy)
- *Psychosomatic*   'I used to get persistent nose bleeds in junior school . . . I kept feeling embarrassed . . . I couldn't face being teased or called names . . . or speaking aloud in class . . . it just became easier for me to stay away and be happy'. (Year 11 girl)

Table 6.9 Distribution of absentees' reasons for first missing school

Factors	Reasons	n	%	
Social	Domestic	20	15.6	
	Peer group influences	13	10.2	28%
	Entertainment	2	1.6	
	Employment	1	0.8	
Psychological	Illness	11	8.6	
	Psychosomatic	7	5.5	16%
	Laziness	3	2.3	
Institutional	School transfers	21	16.4	
	Bullying	19	14.8	56%
	Curriculum and examinations	13	10.2	
	School rules and punishment	7	5.5	
	The teachers	6	4.7	
	Desire to leave	5	3.9	
	Totals	128	100.0	

- *Laziness* 'because I got fed up of getting up early – seven o'clock – every morning'. (Year 9 boy)
- *School transfers* 'I didn't like this school . . . although I loved my junior school'. (Year 9 girl)

  'I liked my other school. I hate the kinds of teachers in this place and I wish my parents had never moved house'. (Year 10 boy)

  'transfer to secondary school. When you're in junior school you stay in the same room with the same teacher. In high school you keep moving around all the time. You know nobody and they don't know you. The teachers don't care either'. (Year 9 boy)

- *Bullying* 'I used to get bullied because I was coloured'. (Year 10 boy)
  'the kids bullied me because of my handicap . . . I was too scared to come to school. Everyone called me names'. (Year 11 girl)
- *Curriculum and examinations* 'because I disliked games'. (Year 11 girl)
  'because I got bored with lessons'. (Year 9 girl)
  'because I had a test and didn't know anything'. (Year 9 girl)
- *Teachers* 'I used to run away from junior school because I didn't like the teacher'. (Year 9 boy)
- *Desire to leave* 'I just felt I had had enough at this school'. (A clear, conscious decision – Year 11 boy)

Table 6.10 shows that when more than one response could be given 40 per cent, 24 per cent and 86 per cent of the 128 absentees continued to miss school for social, psychological or institutional reasons respectively at the time of the study.

It is important to put these findings into their proper context for a variety of reasons. First, the analyses of Table 6.9 were based on the pupils' retrospective interpretations of their earlier actions, some of which had taken place years beforehand.

Second, the researcher himself later recoded the absentees' responses in order to form convenient categories sometime after the fieldwork had been completed. Moreover, this recoding process proved to be an immensely difficult exercise given the degree of overlap between the categories within the pupils' answers. Perhaps this point applied even more in the work undertaken prior to the production of Table 6.10. The basic dilemma within these data which needed to be overcome was that every absentee was unique. Thus it could be argued that every case contained an element of social, psychological and institutional factors within its whole.

Third, both the onset and continuation of the absenteeism behaviour was dependent to a large extent upon the absentees' cognitive processes. All the available evidence suggested that over a period of time many of the absentees

Table 6.10 Distribution of absentees' reasons for continuing to miss school

Factors	Reasons	n	%	
Social	Domestic	32	25.0	
	Peer group influences	7	4.4	40%
	Entertainment	6	4.7	
	Employment	4	3.1	
Psychological	Illness	4	3.1	
	Psychosomatic	16	12.5	24%
	Laziness	11	8.6	
Institutional	School transfers	9	7.0	
	Bullying	24	18.8	86%
	Curriculum and examinations	21	16.4	
	School rules and punishment	13	10.1	
	The teachers	18	14.1	
	Desire to leave	21	16.4	
	Totals	186		

had used their cognitive processes to justify the original absenteeism. Hence, the increase in the number of reasons given in Table 6.10.

Fourth, it was also likely that the absentees' responses shown in Table 6.10 had to some extent been influenced by the treatment and punishments which their absenteeism had received, particularly from educational personnel.

Fifth, it was significant that in virtually every case the pupils' patterns of non-attendance at school had increased with age.

A number of other factors are related to Table 6.9. Only three pupils started to miss school before the age of eight. However, 18 per cent of the absentees admitted having first deliberately missed school prior to their transfer to the local comprehensive schools. Almost one-third of the absentees (32 per cent) began to miss school in the year immediately following this transfer. Interestingly, only half of these pupils gave this as their initial reason for their absence. Likewise, a very small minority of the absentees (5 per cent) – all girls – started their histories of absenteeism beyond the age of 14. A quarter (25 per cent of the absentees) began to miss school at some point during the third year of their secondary education in Year 9.

All these findings reinforce the fact that the three critical periods for the onset of school absenteeism are the last two years of primary schooling, and the first and third years of secondary education. In the latter instances, the segregation of the students into academic and non-academic groups appeared to have had considerable significance and caused a lowering of morale among certain of the at-risk pupils. The failure of staff to provide less able pupils with homework appeared to be a particularly sore point among some of the disaffected pupils.

The evidence indicated that slightly more boys than girls had early histories of absenteeism (up to the age of 12). A higher proportion of girls than boys gave domestic or curricular reasons for initially and later continuing to miss school. By contrast, more boys than girls were influenced by their peers and what they described as acts of bullying. It may be, however, that these proportions are too small to draw any firm conclusions.

A comparison between Tables 6.9 and 6.10 shows that there was an increase in the number of reasons given by the absentees for continuing to miss school when compared with their initial responses. This applied to each of the three major categories but was most noticeable in the additional number of institutional reasons given for missing school. It is probable that these findings reflect the natural tendency among absentees to blame their schools rather than themselves, their homes or other aspects for their behaviour. Once again the process of self-justification appeared to have been at work. Thus, there may be a danger in schools becoming the scapegoats for absenteeism when in reality the genesis has a very different or partially different cause. It is possible, however, that actions which take place within schools may produce the specific stimuli for the withdrawal. Future researchers will need to take these possibilities into account in their research designs if objectivity is to be maintained.

Even allowing for these possibilities, Table 6.10 shows that there were larger than average increases in the parameters in the domestic, psychosomatic, laziness, curriculum and examinations, school rules and punishment, teachers and desire to leave categories. By contrast, there were fewer peer group influences, illness and school transfer reasons given in the later table.

A further important issue which is not shown in the two tables is worthy of note. The reasons given by the non-white absentees in the sample ($n = 24$) proved to be very different from the rest. The traditional and cultural influences exerted upon these male and female pupils meant that their absenteeism appeared to have somewhat different origins from their peers. For example, one able, female, non-white absentee claimed that she began to miss school as a direct consequence of her parents putting pressure on her to conform to the norms of her gender within their society. The girl, therefore, began to feel that there was no point in her achieving good examination passes as these would be superfluous to her later needs. This situation later resulted in a bitter parent–child conflict and in resentment and withdrawal from school. Eventually, in fact, the girl ran away from home to avoid an arranged marriage. Generally speaking, the non-white absentees appeared to be more influenced by domestic, curricular and bullying factors than the other pupils. Further research is again needed before firm conclusions can be made on this issue.

Some natural caution should be attached to the findings reported here, given that the results are based on the perceptions of a group of deviant pupils in a small-scale exploratory local study although, of course, 128 persistent absentees is quite a lot. After all, finding samples of truants is never easy! However, the categories and emphases shown in Tables 6.9 and 6.10 may need to change in other investigations. In any event, local factors undoubtedly played their part in the findings obtained from this enquiry. The fact that bullying, for example, was so frequently mentioned by the absentees probably highlighted a special problem in one of the two schools rather than a national problem. Evidence suggests that when bullying is rife in schools, there is a strong relationship between this and subsequent truancy.

The implications of the findings are that once pupils have begun to absent themselves from school and the initial 'cause' lies undetected, it is likely that the pattern of absence will continue and escalate throughout the pupils' subsequent school careers. This reinforces the importance of 'treatment' and preventative measures being taken in the primary schools and in the first three years of secondary schooling. Later casework will almost certainly fight either a 'lost' or a more difficult cause. It is probably even too late by the third year of secondary education. Thus, the findings tend to support the widespread belief amongst education welfare officers that appropriate remedial action should be taken with absentees very early in their non-attendance histories or the risk of success will be substantially reduced. The fact that only six pupils began to become persistent absentees during Year 10 of their schooling also suggests that early detection is the key. Detecting pupils as truants in Years 10 and 11 is much too late.

It is vitally important in the future that all professionals who work with persistent school absentees take into account the pupils' personalities and institutional records as well as their social backgrounds. Simply to relate absence to home circumstances may be convenient but it can also be erroneous or misleading. Such approaches cannot explain the possible 'causes' of absence but rather seek to retrospectively blame absence upon familial factors.

Future research may be able to show that absentee pupils will attend and/or return to school when they see it as being relevant to their needs. When absentees regard schools as irrelevant, or as reinforcing outdated concepts and exacerbating their failures, then the institution may unwittingly act as an agent which compounds the absentees' deviance rather than overcomes their unique difficulties.

Taken together, Tables 6.8 to 6.10 show that:

(a) educational reasons given for non-attendance increase with age;
(b) so does persistent absence;
(c) both (a) and (b) apply to boys and girls.

The most important fact however, is that most schools are presently not very good at:

(a) detecting initial absence;
(b) eradicating the initial causes of the absence at source, thereby preventing the drift into long-term absenteeism.

Given that schools are now in the technological age, and most have software on attendance, ascertaining (and acting upon) this initial information should not be as difficult as it has proved in the past.

The causes of truancy in schools in Scotland

The Scottish Council for Research in Education Project (1995) undertook research into the causes of truancy in selected primary and secondary schools. They reported that:

- Primary teachers believed that truants' parents gave regular school attendance a low priority compared with family demands.
- Secondary teachers agreed with this. They also thought some parents passed on the opinion that education was unimportant to their children.
- They believed this view would be stronger in areas of high unemployment.
- Secondary school staff also tended to think that truancy was motivated by dislike of subjects, a perception that some of these were irrelevant, and difficulty with school work.
- Less often, they thought reasons for playing truant included peer pressure, personality clashes between pupils and teachers, intimidation by the size of secondary school, bullying, school phobia and other psychological problems.
- Primary pupils thought being bored at school and not liking subjects were understandable reasons for staying away.
- Many primary pupils would consider staying away from school if their mothers asked for their help.
- Truants in secondary schools said they truanted because they were bored with school. Some of the 'good attenders' said that if subjects were more interesting and more choice was available, pupils would be more likely to attend.
- Primary pupils who played truant were most likely to spend the time at home.
- Secondary pupils who played truant were most likely to gather together and talk.

The statistical link between attendance, truancy and performance

The same study shows that non-attendance is the most significant cause for poor attainment. The findings showed:

- There was considerable variation in the extent of absence among the seven secondary schools in the sample.
- In every school explained absence was greater than unexplained absence.
- During the fist two terms of 1993/4, at least 89 per cent of pupils in each school registered some explained absence.

- In the same period, between 14 per cent and 89 per cent of pupils registered some unexplained absence. Two schools registered absence above 85 per cent, one at 14 per cent, and the remaining four between 40 per cent and 70 per cent.
- Absence rates for boys and girls in the same school were very similar although girls tended to have slightly more unexplained absence than boys.

Comment
These tables suggest that occasions of absence, whether explained (authorised) or unexplained (unauthorised) were relatively common in all seven secondary schools.

- The statistical analyses confirmed that as absence increased, Standard Grade awards dropped: by at least 0.05 of a grade for every 1.9 days' absence above the norm. Mathematics and English results were similarly affected by absence, although mathematics slightly more so than English.
- This general pattern of attainment falling as absence increased held in all seven schools, but the link between attendance and performance varied in strength among schools so that there were considerable differences between them.
- The data showed an overall pattern of decreasing Standard Grade attainment with increasing absence from school, but there was wide variation in absence rates between pupils gaining the same level of award.
- Explained absence was of comparable importance in its effect on performance to unexplained absence, and boys and girls were found to be more or less equally affected.

Comment
Although a drop of 0.05 of a grade may not seem large, for the pupils whose absences add up to more than 1.9 extra days the drop will be greater. For those pupils whose performance is on the borderline between grades, the drop will take on additional significance: the differences between Credit and General, General and Foundation awards are important.

The extent of variation among schools in the strength of the link between attendance and performance suggests that there is something about individual schools which creates those variations.

> The fact that explained absence is comparable in its effects to un-
> explained absence underlines how important it is that efforts be made
> to reduce the extent of absence from school of whatever kind.

Factors which influence pupils to play truant

The Scottish Council for Research in Education Project (1995) reported that
the following factors influenced pupils' decisions to play truant.

- Fewer primary school staff had much experience of truancy.
- However, almost all attributed such as there was in primary schools to
  those parents for whom family needs, such as looking after relatives, were
  more important than making sure their children attended school regularly.
  Some secondary staff also held this view.
- Secondary staff also felt that parents who had a low opinion of the value of
  school were likely to pass this on to their children so that they too gave
  education low priority and began to miss school of their own choice.
  Many staff thought these attitudes would be strongest in areas of high
  unemployment.
- Although such home factors were commonly believed to underlie truancy,
  even more frequently secondary school staff thought truancy was caused
  by dislike of particular subjects, especially if pupils could not see their
  relevance.

> *Comment*
> In this study staff views on the influence of home and social factors on
> truancy are unsupported by other evidence so represent no more than
> opinion. However, their views on the relevance of school to later life
> are echoed by the pupils' views.

- Data from the primary pupils suggest that even as early as P4 children
  think that boredom with school and dislike of certain subjects would be
  understandable reasons for staying away.
- Home factors were important for primary pupils as well: relatively large
  numbers of children in both P4 and P7 would consider staying away from
  school if their mothers or whoever looked after them needed their help.
  Almost all primary pupils were sure their parents would not approve their
  missing school unless they were ill or there had been an important family
  crisis such as a bereavement.
- S4 truant pupils mainly cited boredom with school coupled with a prefer-
  ence for being at work earning money as the chief causes of their truancy.

- Some 'good attender' pupils indicated that if school were more interesting and there were more choice of subjects, pupils would be less likely to truant.

Comment
It is notable that few of the pupils considered that truancy was brought about by parental influence, while only a few teachers offered the opinion that a reason for truancy was that the truant children were bored with school.

The number of parents who condoned truancy was thought very small: both primary and secondary school staff emphasised that most parents valued education and were supportive of schools, and the truants interviewed said their parents were angry that they had truanted. The main cause of truancy seems to be pupils' perceptions of school.

Truant and non-truant pupils alike considered that school was or could be boring, but the fact that they react to this in different ways suggests that boredom with school is not the only factor influencing truant pupils. However, there may be scope for teachers to reflect on their practice, to see if anything can be done to make learning more creative and interesting.

The impact of truancy

On truants

- Staff in both primary and secondary schools thought that one of the most important effects of truancy was that it hindered learning; pupils achieved less at school. However, they also cited other effects, related to pupils' ability to fit into society and develop a sense of self-discipline. A particular concern of primary staff was that pupils who became used to irregular attendance early in school life might develop a lasting habit of non-attendance.
- While teachers in both sectors were concerned about the effects of absence on learning, secondary teachers were more so.
- The truant pupils themselves knew their absences could affect their work adversely and most were uneasy about this. Many felt that because of their truancy, teachers were unwilling to help them catch up on missed work.

> **Comment**
> Staff and truants both believed that skipping school led to pupils doing badly in lessons. While the statistical analyses are compatible with this belief, they also suggest that attendance is not the sole influence on attainment.

On regular attenders

- In neither the primary nor the secondary sector were pupils who attended school regularly thought to be greatly affected by the absences of others, although head teachers shared the staff view that good attenders were deprived of teacher time when teachers helped truant pupils to make up missed work.
- There was little evidence from pupils that young people other than the truants were much affected by truants' absence from classes.

> **Comment**
> Although the impact of truancy on non-truant pupils in the schools was not great, the fact that there were pupils who reported a degree of frustration is important for those individuals.

On the staff and on the schools as a whole

- In general, primary staff were less affected by pupils' truancy than were secondary staff because their experience of it was more limited.
- When truancy was encountered in primary schools, head teachers reported greater administrative burdens. Classroom teachers reported frustration in going over old ground, and an extra workload as they tried to tailor lessons to the needs of returned pupils.
- In the secondary schools, the main effect of truancy on guidance and subject teachers was the stress of the added workload it brought, caused by the need for more complex classroom management and difficulties with lesson planning. As with the primary staff, teachers found it frustrating to go over old work.
- Head teachers in both primary and secondary schools were aware that high truancy rates would give a school a poor public image, but for most the problem of truancy was not great enough to cause undue concern.

Comment
Although truancy was not a major problem in most of the schools that took part in the study, the degree of frustration and sense of added work-load reported by staff who had to cope with it emphasise the value of reducing the incidence of truancy wherever possible.

In conclusion, perhaps the two key findings in this chapter are those presented in Tables 6.9 and 6.10. Both show that a majority of persistent absentees first missed school and continued to miss school because of factors which were influencing them within their particular schools. These findings pose a real challenge to teachers, and discovering solutions to this problem is the key theme of the rest of the book.

7   Government initiatives

Since 1997, the Labour Government has made a priority to tackle truancy, exclusion and disruptive behaviour in schools a key part of its strategy to raise standards and improve pupils' performance in schools. This chapter focuses upon the following recent initiatives aimed at tackling truancy and, to a lesser degree, social exclusion. These include:

1 the concept of setting schools clear guidelines at all phases of schooling to raise standards and set clear targets for improving literacy and rates of truancy;
2 the link between truancy, literacy and attainment;
3 the establishment of local homework clubs, homework guidelines allied to the development of pupils' information and communication technology needs;
4 introducing the idea of pupil panels to tackle truancy and the use of classroom assistants;
5 providing guidance on standards and special educational needs;
6 the relationship between truancy and exclusion;
7 tackling social exclusion;
8 summer school initiatives;
9 second chance schools;
10 the inspection of local education authorities;
11 the privatisation of state schools.

Standards and truancy: nursery and infant provision

The Government's initiatives designed to improve standards in schools are focused on all phases of schooling and begin with nursery, infant and primary education. The key ideas behind these targets for the early years are now presented as they all have a knock-on effect and relationship with the antecedents of truancy.

Key principles

- Good quality early years learning opportunities, alongside childcare and support for family learning where appropriate;
- thorough assessment of children when they start primary school;
- a concentrated drive to raise standards of literacy (with proper regard for oral expression) and numeracy, and develop positive attitudes to learning;
- smaller infant classes to support more effective teaching and learning.

Specific measures

- The establishment of early years forums representing the full range of providers and users of early years education in their areas. The forums will review the services available, including the provision of advice to parents before children start school, and devise early years development plans;
- improving quality and quality assurance procedures in schools by:

  (a) introducing common standards of regulation and inspection;
  (b) improving staff training and qualifications;
  (c) making better use of the role of parents;

- setting specific targets and standards for outcomes in early years education. These desirable learning outcomes will emphasise early literacy, numeracy, personal and social skills and learning through play;
- introducing common assessment schemes for children starting school.

The Government's view is that the better the start pupils make when first going to school, the better will be their long-term educational achievements. The greater the number of pupils who succeed; the fewer who will fail, drop out or need to truant.

Standards and truancy: primary school provision

Primary school education is arguably the, or one of the, most important phases in the long-term potential of human beings. Primary education is about more than literacy and numeracy. Yet, these core skills are at the heart of what is done in primary schools. They are also fundamental to all future learning. There is a clear correlation between underachievement in primary school and failure in adult life as well as with truancy.

It is now considered essential that:

- all primary schools primary schools regularly set and review their own targets for improvements in the basics;
- every school has a development plan;

- each school emphasises the importance of attendance and good behaviour for consistent learning to take place;
- every teacher understands the clear link between attainment and attendance.

For purposes of monitoring and accountability, national data on performance as well as for schools' own target setting should relate to agreed national targets. In this, there is a similar strategy in place for secondary schools. For example, local authorities and OHMCI will be invited to focus attention on the performance of schools where results fall in the bottom 25 per cent following statutory assessments at 11 and 14. The aim is to promote better results and raise standards.

All primary teachers need to know how to teach reading and maths in line with proven best practice. Quite often, teachers find that a successful approach includes:

- dedicated time given daily to aspects of literacy and numeracy in which a balance of whole-class, group and individual teaching is used under firm and rigorous teacher direction to enthuse and engage children;
- regular assessment of pupils' progress to enable the teaching to be tailored precisely to their stage of development;
- systematic teaching of phonics in reading as well as sentence and text level skills;
- constructive development of pupils' capacity in mental arithmetic and of applying mathematics in practical and lively ways.

Below are listed a series of other new initiatives which taken collectively should help to raise standards in primary schools, improve pupils' performance and, by so doing, help reduce the antecedents of truancy:

- local plans from schools to propose innovative new ways in raising standards while, at the same time, improving levels of literacy and numeracy;
- improved time management in schools, e.g. finding ways of spending more time to help some of the most disadvantaged and underachieving pupils, e.g. truants;
- providing guidance on good practice in target setting for primary schools;
- improved guidance for teachers on administering reading tests within schools. Schools will be encouraged to analyse results systematically, setting targets for improvement and reporting results to parents;
- providing better guidance to governors. Involving governors in school standards and school improvement issues, including performance indicators, e.g. school attendance, pupils' overall reading scores by comparison with local and national norms;
- supporting family literacy schemes and promoting educationally worthwhile out-of-hours activities to raise:

- standards
- literacy and numeracy
- pupils' cognitive and non-cognitive skills
- community appreciation skills
- recreational and sporting achievement.

- using TECs and other voluntary educational groups wisely;
- LEAs giving priority to professional development activities within nursery, infants and primary schools;
- improving educational/business links for primary schools thereby ensuring that more primary schools benefit from employer support;
- using out-of-hours childcare programmes wisely, e.g. in summer holidays;
- reducing class sizes for the youngest age pupils. Research shows that while smaller classes among early age pupils do not guarantee good results, they can make a significant contribution. They enable classroom teachers and/or classroom assistants, parent helpers, student-teachers, to spend more time with each child, to identify individual pupil needs and difficulties early on, and to offer the help children need to master the basics.

Wragg *et al.* (1998) undertook a project aimed at improving literacy in the primary school. Their research reported that there are ten signs of a successful teacher in primary school. These are:

- a high level of personal enthusiasm for literature, often supplementing the school's resources with their own books;
- good professional knowledge of children's authors and teaching strategies;
- importance of literacy stressed within a rich literacy environment;
- progress celebrated publicly and children's confidence increased;
- teaching individualised and matched to pupils' ability and reading interests;
- systematic monitoring and assessment;
- regular and varied reading activities;
- pupils encouraged to develop independence and autonomy, attacking unfamiliar words, or teachers backing pupils' judgement as authors;
- a high quality of classroom management skill and personal relationships with pupils;
- high expectations, children striving to reach a high standard, whatever their circumstances.

Truancy, literacy and attainment

There is little doubt that many truants have serious problems with literacy. Pupils with low literacy levels tend to perform poorly in formal assessments. They are also inclined to develop low academic self-esteem. Studies show that the reading scores for truants are often well behind the levels for the average population of schoolchildren.

There are probably several reasons which account for the difficulties which truants experience. First, they often emanate from homes where there is little encouragement for schooling. Second, many truants are brought up by parents who were themselves truants while at school. Third, parents of truants often read less to their offspring in the early years. Fourth, the homes of truants are often overcrowded and not conducive to quiet reading, study or homework. Fifth, research shows that as pupils fall behind their peers in terms of literacy and numeracy levels, they are likely to fall further and further behind as they grow older. Sixth, as truants, by definition, tend to spend less time in school, they receive less help with their learning needs. Similarly, because truancy is a sign of school rejection, teachers are often understandably less enthusiastic towards truants than their other regularly attending peers. Teachers also tend to spend less time in discussion with the parents of truants on academic-related issues. Parents of truants visit schools and attend formal parents' evenings less than the parents of good attenders.

For all these reasons, truants tend to be located in the lower sets/streams within schools. Research shows that regular attendance is the prime requisite for ensuring positive long-term academic attainment.

The Scottish Council for Research in Education Study (1995) reported the following correlation between attainment and attendance:

- the best attenders tended to perform best in school;
- as the level of absence increased, the level of standard grade award decreased – this was true for both mathematics and English language, but absence had a greater bearing on attainment in mathematics possibly because this is a sequential subject;
- boys and girls were almost equally affected by absence;
- in general, for every 1 per cent rise in absence, standard grade awards for both English and mathematics dropped by 0.05 grade points;
- the effect of explained absence was comparable in importance to the effect of unexplained absence;
- absence rates between schools showed considerable variation;
- apart from absence, there were no other factors affecting attainment;
- primary and secondary school staff believed that missing school would lead to poor performance;
- primary teachers were concerned that lasting habits of non-attendance might develop from early irregular attendance;
- despite evidence to the contrary, teachers tend to believe that apart from attendance, social and personal factors also affect pupils' performance at school;
- secondary teachers were more concerned about the effects of absence on learning than primary teachers;
- the truants themselves realised that their absence might make them fall behind and get lower marks; they also felt uneasy about the consequences;

- truants felt that when they returned to school, staff did not want to help them, and some secondary teachers agreed with this sentiment;
- primary and secondary staff thought that good attenders were not much affected by truants or truant behaviour – but good attenders would have less of the teachers' time if they had to spend more time with truants;
- most good attenders feel unaffected by truants and truant behaviour;
- some primary teachers thought failing to fit into society was as important an effect for truants as falling behind in work;
- headteachers thought high truancy rates gave schools a poor image;
- truancy was a major problem in only a few schools.

Setting schools' truancy targets

Schools will be obliged to meet attendance targets as part of the Government's initiative to cut truancy. Presently, schools have to reduce their levels of absence by one third by the year 2002.

Methods being considered to cut truancy include:

(a) home–school agreements. Under these schemes parents will be reminded of their responsibilities for ensuring regular and punctual attendance;
(b) the launch of homework clubs;
(c) forcing schools to reduce their levels of truancy by one third between OFSTED inspections;
(d) discouraging parents from taking their annual holidays with their children during school-time;
(e) providing pagers to the parents of constant offenders;
(f) introducing an electronic attendance system that marks pupils present at the beginning of every lesson;
(g) forcing schools to show their 'real' rates of truancy rather than 'fudging the figures' in order to improve their league table position;
(h) encouraging more truants to sit GCSE subjects by ensuring they can make up for lost time through the use of classroom assistant or parent-helper schemes.

These and other schemes will be discussed in more detail in Chapter 8. Briefly, at this point, other ideas for schools to consider include:

1 reducing levels of physical and mental bullying within their schools;
2 establishing a family literacy scheme organised by the school at a time convenient for parents and their children;
3 emphasising the importance to parents of good quality homework in raising standards;
4 advising parents on the needs of their children when undertaking home-work tasks (e.g. need for a desk to write on; ensuring children can work in a different room from the television; providing adequate lighting);

5   the use of home–school associations in every school;
6   better support within schools in providing for pupils with behaviour problems;
7   ensuring pupils with behaviour problems do not interfere with the learning of well-behaved pupils – otherwise some may vote with their feet;
8   excluding fewer pupils for truancy *per se*;
9   providing a more welcoming atmosphere where less able and disadvantaged pupils feel able to approach and discuss their concerns with staff.

Homework clubs, ICT and truancy

Homework guidelines

In theory, the development of homework clubs provides an opportunity for disadvantaged and underachieving pupils to have every chance to develop their learning skills and academic performance. The guidelines on homework clubs provide practical advice for parents and teachers about how much time children at different ages and stages should on average spend on reading with their families and on other forms of homework. For younger children, the emphasis is very much on reading and less formal tasks, whereas formal homework will usually come into play for older primary and secondary pupils. The lottery-funded study support centres are designed to offer facilities for homework, sports and arts in environments which are connected to 8,000 schools throughout the UK.

Research has previously suggested that more than two out of five 10-year-olds previously received no regular homework. By contrast, more than half this age group spend three nights or more watching television. The DfEE guidelines provide teachers and parents with sensible and realistic benchmarks on the amount of homework different age groups at primary and secondary levels might be expected to undertake. Homework policies should also be incorporated into home–school agreements.

The DfEE consultation documents suggest that the recommended time for daily home learning-based activities are:

	Reading	*Other home activities*
Reception class	10 mins	10 mins
Years 1 and 2	20 mins	10 mins
Years 3 and 4	20 mins	20 mins
Years 7 and 8	45–90 minutes per day	
Year 9	1–2 hours per day	
Years 10 and 11	1.5–2.5 hours per day	

The new homework guidelines are intended to give parents a clear idea of what is reasonable to expect at different ages. At the time these were issued in 1998, parents had been responding positively to TV advertising which encouraged more reading at home by parents with children. The homework guidelines are also part of new home–school agreement guidance which is being issued to schools to encourage improved co-operation between teachers and parents – and which will also tackle standards, truancy and discipline issues.

For younger-age children other home activities could mean reading and tackling sums with parents/carers. This would then become more formal home-work as the child grows older.

Homework clubs

Education and Employment Secretary David Blunkett announced plans in November 1998 to ensure that over 6,000 schools in England have homework and study support centres over the next three years. On a visit to West Ham football club to launch a new study support centre linked to the Premier League football club with Sports Minister Tony Banks, Mr Blunkett announced that there would be £220 million available – including an extra £80 million from 2000 from the Standards Fund. Ministers have already pledged £180 million across the UK – £140 million in England – for the New Opportunities Fund from the National Lottery to provide out of school hours learning opportunities.

The new centres targeted at children of 7 and over will provide a quiet place to do homework as well as offering sports and arts activities and access to computers.

Mr Blunkett was quoted at the launch as saying:

> 'Homework is an essential part of every child's education. It is right that parents should have a clear idea of what it is reasonable to expect for their children so that where no regular homework is given, they can dis-cuss this with teachers. But it is also essential that we provide the space and facilities to enable youngsters to do homework where it is difficult to study at home. Study centres will also improve access to sport, arts and computers for youngsters. The extra money we are announcing today – and the partnerships we are developing with football league clubs – will widen that access to many more children. I am very pleased that we have already got 29 football clubs on side. Clubs like this one at West Ham United are right on target when it comes to getting youngsters moti-vated to do their homework, and helping raise standards of literacy. Homework is one of many areas where partnership between parents and schools is essential. Homework does more than just reinforce what goes on in schools during the day, it also helps develop important skills like

independent learning and enquiry, as well as self-discipline. These are skills that will remain relevant throughout a person's life. Good schools have always had clear, well thought out arrangements for homework.'

For example, Huntingdon Secondary school in York uses its homework programme to develop the skills of independent learning in a systematic way. Coppermill Primary in Walthamstow takes a whole school approach to homework starting with reading, adding spelling in Year 1, and a fortnightly task in Year 5.

Playing for Success is part of the Government's drive to expand study support and out of school hours' provision generally. The study support centres will offer programmes focused on improved literacy, numeracy and ICT skills mainly for 7–14-year-olds who are disaffected or likely to become so. Other clubs signed up include: Barnsley, Blackburn, Bolton, Bradford, Charlton, Crystal Palace, Derby, Everton, Huddersfield, Leeds, Leicester, Liverpool, Manchester City, Middlesborough, Newcastle, Norwich, Nottingham Forest, Port Vale, Portsmouth, QPR, Reading, Sheffield Utd, Sheffield Wednesday, Stoke, Sunderland, Swindon, West Bromwich Albion and Wolves.

The development of a national grid of homework clubs will interface closely with other new learning and technological developments. These include:

- ICT for work on literacy and numeracy targets;
- the 'interchange of pupils' between schools and other learning centres, including the provision of master classes to stretch gifted (and under-achieving) pupils to their full potential;
- home learning schemes via the Internet or other ICT links;
- the sharing of teaching materials and best practice in teaching and learning with neighbouring schools;
- by removing barriers to learning, ensuring equality of access, notably for those in rural areas, those with special needs and those in areas of deprivation;
- the development of summer schools;
- extending school sporting opportunities for all;
- improving and developing the work of the Education Action Zones. Education Action Zone status is linked with action to support literacy and numeracy schemes, homework and study revision clubs, family learning, together with housing, health and social services initiatives locally.

It is too early to speculate on the positive effects which the development of homework clubs, ICT and the other initiatives will make on truancy. At the very least, they are bound to impact on the cycle of disadvantage, under-achievement and disaffection on which truancy thrives.

Home–school agreements

The DfEE's guidance for schools on home–school agreements was also published in November 1998. Schools and parents have a common interest: the child. It is important that parents know what to expect from their child's school who, in turn, are aware the school knows that their parents will support them. These agreements will cement that link. The agreements normally cover the ethos of the school, attendance, discipline, homework and any other information which the schools and parents feel they should give one other. In signing these agreements parents will be acknowledging the essential partnership needed between them and the school to educate their child.

Mr Blunkett stated:

> 'Taken together these initiatives are about partnership and opportunity. That partnership clearly chimes with what parents themselves want. Indeed we have had distributed over 1.5 million copies of the National Year of Reading leaflet which gives hints for parents on helping their children to read. We are helping children and young people to make good use of the time they are not at school as well as the time they are.'

Home–school agreements were introduced by the School Standards and Framework Act 1998. The DfEE issued draft guidelines for consultation in July 1998. Every school had to have home–school agreements as from September 1999. Where a registered pupil of compulsory school age is attending irregularly, the parent is guilty of an offence (s444, Education Act 1996) and can be fined up to £1000 per parent, per child. In addition to a fine, magistrates also have the power under s8 of the Crime and Disorder Act to impose a parenting order. Standards Fund money will be in the region of £20 million for 2000–2001 and £60 million for 2001–2002. Figures are for a grant rate of 50 per cent.

The New Opportunities Fund was created by the National Lotteries Act 1998. It distributes money to health, education and environment initiatives. It has £400m to commit to the out of school hours education and childcare initiative. The New Opportunities Fund (NOF) will commence its funding in 1999.

The National Year of Reading ran from September 1998 to August 1999. It aimed to encourage people of all ages to read more. People could telephone for the leaflet, 'A little Reading Goes a Long Way', containing tips on reading for children. Within the first few weeks, over 620,000 free leaflets were issued, which gives an indication of both the interest and the demand.

Pupil panels to tackle truancy and the use of classroom assistants

Experiments are beginning with pupil panels made up of children who regularly skip school in an attempt to tackle truancy levels in Britain. The scheme was co-launched by UNISON (the Union for Education Welfare Officers) and the National Association of Social Workers. Initial panels were set up in London, Scotland and the North West of England with a view to reporting their findings to the Government's Social Exclusion Unit. It is hoped that the panels will provide more light on why pupils miss school and how they spend their time when they are truanting.

Provisional findings suggest that the main reasons for missing school include:

- bullying;
- pupils finding school to be boring;
- dislike of subjects.

It is widely believed that peer pressure is another cause of truancy.

The concept of pupil panels could be extended locally to schools in the following ways:

- using pupil panels of good attenders to advise non-attendees on how to overcome their problems;
- by mentoring frequent absentees with good attenders to help them overcome their educational problems. This may prove particularly helpful in cases where absentees could be successfully re-integrated back into school provided they are able to catch up with outstanding school work;
- using pupil panels of absentees to advise individual schools on;

  - why they miss school;
  - what would make them return to school on a regular basis;
  - what changes schools could make to help them overcome their particular difficulties.

In the past, one of the main difficulties facing high truancy schools was how to find time to meet the individual and group needs of these pupils. It is suggested that schools could specifically identify classroom assistants and/or parent helpers to work with individual or groups of truants to help them to overcome their difficulties. As many truants suffer from low self-concepts often caused by their acute educational limitations, specific schemes to help these pupils overcome their literacy and numeracy problems can only be beneficial.

Standards, special educational needs and truancy

The Code of Practice on the Identification and Assessment of Special Educational Needs provides a framework for schools, LEAs, social services departments and health authorities for identifying and assessing special needs. Teachers have worked hard with local authorities and others to implement the code, and there have been worthwhile improvements.

There are 10 key areas to address in raising the standards of special education:

- early identification of SEN;
- dealing with disaffection and alienation;
- the professional development of staff;
- information technology;
- partnership with parents;
- the Code of Practice and the SEN tribunal system;
- co-ordination between statutory and voluntary agencies;
- partnership with healthcare professionals;
- securing a spectrum of provision for SEN;
- access to further and higher education.

£65 million to tackle truancy and disaffection

In October 1998, David Blunkett, Education and Employment Secretary announced a new programme worth nearly £500 million to cut truancy, unruly classroom behaviour and unnecessary exclusions.

The first steps in the Government's £500 million campaign to improve pupil behaviour were taken in January 1999, when Schools Standards Minister, Estelle Morris, announced £65 million for tackling truancy and disaffection and launched guidelines for schools on improving discipline.

Ms Morris announced Local Education Authority (LEA) allocations under two new Standards Fund grants: £57.4 million is being provided through the Social Inclusion: Pupil Support grant, including £22 million shared automatically between all authorities to provide for the first time, a full-time education for children excluded from school.

Of the £57.5 million available for Social Inclusion: Pupil Support in 1999–2000, £35.4 million is being allocated to 134 authorities on the basis of bids for local projects to tackle truancy and improve pupil behaviour. A further £22 million will be allocated between all authorities to help them move towards providing a full-time education for pupils excluded from schools. Following consultation with local education authorities the money is being allocated on the basis of the total number of pupils in the authority, weighted by the number of pupils entitled to free school meals. The LEAs will contribute half the amount of the grant. The remaining £0.1m will be used to evaluate the programme. This is the first year of funding under the programme of nearly £500m over 3 years which David Blunkett announced on 1 October 1998.

Another £4 million is available to enable 14–16-year-olds to study at college or gain work experience. The Work Related Learning grant will support over 100 high quality projects to regain the interest of disaffected and under-achieving pupils.

Examples of initiatives being supported include:

- a Gladiator Challenge in the Midlands leading to a Gladiator Event Day for primary school children whose attendance is good enough;
- a new engineering centre in Birkenhead to take up to 50 disaffected pupils from Wirral schools;
- schemes in Kirklees and Manchester involving pupils working with their peers to discourage them from skipping lessons and help prevent bullying;
- programmes in Greenwich and Barking and Dagenham to help youngsters who have been truanting in the last year of primary school make a smooth transition to secondary school with intensive summer school activity;
- the John Bunyan Pyramid in Bedfordshire which will link 13 schools with truancy problems and through home–school liaison, use of computerised registration schemes to monitor attendance, and mentoring programmes will tackle their problems together;
- an initiative in Hull City centre to develop vocational courses with the local FE college to help motivate pupils at risk of exclusion.

The Work Related Learning grant is targeted at geographical areas of social disadvantage and low educational attainment. Its priority will be to support further education provision for 14–16-year-olds, particularly those courses of study leading to approved qualifications; and Bridging Courses into employment or training. Money will come on stream in April 1999 with the DfEE providing 50 per cent. Ms Morris said at the press launch:

> 'Today's habitual truant will be tomorrow's criminal unless we act decisively now. Research shows that 65 per cent of school-age offenders sentenced in court had been excluded from school or were persistent truants. Similarly, schoolboy truants are more likely to be the unemployed adults of tomorrow. That is why we have given the police new powers to pick up truants and are providing £500 million over the next three years to improve behaviour and reduce both truancy and exclusions by a third by 2002.
>
> We must crack down on truancy and classroom delinquency. The guidance we are issuing today, for consultation, shows teachers what is successful in improving pupil behaviour and attendance, preventing avoid-

able exclusions, and how to provide an education for children who have been excluded. Serious misbehaviour should not be tolerated nor seen as inevitable, even in the most difficult circumstances. With the money we have announced today the guidance will give teachers practical ideas to beat the troublemakers.

We are working towards a simple but challenging goal: to raise educational standards for all our young people. But you can't do that if the children are not in school or are misbehaving. It isn't just their education which suffers. Keeping children in school and off the streets helps stop them drifting into crime. For example, in London, it is estimated that 5 per cent of all offences are committed by children during school hours.

In today's society what you earn depends upon what you learn. For their sakes, that means that we cannot let children waste their time in school. And the costs of crime which we all have to share mean we cannot afford the "out of sight, out of mind" approach to truancy.'

At the same press conference launch, Ms Morris also announced that a further £4 million would be spent in schools as part of the Crime Reduction Programme which the Home Secretary announced in July 1998. The money will pay for, and evaluate, projects to improve schools' management of attendance, behaviour and bullying and provide extra support for pupils at risk of exclusion, so as to reduce the risk of future offending. The plan is for the Government to support about thirty projects in the first instance.

Tackling truancy and exclusion

The new Pupil Support Grant to promote social inclusion will be available to all local education authorities (LEAs), but will be focused on schools which are well managed and which have significant numbers of pupils 'at risk' of disaffection, exclusion or truancy. It targets money at schemes that stop children truanting and help schools to cope with disruptive children with on-site units and other support. Where expulsion is necessary, full-time education will be provided. The money will also be expected to have an impact on youth crime.

The Pupil Support Programme will provide for schools and LEAs in partnership with others, such as social services, health services and the voluntary sector to build on the successful approaches that have been implemented under the Improving Attendance and Behaviour Grant and round 1 of New Start.

Mr Blunkett was quoted as saying:

'Figures published yesterday show exclusions rising to 12,700. That is the situation we inherited. Far too many children have been losing out on education each year because of truancy and exclusion. Not enough has been done to help schools cope with disruptive pupils. Following the Report by the Social Exclusion Unit, the Government set itself ambitious targets: a reduction, by 2002, of a third in the numbers of children who truant or are expelled without good reason. For those that are excluded, LEAs will provide a full timetable.'

The new 3-year fund will bring co-operation between schools, local councils and police in a package of measures, including:

- computerised registration facilities to help monitor attendance;
- more home–school liaison, and extra school staff to follow up non-attendance;
- truancy watch and pupil pass schemes;
- in-school units where disruptive children can be taught;
- extra cash, or 'dowries', for schools that accept excluded pupils;
- mentoring for difficult pupils;
- school plans for tackling bullying.

The programme will also introduce progress checks so that disruptive children who risk achieving very little at 16 are identified early so effective action can be taken. The Government is separately providing increased opportunities for a more work-related curriculum to re-engage youngsters at risk of disaffection.

This programme will help to prevent problems before they arise. It will support children who are finding school difficult and it will stop others wandering the streets who might be tempted into crime. The Minister stated: 'Too often it is those that get least from school that end up permanently on the margins of society. Their life chances wasted because with no qualifications they can't get work.'

Truancy and School Exclusion Report, 1998

The Government's first Truancy and School Exclusion Report was published in 1998. Below are reproduced its key recommendations.

The measures

- Targets for reducing truancy, focused on the worst performers;
- help to schools for achieving these targets and spreading best practice;
- giving priority in Education Action Zones to plans for achieving serious reductions in both truancy and exclusions;
- tackling disaffection with more imaginative approaches to the curriculum;
- a tougher approach to parents who fail to fulfil their responsibility to ensure that children are in school;
- a new power for the police to pick up truants.

On *school exclusions*, the measures include:

- targets for local education authorities to cut the numbers of exclusions;
- more resources focused on preventative work with children at risk of exclusion;
- clearer guidance, with legal force, to cut down on inappropriate exclusions;
- some Education Action Zones to focus on areas with particularly high levels of exclusion;
- special OFSTED inspections for high-excluding schools;
- a requirement that, by 2002, all excluded pupils receive full-time education;
- changes to performance tables, so exclusion cannot be used as a device to manipulate the reported figures;
- a major push to improve the school performance of children in care;
- measurement and reporting of the number of children from ethnic minorities who are excluded, as well as support for mentoring schemes.

The package of measures is designed to bring all agencies together with parents and pupils to cut time lost from education. They will re-establish the principle that education should be universal not optional. It underlines the Government's commitment to raising educational standards and to be tough on the causes of crime. It is a crucial part of the Government's wider strategy to tackle and prevent social exclusion. Levels of truancy vary greatly between schools and local authorities. To make a real difference there is a need to bring the weaker performers up to the level of the best.

Local targets

The first step is to turn the national target of a one third reduction into a series of targets for improvement at local authority level. These have been set out in LEAs' Education Development Plans, as attainment targets, and have applied since September 1999. Like the attainment targets, the improvement required should be most demanding for those who were the poorest performers in 1998.

The measurement of performance is a particular difficulty, given the concerns about the extent of post-registration truancy and therefore the accuracy of schools' reporting data as indicated earlier in the book. The DfEE is keen to establish accurate local figures on non-attendance. Therefore, LEAs are being encouraged to undertake their own supplementary surveys or other audits in order for accurate local targets to be set and met.

School-based targets

Another issue is that setting too many targets at school level could lead to unnecessary bureaucracy. But schools are already required to record attendance twice daily, and follow up unauthorised absence, and the best schools give this high priority. The Government requirement is for school-level truancy targets to be set, to ensure that improvement takes place where necessary. This will be used where a school's attendance record is significantly below average and this statistic will be linked to OFSTED's inspection process and range of reporting duties.

League tables

The Government will publish data on schools' performance on truancy in the same way as performance on attainment targets (down to school level for secondary schools and LEA level for primary schools).

Help for schools with truancy problems: Education Action Zones

Schools will be better able to play their part in achieving the national targets if they are properly supported. The Government already does a great deal to disseminate good practice and support projects through the Standards Fund. But the Government also proposes to make attendance issues central to the programme of *Education Action Zones* (EAZs) by making high levels of truancy and exclusion an explicit feature of the bidding guidance.

Planning for the first 25 zones began in 1998. Truancy was not an explicit condition of the bidding round but many bids include schools with high levels: the average level of truancy across all bids is almost three times the national rate. The EAZs' emphasis on educational underperformance will help to break the vicious circle of learning and attendance problems, while the community focus of zones will help to draw in other partners to bolster the efforts of the schools.

The curriculum

Research on truancy reports that some children say they truant because they see the National Curriculum as irrelevant. Alternative approaches, especially those which are more work-based, can be successful in preventing truancy.

The DfEE was in 1998/99 in the process of opening up opportunities for the wider use of work-related learning at Key Stage 4 (age 14 to 16). In addition, the Government is issuing clarifying guidance on the position for younger age groups, where head teachers currently have the power to disapply the curriculum for a limited period if they believe the child will then be able to return to the curriculum. It is important to ensure this power does not weaken literacy or numeracy teaching. Subject to this, it could offer a useful way of re-engaging some pupils at risk of disaffection.

Parents

Research indicates that 44 per cent of truants believe their parents know they skip school, and 48 per cent of non-truants were deterred by fear that their parents would find out. There can be no greater testimony to the importance of parental supervision and attitudes in preventing truancy. It is intensely demoralising for schools if parents condone truancy – or indeed actively encourage it by taking children out of school, for example for family shopping trips or on extended holidays.

Home–school agreements should help with this, but for more serious problems, more serious sanctions are needed. Where parents fail to ensure that their child attends school, they – not the child – commit an offence. But many schools and local authorities complain that when cases are taken to court and a conviction obtained, the fines imposed are very low. There is the question of the parents' means to consider and the courts may also have to take other factors into account. The Government is anxious that the issue should be taken seriously, and the DfEE is encouraging local education authorities to inform magistrates of local truancy problems so they have them in mind when considering cases.

In this context, the Crime and Disorder Bill, 1998, gives Courts an additional option. Where a parent has been convicted of failing to secure a child's attendance at school, the Court will be able to impose a Parenting Order for up to 12 months. The Order will be able to include specific obligations upon the parent, for example, that the parent escorts the child to school.

The police: new truancy powers

Schools need help from all local agencies, if they are to reduce truancy. The police are sometimes held back when dealing with truancy by the lack of an explicit power to pick up truants. The Government decided to give the police such a power and this was included in the Crime and Disorder Bill which came into force in July 1998.

This will enable the police to take truants back to school or to such a place as the local education authority may designate. The powers are framed in such a way as to reinforce multi-agency working and local truancy reduction schemes, thereby avoiding the risk that it will be seen as passing the responsibility for the problem on to the police alone. It should be stressed that this enabling power is restricted to the police and should not be attempted by other professionals. This is especially true in the case of delinquent truants who may be violent under certain circumstances.

The police's new truancy powers came into effect in February 1999. One of the first boroughs to introduce new 'truancy patrols' was Haringey where absenteeism from school stands at almost twice the national average. The police 'truancy patrols' work closely with education welfare and social services and tour the Authority in a specially designated van.

In the past, nosy neighbours, off-duty teachers, worried shopkeepers and the 'boardy man' were the only 'spies' on the streets as far as truants were concerned. But now, the police are in the front line. Previously, the police needed evidence that children were at significant risk of harm before they could pick them up. For example, this could mean standing around in a rent-boy area or sniffing glue by a canal. Today, under Section 16 of the Crime and Disorder Bill, 1998, the police are empowered to pick up children they believe are absent without authority and take them back to school.

Early evidence from Haringey suggests that truants who are being picked up on the streets and returned to school often have social or medical problems in addition to missing school. One boy, for example, was found to be experiencing severe stomach pains when apprehended. Others are carrying around false sick notes or other notes excusing them from school on the grounds of a sick note or a doctor's appointment.

Some of the pupils approached by the police were not truants. Two girls, for example, on bicycles outside the grounds of Tottenham Hotspur Football Club turned out to be refugees recently arrived from Mozambique and still without school places. Another pupil was found to be excluded from his primary school without any alternative provision having been provided. Another presumed truant turned out to be a young teenage mother. And, finally, another pupil turned out to have run away from home in a different part of the country. Clearly, the range of problems which the 'truancy patrol' in Haringey, and in other parts of the UK will find, will vary day by day, region by region. But even though the scheme is in its early days, the number of social, psychological and educational problems which are being uncovered on a daily basis are enormous and highlight the necessity for close links to exist between the police, social services, schools and the local education authority.

Changing the culture

With the measures set out in the Truancy and School Exclusion Report, the Government has in place the tools to achieve a step-change in truancy. Hopefully, this may help to end a situation in which failure to attend school is tolerated and sometimes condoned. Schools and LEAs will have to meet tough targets for cutting truancy. Police will be able to pick up children who fail to attend school. Courts will be able to fine parents and in some cases subject them to Parenting Orders. Parents already have a legal duty to ensure that their children attend school; the Government will ensure that this duty is reinforced. Together these measures will also have another important effect: they will change the attitudes of children themselves, as children learn that there is zero tolerance of truancy. This should achieve the step-change the Government seeks. However, the effectiveness of the strategy will be monitored carefully by all interested parties including the Government.

Summary of key recommendations

Below is listed a summary of the key recommendations of the Government's first Truancy and School Exclusion Report.

Truancy

- The overarching aim of the package is to deliver, by 2002, the target of a reduction of a third in the amount of time lost to truancy.
- The national target will be broken down into a series of targets for improvement at local authority level. The improvement required should be most demanding for those who are the poorest performers now. DfEE is consulting with local authorities over the procedure for setting the targets.
- The measurement of performance is a particular difficulty, given the level of concerns about the extent of post-registration truancy and, therefore, the accuracy of schools' reporting. The Government is considering how this can be addressed, whether through supplementary surveys or other audits.
- The Government is taking powers to require school-level truancy targets, to ensure that improvements take place where necessary. It will be used where a school's attendance record is significantly below average.
- Data will be published on schools' performance on truancy in the same way as performance on attainment targets (down to school level for secondary schools and LEA level for primary schools).
- Attendance issues will be made central to the programme of *Education Action Zones* by making high levels of truancy and exclusion an explicit feature of the bidding guidance.
- The DfEE is to open up opportunities for the wider use of work-related learning at Key Stage 4 (age 14 to 16) and issue clarifying guidance on appropriate circumstances to disapply the national curriculum for younger age groups.
- The DfEE will encourage local education authorities to inform magistrates of local truancy problems so they have them in mind when considering cases.
- The Crime and Disorder Bill gives Courts the option, where a parent has been convicted of failing to secure a child's attendance at school, to impose a Parenting Order for up to 12 months.
- The police have been given an explicit power to pick up truants in the 1998 Crime and Disorder Bill.

Exclusions

- The overarching targets of the strategy are that by 2002 there will be a one third reduction in the numbers of both permanent and fixed-term exclusions from their current levels. All pupils excluded from school for more than three weeks will receive alternative full-time and appropriate education.

- The national target of a one third reduction will be broken down into a series of targets for improvement at local authority level. The improvement required should be most demanding for those who are the poorest performers as measured by 1998 rates.

- To improve the knowledge base about exclusions, schools will have to notify LEAs of all fixed-term exclusions of one day or more. The Government is commissioning a major research study on the reasons for exclusion. From September 1999, the Government will collect aggregated data on the educational achievement of children being educated out of school.

- The Government will publish data on performance on exclusion down to school level for secondary schools and LEA level for primary schools. Since the problem of exclusions of ethnic minorities is so serious, the Government has decided that published performance data on exclusions should be broken down by ethnic group.

- The Government has amended the Schools Bill 1998, to give more guidance on exclusions. They have created new grounds for appeals against exclusions, and ended the inappropriate use of exclusion for very minor incidents. The new guidance focuses more on prevention, and covers all the reasonable steps that should have been taken by the school to avoid excluding the child. The Schools Bill has been amended to give LEAs the right to be represented and heard at governors meetings.

- The Government plans to change the procedures for calculating the performance tables to ensure that exclusion cannot be used as a device for manipulating the reported figures. One option would be for pupils who were in school at the beginning of Year 10 to continue to count on the school's roll until the end of Year 11. The Government is consulting on the best way to achieve this objective.

- The Secretary of State for Education and Employment has asked OFSTED to conduct special inspections of ten schools each year which have disproportionately high levels of exclusion or truancy, either overall or among specific groups, and particularly of those with African-Caribbean children. This will be outside their normal 6-year scheduled programme. Local authorities can also ask OFSTED to investigate if they have similar concerns, and the independent appeal panels which meet to consider disputed exclusions should draw to the attention of the local authority concerns they have about high-excluding schools.

- Exclusion issues will be made central to the programme of Education Action Zones. Combating high levels of exclusion is one of the Government's priorities.

- The DfEE is providing advice on specific measures to target funds for schools on preventative work with children at risk of exclusion and schools that receive excluded children: such funds will be conditional on there being joint plans and partnerships locally to engage all the relevant agencies.

- The requirement to provide out-of-school education for excluded pupils will encourage LEAs to support schools better in holding on to children at risk of exclusion: a logical system is for them to offer 'dowries' to schools as a support package to receive or hold on to children at risk of exclusion.

- The Government is ensuring that equal opportunities issues, as well as behaviour management, are adequately incorporated into the requirements for initial teacher training and in-service training. The DfEE Task Group on raising achievement of ethnic minority pupils is considering what can be done to promote community mentoring in ethnic minority communities.

- The Government is setting targets for the educational attainment of children in care. A starting point might be that 50 per cent of all children in care should achieve a qualification by 2001, and 75 per cent by 2003. In addition, effective education should be considered a key outcome of relevant social services work involving school-age children.

- LEAs will be obliged to provide every child who is excluded for more than three weeks with full-time and appropriate education. This will be imposed through changes in guidance. It is a new burden on local authorities and the resource implications are being considered in the Comprehensive Spending Reviews. Full provision is being phased in, and this should take no longer than three years. Once this pledge has been implemented, all children should have a clear individual plan, including a target date for re-integration.

- The Minister for School Standards will lead a Ministerial task force to review progress in tackling exclusion and truancy, and monitor the follow-up to the first Truancy and School Exclusion Report. In its further work on better integration, the Social Exclusion Unit will look at some of the 'joined-up Government' issues underpinning exclusion and truancy, including the multiplicity of statutory plans affecting young people, arguments for joint audit and inspection of different services as they bear on the same client group; the need for better information sharing between professionals, training to produce better understanding of inter-professional interfaces, and joint dissemination of the lessons of different departments' programmes to fund anti-exclusion and truancy work. This should include an examination of the case for a single consultancy resource within the DfEE to spread good practice and provide field support to aid the introduction of the new targets.

The link between truancy and exclusion and minority groups

Evidence shows that some groups within the community have well above average rates of excluded pupils; many of these pupils are also truants. One reason for this is the undoubted racism and racist attitudes which can be either endemic or beneath the surface in schools as the Lawrence Report (1999) highlighted.

Ethnic minorities

Sixteen per cent of permanently excluded children are of ethnic minority origin; and nearly half of those are African-Caribbean. Yet African-Caribbean children make up only a little over 1 per cent of the school population. One study found that African-Caribbean children who had been excluded had different characteristics from other excluded children in the study: a higher proportion lived with a lone parent, and they also tended to be of higher or average ability (but said by schools to be underachieving). They had not usually shown disruptive behaviour from early in their school career, and showed less evidence of deep-seated trauma. Statistically, African-Caribbean children are no more likely than other children to be persistent truants: this suggests that they are not disaffected with education.

A 1996 OFSTED research review explored the issue of ethnic origin and teacher–pupil interaction. It concluded that qualitative research has frequently pointed to a relatively high level of tension, even conflict, between white teachers and African-Caribbean pupils. Examples quoted varied from teacher complaints about 'troublesome' black pupils, disproportionate levels of criticism and control of black pupils, negative stereotypes, and a 'stimulus–response' situation where pupils identified and responded to expectations of low ability and disruptive behaviour.

African-Caribbean children

Successful projects work with parents and the wider African-Caribbean community. Mentoring programmes can be successful when they are part of a wider school strategy, when there is commitment from senior managers, well-trained mentors and good links with teachers and parents. As well as providing role models, mentors have an impact more widely in the school.

- *KWESI* This is a rapidly growing project in Birmingham. It was started after concern about high exclusion rates and low attainment of African-Caribbean children. KWESI largely provides mentoring support to schools. The project has won the support of both schools and the LEA; successfully recruited from the community, trained and put in place mentors; and has seen exclusion rates falling by 23 per cent. Two thirds of this reduction comprises ethnic minority pupils.
- *Lifting the Exclusion Zone* This is a partnership project of Divert, three local schools in Nottingham, local black-led churches and statutory agencies. Its aims are to reduce exclusions of African-Caribbean and mixed race children, to provide support for their families and to improve self-

- esteem, behaviour and school attainment. The project has recruited and matched 14 mentors with children, established a multi-agency advisory group, engaged with schools in case conferences and exclusion panels and won funding from local companies, LEAs and health trusts.

Children in care

There is a great shortage of data about the educational circumstances and achievements of children in care, and this in itself is a symptom of the low priority often given to their schooling. However, different small studies have shown that:

- the permanent exclusion rate among children in care is 10 times higher than the average;
- perhaps as many as 30 per cent of children in care are out of mainstream education; whether through exclusion or truancy.

Some of this may be attributable to poor communication between professionals. Studies have shown that social services staff are often vague about the exclusion status of children in their care or how to appeal and that schools do not always know that a child is in care. But other relevant factors include the influence of family relationships before the child entered care, and the frequency of placement breakdowns. A new placement in a new area disrupts education through a change of school. Exclusion can add to this vicious circle: many foster parents cannot cope with a child at a loose end all day so exclusion often triggers a breakdown in care placement.

The Truancy and School Exclusion Report (1998) showed that joint planning between LEAs and social service departments was now happening in quite a number of authorities, and can help to reduce the excessive numbers of children in care who are excluded. It needs to become the norm.

Hampshire Social Services Department, for example, provides a model of good practice. It has a specialist service, involving nine qualified teachers, who make sure the 700 children in care have access to the best educational opportunities. They work with social workers, young people and the schools. Each young person has his or her own education plan, which is actively monitored and followed up. This service produces regular reports showing:

- attendance levels;
- numbers permanently excluded;
- numbers in mainstream, special and other education;
- areas of concern and good practice.

In 1997, children in care in Hampshire achieved the following results:

- 56 per cent passed one or more GCSEs;
- 14 per cent passed five or more GCSEs at A to C;
- 27 per cent in mainstream schools passed five or more GCSEs at A to C.

What happens to children who are excluded?

Children who are permanently excluded should be quickly re-integrated back into school wherever possible. But this happens in only about a third of cases. The rest lose their entitlement to full-time education and receive what is known in education law as 'education otherwise'. This is arranged by LEAs in most cases, either in special centres known as Pupil Referral Units (PRUs), through home tuition which may only be for a few hours per week, or in a further education college. Current guidance recommends that teachers set work for children who are excluded for a fixed term. However, the guidance is not statutory and evidence suggests this does not happen.

There are about 25,000 children receiving education otherwise. One survey suggests it costs about four times as much to provide as mainstream schooling but that children receive on average only 10 per cent of full education. OFSTED's report on the first 12 inspections of PRUs painted a generally poor picture: a full timetable was rarely provided. Once it had inspected 100, five had been found to be failing and in need of special measures. However, more recent inspections show that PRUs are becoming more successful in improving attendance and stimulating positive attitudes to learning and behaviour. They are less successful in their assessment of children's prior attainments and monitoring academic progress.

Preventing and managing exclusion

The best approaches to exclusion ensure that problems are prevented and dealt with quickly, and that when children are genuinely disruptive they are not abandoned but provided with help and education outside the school environment. The best approaches always include some or all of the following:

- unambiguous rules, a clear hierarchy of sanctions, applied consistently when the rules are broken. Parents, staff and governors need to stand shoulder to shoulder on discipline, and children need to be in no doubt about the consequences of bad behaviour. Where this is done, schools see fewer disruptive incidents, and more class time is spent learning;
- behavioural problems need to be identified at primary school or early in secondary school and teachers need to be well trained in behaviour management with an equal opportunities perspective;
- where necessary, help available quickly from specialists, perhaps educational psychology service or child and adolescent mental health services;
- good arrangements for sharing information between services and for joint working more generally, overcoming agency and professional boundaries;

- early involvement of parents, good community links, role modelling and mentors;
- a more flexible and creative approach to the curriculum, particularly for older children.

When children have to be disciplined for bad behaviour this may lead to exclusion. Evidence on good practice suggests that:

- a very clear process, case conferences and mediation give an opportunity for other agencies and the parents to get involved;
- 'internal exclusion' from, for example, part of the school or a particular lesson, can be useful. It ensures children are on site all day, learning, rather than roaming the streets. Some schools have 'sanctuary' rooms, where children can be sent to cool off, under supervision, for a lesson or two;
- dual registration at school and a PRU can mean the child gets specialist support without having to be excluded from the school. It can help if the PRU is on the same site as the school;
- if groups of schools work together to run informal 'one in – one out' arrangements for excluded children, time out of school is minimised;
- when a child already has special educational needs, it is generally better to hold a review to find alternative or additional resources rather than to exclude.

The London Borough of Newham has succeeded in reducing the numbers of children excluded from school, including black and other ethnic minority children, children in care and children with special educational needs. Its policies have been agreed corporately by the council. The numbers of permanently excluded children have decreased across the authority in secondary schools from 76 in 1993–94 to 31 in 1996–97.

Langdon School is a large comprehensive in East Ham which did not exclude any pupils in 1996–97 and only one pupil in 1995–96. It has a whole-school approach that includes:

- very clear preventative policies;
- early help for behaviour and learning;
- home–school agreements;
- targets for each pupil;
- a sanctuary room for children.

Alternative education

When children do have to be permanently excluded, the best provision has a number of common features:

- for all pupils there should be a very clear learning plan, with objectives and targets, time scales for achievement, overseen by a named worker. Attendance at a pupil referral unit needs to be enforced as rigorously as at mainstream schools;
- for younger children, there should be a very clear plan and time scale for re-integration, with good links back to mainstream provision. This could be from a PRU or from home tuition with opportunities for group work. A key worker who takes a special interest in the child and who has responsibility for following up progress helps a great deal;
- if reintegration really is not possible, plans for a permanent satisfactory solution should be in place, with clearly allocated responsibility to make it happen;
- some older children need, and respond better to, more flexible and vocational learning than to the National Curriculum. Work experience and further education leading to further training or employment are very positive;
- a mentor, perhaps a university student, someone from the local community or business, or someone who has overcome earlier school difficulties, can help to remotivate young people and turn them away from anti-social behaviour.
- Include (previously called Cities in Schools) works in partnership with 25 local authorities to help over 1,000 young people who are all either excluded or long-term non-attenders. Of these, 40 per cent are persistent or serious offenders and 33 per cent are in care. Includes bridge courses for 14 to 16 year olds who have suffered irretrievable breakdown in their education and blend a further education course with work experience and a personal development programme supported by a key worker. The full-time cost is about £5,000, which compares to an average of £8,000 for education otherwise. Include is also developing re-integration and prevention services.

Tackling social exclusion

Social exclusion wrecks lives and wastes resources. This is the mantra of the Social Exclusion Unit (SEU) that gives us all pause to take stock. The SEU is right, of course. Its first three reports – on truancy and exclusion, rough sleepers, and neighbourhood renewal – show a consistent pattern of cause and effect. They identify individuals and communities who are cut off from mainstream services and social networks.

People who are socially excluded are less likely to have ready access to public services and find those services more difficult to use. They are more likely to lack basic literacy and numeracy skills, to be unemployed or in low-wage employment and to suffer disproportionately poorer health. Some may become involved in drugs misuse and crime; many more will be victims of crime or lead lives restricted by the fear of it.

The real tragedy is that lives need not be wrecked, nor resources wasted on repairing the damage, were we systematically to apply what we already know. The SEU in its reports – and the Government in many of its White Papers has gathered together many examples of public, private and voluntary sector interventions. Community, self-help, caretakers and neighbourhood wardens, for example, have increased local surveillance, reduced crime and brought neighbourhoods back into good repair. Adult mentors and work-based curricula for 14 year olds have played their part in greater staying-on rates and higher educational attainment and rates of employment. Local authorities have brokered agreements with key commercial services to have them return to socially excluded communities.

So the question for public sector managers is not 'How can we tackle social exclusion?' but 'Why aren't we doing so?'

Work being done shows that a major barrier to tacking social exclusion is that people who hold the responsibility often don't have the power to act. Many organisations now have designated posts focusing either on the overall issue or on key parts of it such as community security, educational attainment and regeneration. The problem is that these posts are generally on the edges of organisations and, despite the efforts of very able staff, they can easily become detached from the organisational mainstream. There is little chance for people in these posts to make much headway, for instance, by achieving major turnarounds in the use of mainstream budgets and services.

Part of the problem originates from the way Government works in vertical departmental 'silos'. At the national level, this is something that the SEU, actively chaired by Tony Blair, is trying to change. Examples of early successes include the immediate amendment of education legislation to include recommendations from the truancy and exclusions report and the publication of joint health and social services priorities, underpinned by an explicit aim to treat the two sectors as one.

Locally, too, there is much that can and is being done. Early studies identify seven key areas for action and, more importantly, show how they must be linked together to ensure a coherent and effective joint attack on the problem. They are:

- *the identification of positive social outcomes* enabling people to see that life can be different and to identify what they want from it – the essence of community planning;
- *community self-help* recognising the abilities and resources of people who are socially excluded and enabling them to use these to rebuild social networks, restore community confidence and make effective use of democratic processes;
- *the restoration or remodelling of private sector services* such as stopping whole areas being 'redlined' and so being unable to get insurance cover, and connecting people into the informal networks through which many employers recruit;

- *the improvement of public sector services*   such as targeting and siting services to increase access and providing community leadership to help communities and excluded community leadership to help communities and excluded individuals to gain a voice and get a response from key organisations;
- *collaborative community and organisational action*   working through zones, partnerships, joint service management, one-stop shops and pooled budgets to ensure services dovetail with one another and with local communities;
- *the re-gearing of local public sector management*   rethinking the way public services are planned, commissioned, provided, managed and quality assured to provide a consistent, mainstream focus on building social cohesion;
- *regional, national and European action*   using the appropriate levers to bring about local change, and working with others to create a favourable policy environment within which to tackle social exclusion.

The summer school initiative and the Internet

Mr Blunkett announced in 1999 there would be twice the number of funded summer schools as previously, with some 1200 schools participating, and an extra £105 million for the National Grid for Learning Initiative, the network which links schools via the Internet to curriculum materials. There were, for example, 900 literacy and 300 numeracy summer schools in 1999. He said,

> 'The summer school initiative has proved a real success. The teachers are enthusiastic, the children are learning and parents have become involved too. In the first year, there were just 50 schools. In 1999, there will be 1200, providing lessons for over 40,000 children. These schools play a crucial role helping those children who need extra help in either literacy or numeracy before they go on to secondary school.'

Commenting on the investment in the National Grid for Learning Mr Blunkett said,

> 'The world does not stand still. We can get more from the money we are investing in education if we harness new technologies. That is why we are modernising the classroom through the National Grid for Learning. The extra £105 million will help it to develop its content and the infrastructure.'

Second chance schools

The Government is providing opportunities for second chance schools for pupils aged between 14 and 17. The aim is to provide pupils who have dropped out of school early, and who are finding difficulty in obtaining regular employment, to be given a second chance as part of New Deal opportunities. These pupils will be paid for studying. They will mainly follow GNVQs which it is hoped will provide the students with the necessary skills to obtain meaningful employment.

European money is also likely to be sought to provide second chance opportunities for disaffected youngsters who have failed in mainstream schools. Yorkshire is the site for the proposed first school of this type.

In Scotland, the Government is proposing establishing new multi- and inter-disciplinary schools to work with socially disadvantaged, underachieving and failing pupils. As part of this scheme, teachers in schools will work alongside social workers, other caring professionals and people in the community to ensure that pupils' social and educational needs are being met at the same time.

First day contact

Worries over missing school children and concerns about child abuse have led to the DfEE issuing new advice and guidelines on how to inform parents. Headteachers are currently concerned about the added pressure this will bring on top of a school's already busy workload.

The publication of the Government's new guidelines coincided with the announcement of £65 million in Government grants to cut truancy. The money, which is the first slice of £500 million announced by Mr Blunkett in 1998, will be spent on schemes including vocational education for disaffected pupils, pagers for parents of persistent truants and summer schools to help absentees catch up with work they have missed.

Ministers are urging schools to contact parents on the first day of a pupil's absence, raising concerns of impossible workloads for headteachers.

The guidelines were published as part of a consultation document on how to cut truancy and support vulnerable children. But the advice gained added significance following the disappearance – and safe recovery – of the two East Sussex 10-year-olds, Lisa Hoodless and Charlene Lunnon in 1999. The girls' school, Christ Church in St Leonard's, was publicly criticised for waiting a whole day before the parents were informed.

The Government's draft guidance on pupil support says: 'If a pupil is absent without explanation when the register is called, school staff should wherever possible contact the parents that same day'. This would make it clear to families that absence is a matter of concern.

Manchester became the first LEA to recommend first-day absence checks for all its schools. A spokesperson for Manchester stated:

> 'While we can't require schools to do this kind of thing, we can encourage and demonstrate the benefits. If we can put before them [the schools] both the attendance issue and the child protection issue, then these are compelling grounds.'

Consequently, Manchester has given this advice to its 200-plus schools.

Manchester moved quickly to follow the Government's advice partly because of the death of Suzanne Ravity, aged eight, who died at the hands of her mother's lover in 1997. Despite missing thirteen consecutive days at school, she was never checked on by teaching staff. By the time her case was referred to welfare officers, she was dead.

But headteachers' leaders have described immediate attempts to locate absentees as often being unrealistic. David Hart, the General Secretary of the National Association of Headteachers, said

> 'It will impose considerable pressure on schools not only in normal cir-
> cumstances but particularly where schools are suffering from large-scale
> absences during incidents such as flu epidemics. We do need to strike
> a sensible balance between the needs of pupils and the needs of schools.'

Education Secretary David Blunkett, speaking on Radio 4's 'Any Questions', struck a more emollient note: 'I understand it isn't possible in all circum-stances. We don't expect the moon'. Parents had to play their part as well as school staff.

Anne Hanney, Head of Christ Church School, said she attempted to account for all children within the first day. But on the day Lisa and Charlene disappeared, 32 children were off sick and 17 pupils late, making an immediate response very difficult.

> 'At the moment, this is a school of 480 children with two telephone lines.
> One mother wanting to talk to us has not been able to get through until
> 10.30 am.'

She said the idea of recruiting parents to ring round absentees had been considered but rejected because many absences were for confidential reasons.

The Government's advice could present headteachers such as Maggie Terry, the Head of Ambler Primary School, Islington, North London, with a compli-cated 'ring round' every morning. The school draws 48 per cent of its 435 pupils from homes which either do not speak English or speak it as a second language. She said,

> 'In theory, it is a very sound idea. In practice, there are difficulties. I would
> have a problem with interpreters. I have someone from virtually every
> country in the world in this school. Contact will be made even more diffi-
> cult because many families are living in accommodation for the homeless,
> without immediate access to telephones.'

Wyn Morgan, Head of Kings Houghton Middle School, Houghton Regis, Bedfordshire, says he is lucky to be running a school with a relatively low absence rate. But the prospect of first-day contact still raises problems. Many children come from families with two working adults and the school may often be ringing back-up contacts, such as grandparents who live out of the area, to find out why a student was not in school. 'We have about 509 children, so you can imagine what it would be like trying to ring round in the morning', Mr Morgan said. The onus should be on parents to contact the school. 'They usually have only one or two children, so it is easier for them to ring us, than for us to ring them'.

Mick Bucktrout, head at Airedale High School, Castleford, Wakefield, believes immediate contact with the parents of all unexplained absentees will be impossible without more money.

> 'We adopt a policy of first-day response for children that have a history of absence which suggests that they might be truanting. However, we don't have such a policy for all children because in a school of more than 1,000 with an absentee rate of, say, 10 per cent, we would have 100 off.
>
> Some families are not on the phone. In order to get in touch, we would have to have a full-time worker. My suggestion would be: if the Government feels that it is a good idea then it needs to allocate funds.'

In Manchester, the LEA admitted that first-day contact had significant implications for resourcing and staffing. The LEA believed that reallocating and re-examining the responsibilities of non-teaching staff could be a useful first step in the process.

The inspection of local education authorities

The Government's Consultative Document published in January 1999, proposed a framework for the inspection of local education authorities commencing in September 2000 onwards. It is likely to prove extremely beneficial in co-ordinating attempts to combat truancy, disruptive behaviour, school exclusions and other forms of disaffection. LEAs will be inspected every two years. Key themes in the inspection will be raising standards in literacy, numeracy and/or information and communications technology (ICT).

The framework includes the inspection of LEA documentation, performance indicators, guidance notes and approval of schools' development plans. Visits to schools and other educational settings will take place as part of the overall assessment. Further evidence of LEA effectiveness will derive from, for example:

- the evaluation of the standard of pupils' work and the quality of teaching;
- discussion with pupils, teachers, headteachers and governors;
- examination of pupils' assessment records, school reports and individual education plans;
- assessment of the quality of links with support services;

- the evaluation of the sufficiency and adequacy of school buildings and resources.

One key part of the OHMCI and Audit Commission visits will be on the extent to which LEAs and schools are not only raising standards but reducing previously published levels of truancy, exclusion and disruptive behaviour. Based on the findings from all the above elements, LEAs will be deemed to be more or less successful. LEAs will have to prepare and publish an action plan within seventy days of receiving their report in England and eighty days in Wales if a translation of the action plan into or from Welsh is deemed by the LEA to be necessary.

The OFSTED (1999) Report on *Raising the Attainment of Minority Ethnic Pupils* came to the following conclusions on the link between guidance and support on school attendance.

> Practice varies, but most LEAs do not monitor their attendance data by ethnicity unless there is a significant issue such as the impact of extended holidays to the Indian sub-continent, and even then LEAs respond in different ways. A few LEAs have identified extended leave as a significant factor in depressing the attainment of minority ethnic groups and can produce research evidence to support this view. However, the picture is far from simple and attainment is not depressed for all pupils. Some schools have better 'catch-up' strategies to minimise the impact of extended leave. These LEAs issue guidance to schools on liaising with families about such visits. Procedures emphasise that families must ask schools for permission for absence and must set a return date if pupils are to remain on roll. One north east LEA which does not monitor attendance by ethnicity is nevertheless concerned about the impact of extended leave and has raised the issue with the local Race Equality Council in order to make families aware of the educational disadvantage posed by such visits. Schools in this LEA maintain pupils on roll regardless of the length of their extended absence.

Research also indicates that fewer parents from some ethnic minority groups attend school events such as parents' evenings. One study reported, for example, that very few Bangladeshi parents attended local schools' parents' evenings. Only 11 per cent of the parents of Year 7 Bangladeshi pupils attended parents' evenings. However, as a result of a number of actions led by a Bangladeshi science teacher in the school, including telephone calls, letters of encouragement and offers to accompany parents, the attendance of the parents of these same pupils (then in Year 9) rose sharply to 74 per cent. Similar initiatives may be required with ethnic minorities in some schools to provide appropriate study support; monitor literacy and numeracy; promote good standards of behaviour, pastoral care and mentoring, as well as to monitor equal opportunities issues.

Failing schools and privatisation

A specialist comprehensive school in the West Midlands – which OFSTED lauded as only one of 40 improving secondary schools in England to have made significant progress between inspections – was chosen in early 1999 to lead the first private sector takeover of a failing state secondary school. The City Technology College in Kingshurst, Solihull, through its commercial arm 3Es Ltd, won the bid to run the failing King's Manor School in Guildford, Surrey.

King's Manor, a 1950s red brick structure, lies in one of the most depressed areas of Guildford. Externally, the school appears successful. There is no vandalism, litter or decay in the buildings. However, King's Manor has been under-subscribed and was used by the local authority as a 'dumping ground' for excluded pupils from other schools. The school was regarded as failing and the LEA wished to close it.

The King's Manor Project will be reviewed with interest by all involved in education. The Government currently proposes that this first privatisation may be the forerunner of many more. Although truancy *per se* was only one of the problems faced at King's Manor, it is the solutions as much as the causes which will interest the Government in this experiment.

8　School-based initiatives

This chapter focuses upon over thirty different and practical schemes which schools can implement to help combat truancy. These ideas are provided as a result of:

(a) evidence obtained from the literature;
(b) feedback from teachers in schools in England, Scotland and Wales on in-service training events;
(c) data obtained from master's degree (taught and research) students under the supervision of the author at Swansea Institute;
(d) school-based research projects.

Headteachers and teachers reading these ideas may wish to use one or more or a combination of some or most of them as befits the needs of their individual schools. Ideas included in this chapter are:

1　personal and social education programmes;
2　use of foundation programmes;
3　corrective schemes to overcome literacy and numeracy problems;
4　suggestion box schemes;
5　use of classroom assistants;
6　home–school, parent, pupil contracts;
7　use of security firms;
8　use of role play;
9　formation of anti-truancy teams;
10　positive reinforcement and lottery-type schemes;
11　the place of at-risk registers;
12　combating lateness;
13　combating post-registration truancy;
14　return to school policies;
15　managing school transfers properly;
16　clarification of staff roles;
17　use of paging systems;

18 improved recording of attendance;
19 inter-agency co-operation;
20 disaffection: truancy, behaviour and exclusion in relation to alternative curriculum provision;
21 improving home–school communication;
22 use of social workers in schools;
23 second chance opportunities;
24 use of private schools;
25 improved health checks;
26 appointment of attendance support teachers;
27 appointment of an attendance support secretary;
28 extension of primary school practice;
29 compensatory programmes;
30 supporting teachers and schools in preventing exclusions;
31 mentoring of truants;
32 flexibility of approach.

Ideally, these ideas need to be read alongside the Government's initiatives in Chapter 7 and the ideas contained in the remainder of this book from Chapter 9 onwards. Taken collectively, they provide schools with an abundance of up-to-date information and schemes which really do work when put into practice effectively.

Personal and social education programmes

Few schools presently include the topic of truancy, parental-condoned absenteeism, specific lesson truancy, etc. as a key part of their personal and social education (PSE) programmes. An examination of PSE programmes in Years 7 to 11 in selected comprehensive schools in England and Wales, specially undertaken for this text, revealed that popular topics for inclusion included: settling into secondary school, codes of behaviour, study skills, first aid, health hazards (AIDS, smoking, etc.), exam techniques, insight into industry, the changing body, sex education, gender, bullying (and/or bullying initiatives), records of achievement, the consequences of crime (shoplifting, joyriding), health and safety, alcohol abuse, child abuse, relationships, home school responsibilities, dress sense, drugs, action planning in careers, youth enterprise, the community and local environment, equal opportunities, disabilities, religious toleration, ethnicity, meningitis, etc. Quite a list! Yet, of all the schools' PSE programmes examined, only one included truancy on its contents list – and this only in Years 10 and 11; far too late.

Truancy is an important issue for pupils to understand. Understanding can lead to rejection – the same theory as in educational programmes about drugs and alcohol abuse. When pupils are confronted with the realities of truancy – poor jobs in later life; lower wages; links with criminality; social and psychological distress – they are much more likely to think twice about truanting.

Enabling pupils to understand the short- and long-term consequences of their action is important. Truancy education should start as young as possible – early in Year 7 would be best in secondary schools. Truancy as a topic can be closely related to programmes on behaviour, discipline, disruptive behaviour, codes of practice and bullying which are already key themes in many schools' PSE programmes.

Foundation programmes

Research shows that there is often a considerable gulf between pupils' attainment and achievements in primary schools at the point of their secondary school transfer. Often these divides are not due to innate intellectual differences but to measured differences between primary schools' outcomes even in homogeneous areas, weak or very good teaching (by subject or across the board) or due to a wide range of other local, social and educational factors.

Some schools are beginning to find that the use of foundation programmes can help all pupils in Year 7 to start from the same baseline. For example, using the first six weeks of Year 7 to ensure pupils are ready to advance into the National Curriculum. Alternatively, using periods of time in Year 7 or later to boost pupils' reading and/or literacy and numeracy levels.

Research suggests that it is pupils who have fallen two or more years behind their own reading ages at the point of secondary school truancy who are more likely to continue to fail in school and to truant. Successful pupils rarely persistently truant. Enabling pupils to catch up with their numeracy, literacy and reading abilities should be a key strategy in the prevention of truancy especially for schools with a high proportion of pupils emanating from socially deprived and disadvantaged communities. Some educationalists believe that each new year should begin with a 2-week foundation programme based on pupils' individual and collective needs.

Corrective schemes to overcome literacy and numeracy problems

Research shows that it is possible to reduce pupils' literacy and numeracy problems in comparatively short periods of time by concentrated efforts. For example, a learning support department can introduce a Corrective Reading Scheme aimed at raising basic literacy levels through the use of a daily structured group reading programme. Such programmes are designed to be positive and supportive for pupils. The need to attend on a regular basis should be emphasised. Success in a programme can also be linked in with a reward system.

One study found average gains in reading ages on the New MacMillan Reading Analysis Scheme of between 18 months and 2 years over a 3-month period across all four levels of the programme using a Corrective Reading

Scheme. There were specific cases of persistent absentees attending for the research programme who missed the rest of their schooling. This must say something about *relevance* within the curriculum; not least related to pupils' aptitudes.

Suggestion box schemes

The use of the suggestion box scheme originates from the United States and from initiatives on bullying such as the Childline movement. The use of suggestion boxes in schools can be widened to include a whole range of problems which put pupils at risk. It is imperative that such schemes follow these principles:

(a) the box should *not* be placed at the end of a long corridor;
(b) the box should not be placed outside the office of the head, deputies, heads of year, etc.;
(c) the ideal location is in a quiet spot close to a busy part of the school which all the pupils tend to use. This means the pupils can easily gain access to the box while, at the same time, not drawing attention to themselves;
(d) the information given should be anonymous;
(e) staff should not overact when/if the box is used for trivial and/or different purposes from the ones intended.

In schools where suggestion boxes have been used the following outcomes have been found:

(a) the boxes can be more or less frequently used, often dependent upon the amount of publicity given to their use;
(b) the boxes tend to be used more by Year 7 and 8 pupils rather than older age groups. However, when the boxes are used by older age pupils (including sixth formers) the issues can be serious. For example, the use by a pupil to indicate that her friend is pregnant and needs help; or, a pupil is not a truant but is being abused at home. Or, there again, a pupil is staying at home to comfort the mother (following a separation and/or divorce) or because the mother needs company and/or protection.

Suggestion boxes are unlikely to help in trivial cases of non-attendance. They can however, be 'life savers' in potential or actual serious cases. Many pupils exhibit deep concerns about their friends in need or trouble but are reluctant to speak to staff in authority about them. Suggestion boxes, appropriately used, can form a convenient half-way house. They are most useful in potentially the most serious cases and can be life savers, e.g. when a person is truanting because of the severity of his or her bullying.

Use of classroom assistants

Many teachers are simply too busy to give pupils in need the attention they require. In primary schools, the use of classroom assistants in some LEAs is commonplace. Similar schemes need extending to secondary schools.

Classroom assistants can be paid or unpaid, trained or untrained. They might be parents, mature (even retired) people, personal tutors, mentors or simply volunteers. The use of classroom assistants can be particularly beneficial with pupils who have reading, literacy or numeracy difficulties, special needs, behavioural problems and who need to catch up with missed work such as truants.

The use of classroom assistants on a national basis at all levels of the education service could be especially beneficial in combating inequality especially for those pupils who emanate from socially disadvantaged backgrounds.

Home–school, parent, pupil contracts

As mentioned in Chapter 7, the Government intends to introduce home–school contracts for all pupils by the year 2001. The aim is to encourage parental, pupils' and schools' responsibilities. Whether and how such contracts can be made legally binding is a question requiring further research. In any event, they can only be helpful.

Pupil–school contracts can be equally helpful. Although a number of schools already have such contacts, they tend to be in their infancy. The use of home–school and pupil–school contracts is considered to have considerable potential in the fight to reduce truancy.

Use of security firms

Some schools currently use security firms to patrol main entrances and boundary perimeters before and/or during and/or after the end of the school day. Such schemes can be costly. They are often used at the expense of the remaining teaching and support staff in the school.

There is no doubt that the use of security firms can reduce the amount of specific lesson absence. Another tactic used by some schools is to ensure that the exterior boundaries are secure through, for example, the building of high walls and/or secure fences around the entire perimeter of the school. Such schemes can be helpful; but they are also a last resort and a sign that the school is failing in its intention to reduce its truancy.

Use of role play

Some schools have found the use of role play, either in assemblies, in class time or as part of the PSE programme, to be an effective means of preventing or combating such issues as bullying, extortion, racial or gender inequalities, indiscipline, violence, drug-related activity as well as truancy. Some schools produce plays and/or videos as part of this preventative work. It is believed that the therapeutic effects of this approach can be especially beneficial to pupils at risk, particularly those who are vulnerable to peer pressure.

Formation of anti-truancy teams

Teachers and social workers in Milton Keynes are an example of an anti-truancy team. They take part in a scheme which could serve as a model for cross-departmental co-operation in the organisation of services for children. The Close to Home project follows repeated demands for such integration. Teams of social workers, youth workers and teachers go out into the community from their school base. The intention is to reduce truancy and exclusions. The teams also include careers staff, educational psychologists and education welfare officers. They operate in the catchment areas of two local secondaries, the Leon School and the Sir Frank Markham Community School.

The new youth offender teams in the Crime and Disorder Bill, 1998, require schools to work with social services, probation officers and the police. A total of 70 per cent of young offenders are either regular truants or have been excluded (see Chapter 5).

Positive reinforcement and lottery-type schemes

Many, if not most, schools now use various forms of positive reinforcement and rewards to promote good school attendance. A positive form of reinforcement and praise for pupils who attend school regularly – however this is done – can work wonders. A system of rewards and/or incentives will show the whole school community how highly attendance is valued and will demonstrate to pupils and their families that the school values and appreciates their efforts. Promoting this policy should be the responsibility of the entire school staff not just pastoral staff and/or form tutors.

Pupils worthy of recognition include:

- 100 per cent attenders and other excellent attenders (over a term, a year);
- consistently good attenders;
- poor attenders who show a significant/any improvement;
- those from a year group with consistently good attendance;
- those from a year group who show a marked improvement;
- Year 7 pupils who begin their secondary career with a good attendance record;
- the whole school.

Traditional forms of reward include:

- letters to parents;
- personal congratulations from the headteacher, head of year or other senior staff;
- photo-display, featuring named pupils;
- stickers in homework diaries;
- regular features/presentations on an attendance notice board in school corridors/form or staff rooms;
- presentations at assemblies, parents evenings, etc. (e.g. for the most improved attender in the year, form, school);
- linking attendance to a school's merit/credit/reward (e.g. mug, crayons) system;
- the use of badges or special privileges.

More recently, some schools have begun to extend these schemes to include:

- monthly prizes for form, year for best attendance;
- termly prizes for best attendance;
- annual prizes for best attendance.

Rewards can include winning ghetto-blasters, videos, televisions, radios, computers, etc. One school arranges for the best attending form in each year to be given an annual visit to Alton Towers. Similar schemes at other schools make the major prize a visit to Euro Disney, a week's holiday in France, a trip to see England play at Wembley. The best prize for individual attendance found to date is for an all expenses paid trip to Disney in Orlando for a family of four for two weeks – all out of school funds. Put like this, good attendance is fun and makes sense!

Other interesting rewards which have been brought to my attention include: an evening out in a restaurant with Ryan Giggs and Sporty Spice, a visit to see Boyzone, U2 and the Manic Street Preachers and a photograph taken with Caprice!

Some schools have begun lottery-type schemes to reward good attendance. Thus, every pupil, every form which makes 100 per cent attendance in a week/month/term/year enters a weekly/monthly/termly/yearly draw for a prize. Weekly prizes tend to be small. Monthly prizes a little bigger. Termly prizes are often quite significant, while annual prizes are very significant to the extent that they would be valued by everyone.

Paying for these schemes often requires ingenuity and extra funding activity on the part of school staff and/or parent teacher associations.

At-risk registers

The use of at-risk registers by schools can help to identify potential truants at an early stage. Potential pupils included on such registers can include those with siblings who have previously or are actually truanting; pupils from one-parent families; pupils whose academic performance is causing concern and whose progress is well behind; pupils with known serious problems at home and who may be involved with the social services, etc.

The implementation of an at-risk register in primary schools can alert teachers to give special attention to their pupils with particular academic, social or psychological needs. In secondary schools, at-risk registers should be in use by the beginning of Year 7 to be really effective. Thereafter, pupils remain on the register, or others are added to the register, dependent upon personal progress and need. Pupils on the 'at-risk' register are carefully monitored throughout their school careers and appropriate action taken as necessary.

Combating lateness

Lateness on the part of teachers or pupils can lead to indiscipline and truancy. In both instances, it gives the wrong message. Repeated absences at the beginning of a school session can amount to failure to attend regularly for the purpose of Section 199 of the 1993 Education Act.

In addressing lateness schools must:

- have a clearly-defined and consistently applied policy on lateness. This must be precise in terms of the times when registers will close and the sanctions that may be applied;
- publicise this policy in school and communicate it to parents;
- balance any sanctions with positive encouragement;
- praise and acknowledge punctuality;
- praise and acknowledge latecomers who improve;
- ensure that teachers set a good example by arriving punctually for lessons;
- follow up the reasons for lateness and be alert to any emerging patterns or problems;
- set in place systems for effectively monitoring lateness – latecomers should sign a late-slip or a late-book;
- never cover for lateness (if a pupil is absent when the register closes he/she should be marked absent – to leave a gap in the register and then to mark a pupil down as present when/if he/she eventually arrives is to disguise any difficulty which that pupil might be experiencing and to delay any support which might be offered).

A school policy on lateness

A school policy on lateness will:

- be firm but fair (an approach which tends to be over punitive may well have the effect of discouraging the latecomer from attending at all);

- balance sanctions with positive encouragements;
- bear in mind the school's geographical setting (the vagaries of public transport, etc.);
- consider how far the responsibility for pupils failing to arrive punctually rests with them personally or with their parents.

Example:

> Lateness will be defined as any arrival ten minutes later than the bell for the start of the session. A pupil arriving more than ten minutes late will be given a late mark. More than three late marks in a week will result in a detention.

Combating post-registration truancy

Post-registration truancy is not reflected in most published figures of unauthorised absence yet it probably accounts for most of the truancy that actually takes place in some schools. Most schools underestimate the extent of their own post-registration truancy rate and would probably be surprised if they realised its true extent.

Some teachers may secretly be quite pleased when certain disruptive or difficult pupils fail to attend their lessons. This is understandable but to, in effect, condone post-registration truancy can be a very dangerous business as it may place the teacher concerned in a very difficult position should anything happen to that child who is out of lessons. Such an attitude also sends very mixed messages both to the pupil(s) who are not in the lesson and to those who are. There needs to be a clearly-stated school policy on post-registration truancy. Schools should also ensure that the parents of post-registration truants are promptly notified. This is frequently overlooked, but it is vital that parents are kept informed.

Post-registration truancy can be addressed in two ways:

- a reactive strategy;
- a proactive strategy.

A reactive strategy could involve:

- teachers patrolling the school premises during lessons;
- keeping toilets locked during lesson time;
- post-registration truancy spot checks;
- special punishments for those caught post-registration truanting;
- installation of video monitors! (some schools do have them).

Such a strategy may be successful – but perhaps for the wrong reasons. Alternatively, it may convince post-registration truants that there is less chance of being apprehended if they actually leave the school premises.

Some schools will react against the notion of turning their buildings and grounds into fortresses – indeed, it could be argued that it is better to have post-registration truants in the school grounds (say, the school toilets) where at least their whereabouts is known, and they are reasonably safe, albeit unsupervised.

A proactive strategy could involve:

- teachers always carrying out quick register checks at the start of every lesson (many schools insist that this is done as a matter of course but it frequently appears to be a custom more honoured in the breach than in the observance);
- all pupils out of lessons must have signed 'Out of Lesson' slips;
- clear policies supporting teachers who have to deal with persistently difficult/disruptive pupils;
- a lively, relevant and accessible curriculum;
- special support for those pupils who do find certain lessons especially difficult;
- a clear policy which all staff understand and apply.

A school may address the issue of post-registration truancy through a strategy which relies on both reactive and proactive strategies, although the emphasis should be on the latter. But in addressing post-registration truancy schools need to consider whether their attempts to reduce it may lead to an increase in blanket truancy – if pupils are unable to skip individual lessons they may choose not to come into school at all. Some pupils may see post-registration truancy as a form of 'safety valve'. Schools will need to be aware of this and may need to develop strategies for dealing with it.

Return to school policies

One of the most difficult events for a truant is to be made to feel welcome or to be able to relax and re-integrate back into school in a meaningful way, especially after a regular or protracted period of absence. Therefore, schools need to formulate return to school policies. Some pupils who would like to return to school find that teachers inadvertently reinforce their truancy by making ill-judged comments or by singling them out for special attention in an unfortunate way. Making pupils who are already embarrassed feel even more self-conscious is not helpful and should always be avoided.

Schools can apply the following guidelines to ensure they are giving out the right signals:

(a) Always ensure that the school keeps in touch with any pupil who is absent for long periods. (The child and his/her family still need to feel part of the school community throughout the period of absence.)

(b) Always make the child feel welcomed back (even if his/her past behaviour has been difficult).

(c) Never make sarcastic comments (a casual, 'Nice of you to turn up' or 'Had a nice holiday?' can in a moment destroy hours of careful preparation).

(d) Never leave a child feeling dumped in a corridor or outside an office. (There must always be someone to take responsibility for and know what to do with the child.)

(e) Always ensure that the child has someone/somewhere to go if things get difficult.

Pupils returning after a long absence cannot perform miracles – renewing or remaking friendships, catching up in the classroom, readjusting to a structured day – all take time and do not happen overnight. There may be hiccups. But throughout the process pupils must feel that the school is glad to see them and values their return.

Managing school transfers properly

Research shows that pupils are particularly vulnerable at times of making school transfers, especially at the age of eleven; in Year 10 after selecting GCSE subjects; and when moving home or area; or at the beginning of each academic year as they move forms or classes.

Any change of school can be difficult for a child – whether it involves the move from nursery to infants, from infants to junior or whatever. But the transfer from primary to secondary school can be a particularly difficult time for some pupils as they face up to a number of new experiences. By developing effective links with primary feeders, schools will be able to facilitate the smooth transfer of the majority of pupils and to identify those pupils in Year 6 who may appear likely to experience attendance and other difficulties at their secondary school.

A different learning environment

Secondary schools need to be aware that Year 7 pupils may:

- experience difficulty adjusting to a much more complex learning environment;
- lack basic social and interpersonal skills;
- have special educational needs which have not yet been clearly identified;
- experience curriculum discontinuity;
- experience difficulty relating to several new teachers;
- experience difficulty working in a number of different classrooms;

- have a problem with a more structured timetable;
- find it difficult coping with the demands of homework.

A different physical environment

Secondary schools need to be aware that Year 7 pupils may:

- be unused to moving around a large school for different lessons;
- lack basic organisational skills;
- be unused to using public transport to get to school;
- have difficulty adjusting to a large impersonal dining room.

A different social environment

Secondary schools need to be aware that Year 7 pupils may:

- be unused to relating to large numbers of adults and children;
- have to make new friends;
- miss the intimacy of primary school;
- be unused to the demands of wearing school uniform;
- now find it difficult accepting the fact that they are at the bottom of the school's structure (i.e. 'the pecking order');
- feel isolated and lost.

Any combination of the above factors may cause a Year 7 pupil to experience difficulties in attending. It is vital that such difficulties are picked up and addressed sooner rather than later.

Effective primary–secondary liaison

This will involve:

- a clearly identified staff team responsible for maintaining links with feeder primaries;
- a clearly defined and regularly reviewed strategy to facilitate secondary transfer;
- systems to monitor and review the progress of all Year 7 pupils;
- structured visits from primary schools in the summer terms – and follow-up meetings with primary staff;
- measures to ensure curricular continuity (purposeful liaison between Year 6 and Year 7 teachers);
- effective liaison with the education welfare officers attached to feeder primaries;
- special induction programmes for those Year 7 pupils who come from primaries other than the school's usual feeder primaries (this may often be

the odd one or two pupils – precisely those who may find secondary transfer a lonely and difficult time);

- getting the whole school involved in taking responsibility for assisting those newly joining the school;
- involving parents from the very beginning.

Some suggestions

- Ask last year's Year 7 pupils what, if anything, they found difficult;
- 'pair' vulnerable pupils with a responsible pupil from Year 12 or Year 13;
- initiate a mentor scheme;
- use homework diaries to assist organisation skills;
- make sure that the pre-admission visits of Year 6 pupils do not become too formalised – a treasure hunt can enable them to familiarise themselves with the school grounds and buildings;
- send primary feeders details of the syllabus/curriculum which Year 7 pupils will have to follow;
- try to meet all parents of Year 7 pupils.

Primary schools have a huge role to play in preparing children for life in secondary school. The earlier any attendance difficulty being experienced by a child is identified the sooner support can be offered. Practical games can be used to help pupils to adjust to their new school such as the 'Snakes and Ladders' scheme now described.

- Topic 1 – Settling into secondary school
- AIDS – 'Snakes and Ladders' game boards: workbooklet

Introductory activity

(a) Organise class into a circle and ask them to turn to the person next to them, introduce themselves and find out four things about that person. Report to class.
(b) The purpose of this session is to introduce the concept of self-confidence and the kinds of things that make people self-confident, i.e. feeling skilful, feeling appreciated and feeling responsible for your own actions and behaviour.

Building self-confidence is especially important during early adolescence. One way of thinking of self-confidence is to imagine that it is a 3-legged stool – What happens if one leg is damaged or missing? (The stool collapses.) But just as with a broken 3-legged stool it's possible to repair damaged self-confidence by helping people strengthen their 'weak leg'.
(c) Complete Worksheet.

(d) Using a separate sheet of A3 paper explain to pupils they are about to practice focusing on their positive characteristics and past successes by creating a 'Success Lifeline'. 'Success' means something they have done that has given them a sense of pride or accomplishment, no matter how big or small, e.g. a contest they won, a skill learnt, something they made, an award, a special friendship, etc.

(e) On the A3 paper draw a long line. Label the beginning as Birth and the end of the line Present. Ask them to recall 3 successes they have experienced in their life. Locate them on the line using the line as a time line. Date the experience and write a brief explanation of it.

For homework illustrate the experiences, i.e. it may be a photo or newspaper article, or a drawing or a magazine picture providing a visual representation of the event.

Settling in

- To increase pupils' awareness of the school layout they must complete the settling in sheet.
- A discussion of the behaviour expected in Goodacre as described in the Goodacre Code (see Chapter 12).

Clarity of staff roles

Ensuring that the attendance, academic and pastoral needs of pupils are met is one of the key functions of schools. Unfortunately, in too many schools role conflict, or the lack of clear role definitions, can inadvertently hinder effective school polices on attendance.

The form tutor

Schools need to ensure that the form tutor:

- is the key person in the school's pastoral care system;
- has the support and advice of colleagues;
- promotes habits of regular attendance and punctuality both with individuals and with the form group;
- accurately maintains registers and responds to parental notes and unexplained absences;
- is alert to emerging patterns of absence;
- is aware of and consistent in applying school systems for monitoring and promoting attendance.

The subject teacher

Schools should also ensure that the subject teacher:

- sets an example of punctuality by arriving for lessons on time;
- keeps an accurate register of attendance in each lesson and promptly feeds back absences to form tutors and/or year heads;
- deals with lateness to lessons consistently and promptly (action taken immediately is often more effective than a detention at a later date);
- recognises that learning difficulties are an important factor in poor attendance;
- explores methods of making specific provision for children who are frequent or long-term absentees;
- welcomes and values the presence of all pupils in their lessons.

The head of department

In schools, the head of department:

- examines the curriculum in order to develop ways of improving the quality of the classroom experience;
- develops sensitive and effective departmental re-entry strategies which welcome pupils back from a period of absence and offers support in the organisation of missed work;
- regularly liaises with form tutors and year heads on attendance-related matters.

The head of year/house

Schools should ensure the head of year/house:

- assumes a key role in co-ordinating all aspects of attendance-related matters;
- monitors and supervises the work of form tutors in promoting attendance;
- effectively liaises with other senior staff on attendance related matters;
- when necessary, communicates with parents of children experiencing attendance difficulties;
- meets regularly with the education welfare officer;
- consults, when appropriate, with other agencies – social services, child and family clinic, etc.

The headteacher

Through his/her senior management team the headteacher:

- ensures that whole-school policies on attendance-related matters are drawn up and applied;
- consults with the school community in the process of drawing up such policies;

- ensures that these policies are communicated to pupils, staff, parents and governors (via, for example, the school brochure);
- creates a school ethos which values and promotes excellent levels of attendance and punctuality.

Use of paging systems

The concept behind paging systems is to enable schools to alert parent/s to the fact that their child has failed to register, has participated in post-registration truancy or has otherwise left the premises without permission. Informing parents in this way helps schools fulfil their statutory duties while, at the same time, putting indirect pressure on to the parent/s who are often inconvenienced by the notification – especially if they are at work. It can help parents and schools tackle truancy together in those cases where parents are responsive to the educational needs of their children.

Unfortunately, each pager is relatively expensive and many schools cannot afford to equip all parents, or those whose children truant, with them. It may be that if this scheme is to work, some form of Government help will be necessary.

Improved recording of attendance

Recording of attendance

Schools need to develop clear guidelines on methods to:

- record attendance accurately;
- detect absenteeism at the early stages;
- act on absenteeism as soon as it is detected;
- support absentees and their families if necessary;
- work with other agencies that:
  (a) are either involved with the absentee; or
  (b) need to be involved with the absentee in order to support the child and or his/her family;
- let all children know:
  (a) they are part of the school community;
  (b) they will be missed if they are absent from school;
  (c) their parents will be contacted to identify the reason for absence;
- acknowledge and reward excellent and improved attendance.

Registers

In assessing attendance levels, the form register is of paramount importance. Registers are legal documents – should the parents of a persistent non-attender be prosecuted by the Local Education Authority under Section 199 of the 1993 Education Act, then the information which the registers contain would be used in court as evidence (see Boxes 8.1 and 8.2).

While there is a statutory requirement to complete registers, there is another side to the matter which should not be overlooked. The twice-daily requirement to register pupils can and should be perceived as an opportunity for the school to receive children formally from home, and serve as an introduction to the session.

Practice can range from a five-minute session when the roll is called, to an extended form period where registration takes place alongside other activities as part of a structured tutorial programme. The ways in which registration is conducted – for example, the degree of familiarity involved, and the extent to which it is seen as related to pastoral and tutorial matters – not only influence the maintenance of an accurate attendance record but also help to foster good attendance among pupils. It is vital that children are continually reminded that the school takes attendance very, very seriously.

Features of good practice include:

- the use of red and black biro only;
- a consistent adherence to the system of symbols for marking set out in the front of each register;
- clear, neatly written, easily comprehensible personal details for each child in the appropriate space;
- regularly calculated weekly totals;
- school holidays and other occasions when the school is closed clearly marked;
- loose notes, letters and other pieces of paper kept to a bare minimum – preferably none at all;
- alterations made in such a way that the original entry is still clearly visible;
- a clear school policy on registers and registration (included in the school brochure).

Schools will need to be aware that while some personal information about pupils must remain confidential or restricted on a need to know basis, it is nevertheless vital that key staff such as form tutors and year heads have clear access to information on those aspects of a pupil's life (both within and outside of school) which may be relevant to that pupil's attendance and behaviour patterns.

With regard to personal details about pupils' lives, schools need to be clear about:

- *what* is relevant;
- *how* this information is to be used;
- *who* needs to know it;
- *where* such information is to be kept.

confidentiality can and should be mirrored by care and concern.
   Features of poor practice include:

- the combined and varied use of red, black, blue, green, biro, ink, pencil, felt-tip, etc.;
- casual approach to the system of symbols ('b' for 'bunking');
- incomplete, inaccurate, and scrappily assembled personal details for some children;
- lack of weekly totals;
- an ongoing continuous line of marking, without any clear indication of the details (holidays, occasional days, etc.) of the school year;
- a register overflowing with various notes, letters, scraps of paper, etc.;
- unclear amendments, use of Tippex.

Box 8.1 Heads of year register check

FORM _____   FORM TUTOR _____

DATE _____

Please attend to the points ticked below as soon as possible:

1 ☐ Register not marked.
2 ☐ Incorrect colours/pencil/'Tippex' being used.
3 ☐ Weekly/half termly headings incomplete.
4 ☐ Reasons for absence not stated – use correct codes.
5 ☐ Unauthorised absence not followed up (see below).
6 ☐ Unauthorised absence totals not entered.
7 ☐ Daily and weekly totals not being entered.
8 ☐ Attendance percentage not calculated.
9 ☐ Register not always returned promptly.
10 ☐ Register cluttered with notes/circulars. Please tidy.
11 ☐ A very well kept register. Thank you.
12 ☐ Other difficulties encountered (see below).

Thank you for your attention to these details.

_____ Head of Year _____

Box 8.2 Attendance and behaviour: the statutory basis

The statutory basis for the control and management of pupils' behaviour and attendance is set out in the schedule below.

Behaviour

The head is responsible for maintaining discipline, taking the governors' views into account. He/she is solely responsible for excluding a pupil, and must inform the pupil's parents (if the pupil is under 18) and explain why. In the case of exclusions of more than five days in the aggregate in any one term, or consequential loss of opportunity to enter a public examination, the governors and the LEA decide. The parents should be told of the reasons for the exclusion and of their right to take the matter up with the governors and the LEA. The governors and the LEA have the right to direct the head to re-instate the pupil (the LEA does not have this right in cases of permanent exclusions in voluntary-aided schools). In cases of permanent exclusions there is the right of formal appeal, arrangements for which must be made by the LEA (or by the governors in voluntary-aided schools), if the pupil has not been re-instated.	Education (No 2) Act, 1986 [S22–28] Education Act 1993 [S261–262]	WO Circular 12/87 WO Circular 60/94 WO Circular 81/94
In GM schools, appeals against exclusions are made in the first instance to the Discipline Committee of the governing body. In the case of permanent exclusions, further appeal may be made to an independent Appeal Committee. The decision of an appeal committee is binding. The LEA of the area to which the pupil belongs must be informed as soon as practicable once a permanent exclusion has been upheld by the Discipline Committee.	Education Act 1993 [S55–58; Sched 5, 13(4), Sched 6,5] SI 1993/3102	DFE Code of Practice for GM Schools on Establishment and Conduct of Exclusion and Admission Appeal Committees (December 1992).

Corporal punishment has been abolished for all pupils in maintained schools and for pupils in independent schools whose fees are wholly or partly met from public funds. Corporal punishment may be applied to privately funded pupils in independent schools with more than 50 boarders.	Education (No 2) Act, 1986 [S47–48] Statutory Instrument 1987/344 Statutory Instrument 1989/1825 Children Act 1989 [S63] Education Act 1993 [293]	Department of Health Regulations
Child Protection: parents, in effect, give schools the authority to act 'in loco parentis'. Schools should take independent action to deal with emergencies. They have a general duty to act independently in respect of suspected abuse at home.	Children Act 1989 [S2(9), S3(5)] Working Together Under the Children Act 1989	Children Act 1989: Guide for the Education Service (OU) WO Circular 46/88 (signs of abuse) WO Circular 52/95
Schools have a duty to protect children from harm. They are recommended to have designated teachers and procedures to refer cases where they are concerned about a pupil's safety to the investigating agencies according to the procedures established by the local Area Child Protection Committees (ACPC). The designated child protection teacher should receive appropriate training.	Children Act 1989 [S87]	DES Circular 4/88 Working Together (Dept of Health, 1991)

LEAs may apply to the courts for an Education Supervision Order (ESO) where a child of compulsory school age is not being properly educated. Alternatively, LEAs may institute proceedings under S39 of the Education Act 1944 whereby parents may be prosecuted for failing in their duty to ensure their child attends school regularly. While an ESO is in force, parents lose their right to have their child educated in accordance with their wishes.

Children Act 1989
[S36(4)]
Education Act 1944
[S36–40]
Children Act 1989
[Sched 3,13(2)]
Education Act 1989
[S76]
Education Act 1980
[S6,7]

Attendance
Children must attend school from the beginning of the term after they attain the age of 5 until they have reached the age of 16.

Education Act 1944
[S35] as amended by
Education Act 1981
[S17]
Education Act 1962
[S9]

All schools must keep an attendance register in which pupils are marked present or absent at the beginning of each morning and afternoon session. Schools must distinguish in their attendance registers between authorised and unauthorised absences of pupils aged 5–16 and must publish rates of unauthorised absence in prospectuses and annual reports. They may keep attendance and admission registers on a computer, subject to certain safeguards relating to the correction and preservation of the register. Parents may be prosecuted for failing in their duty to ensure that their child is properly educated. In such circumstances the LEA may institute proceedings for a School Attendance Order to be served on a parent, or may apply to the courts for an Education Supervision Order. Where a child is the subject of a School Attendance Order he or she must attend the school named in that order.

Pupils' Registration Regulations, 1956 Statutory Instrument 1956/357
Statutory Instrument 1991/1582
Statutory Instrument 1995/2089
Children Act 1989 (S3694]
Education Act 1944 [S36]
Education Act 1993 [S192–203]
Children Act 1989 [Sched 3, 13(2)]

WO Circular 45/91
WO Circular 53/94

Guidelines on the methods of marking attendance are usually to be found on the inside covers of registers. Individual schools and individual teachers within schools tend to vary considerably in their own interpretation of these guidelines. A school's instructions to its staff on this matter need to be specific and detailed and not liable to ambiguous interpretation. Parents need to be made aware and reminded of the school's expectations with regard to notes explaining absences, etc. Most schools doubtlessly already do this, but reminders need to be constant and fresh. The profile of attendance as an important issue needs to be continually raised. The way in which a school's registers are maintained will reflect the importance which that school attaches to this issue.

A collection of accurate and well-maintained registers provides an ongoing and up-to-date database on the basis of which informed debate about attendance matters can take place. It provides the basic tool with which a school and its Education Welfare Officer can begin to target individual pupils encountering problems in their school lives; and the importance that a school attaches to it can be used to remind pupils, parents, governors and staff that the school regards attendance as one of its top priorities.

The way to better-kept registers

- Make everyone – staff and pupils – aware of how important registers are. They are, after all, legal documents;
- ensure that staff know how to properly maintain a register;
- ensure that there is a clear school policy on what constitutes:

  - authorised absence;
  - unauthorised absence;

- ensure that this policy is clearly communicated to parents;
- ensure that a senior member of staff (or perhaps a governor) is charged with regularly inspecting the registers;
- ensure that registers that fall below standard are brought up to scratch;
- encourage staff to take a pride in their registers – perhaps a half-termly staff room competition for the best-kept register;
- act now – registers should be well maintained at all times for they are a basic tool in addressing attendance matters.

Inter-agency co-operation

Too many cases of truancy are mishandled due to inter-agency conflicts, rivalry and/or poor communication. Within schools it is essential to effect and maintain high levels of attendance, schools therefore need to develop a whole-school policy on attendance. Such a policy will be as follows.

Owned by everyone

Teachers, pupils, parents and governors all need to be involved in drawing up such a policy. A policy devised by just one or two senior staff may be ineffective. Any policy must be periodically reviewed and all parties concerned periodically consulted.

Communicated to everyone

Pupils and parents must be periodically reminded of the school's expectations regarding attendance and punctuality. Governors should be kept informed of the policy and how it is working.

Understood by everyone

Pupils and parents must be clear as to those explanations for absence/lateness which are acceptable/unacceptable. They must also clearly understand what will be the consequences of any unauthorised absence/lateness. Lines of communication and delegated responsibilities within schools must be clearly established. Staff must be clear as to what is classified as authorised/unauthorised absence.

A clear whole-school policy on attendance (see Chapter 9), together with effective systems for monitoring and promoting attendance, can help create a school ethos which:

- values and contributes to high levels of attendance and punctuality;
- reduces levels of authorised absence and lateness;
- reassures parents and the wider community;
- prepares children for the time-keeping discipline of adult life; and, most importantly
- enables children to take the fullest advantage of the educational opportunities which school has to offer them.

While the ultimate responsibility for ensuring that children attend school regularly rests with the parents, schools can do a great deal to encourage and support them to meet this responsibility.

Teachers are in the front line in having to deal with difficult pupils. But neither the causes nor the effects of truancy and exclusion can be understood solely in educational terms. Schools often find themselves having to deal with problems that should have been dealt with by families, or by other public agencies. Similarly, when schools fail to keep children on their premises, or exclude them, the costs spill over on to other agencies and on to the wider community.

What are the costs?

Educational underachievement

The most obvious impact is, of course, on education itself. Truants are more likely than non-truants to leave school with few or no qualifications. The latest Youth Cohort Study showed that 38 per cent of truants reported that they had no GCSEs, compared with 3 per cent of non-truants. Of those who had truanted, only 8 per cent obtained 5 or more GCSEs at grades A to C, as against 54 per cent of those who had not truanted in Year 11.

Unemployment and homelessness

Like others with low qualifications, those who miss school are more likely to be out of work at age 18, and are more likely to become homeless. For example, over three-quarters of homeless teenagers in one Centrepoint study were either long-term non-attenders or had been excluded from school.

Crime

The most striking link is with crime:

- according to the Audit Commission, nearly half of all school-age offenders have been excluded from school; and a quarter truanted significantly;
- Home Office research showed that truants were over three times more likely to offend than non-truants. One study found that 78 per cent of males and 53 per cent of females who truanted once a week or more committed offences;
- a 6-month study by the Metropolitan Police found that 5 per cent of all offences were committed by children during school hours; 40 per cent of robberies, 25 per cent of burglaries, 29 per cent of thefts and 20 per cent of criminal damage were committed by 10 to 16 year olds;
- in 1995–96, the Metropolitan Police arrested 748 excluded children, some of whom had committed between 20 and 40 offences before arrest;
- there is evidence that sentencing of those who have truanted or been excluded is severe: one study showed that pupils who had a poor attendance record were much more at risk of a custodial sentence than those with more positive reports.

Exclusion and truancy have costly effects, whether those costs are borne by the police, courts and prisons; by the social security budget; or by the victims of crime. The Government is already substantially overhauling the system for dealing with young offenders. Tackling exclusion and truancy should contribute to stopping youngsters being drawn into crime in the first place.

Who is responsible?

Both nationally and locally, responsibility for dealing with the problems associated with truancy and exclusions is fragmented. In Whitehall, the DfEE has the main responsibility for policy on truancy and exclusions, but the Department of Health also has a key interest, notably through social services, as does the Home Office for the crime and criminal justice aspects.

Several departments run specialist funds to support exclusion and truancy projects. The DfEE runs two: the Standards Fund, of which £22 million goes to attendance and behaviour projects, and New Start which aims to bring together multi-agency programmes for young people aged 14 and over who are disaffected and at risk. Other projects are funded through the Single Regeneration Budget, on which DETR leads. The Home Office and the Department of Health sponsor projects through mainstream funding. In addition, local projects may get funding from other sources, whether private giving, charitable trusts, the lottery, business or the European Social Fund.

At a local level, responsibility is divided between schools, local education authorities and the police. It is simply not clear who is responsible if overall levels of truancy and exclusions rise.

The professionals who look after children who may truant or be excluded are required by law to produce a range of strategic 'plans' including Children's Services Plans, Behaviour Support Plans, Education Development Plans, Youth Justice Plans, Drug Action Strategies. The purpose of these plans is to focus on particular problem issues. But the number of them runs the risk of duplication and lack of co-ordination. And some children have as many as eight different professionals dealing with them, not always communicating with each other.

A complex set of interrelated problems has not been well-managed by Government, whether at national or local level. Responsibility has been divided and dispersed without sufficiently coherent policies to prevent behavioural problems, and to deal with them when they do arise. 'Joined-up problems' of this kind are one of the main reasons behind the setting up of the Social Exclusion Unit.

Disaffection: truancy, behaviour, exclusion in relation to alternative curriculum provision

Alternative curriculum provision

A wide variety of arrangements are made within LEAs to cater for disaffected pupils, particularly in KS4, many of whom are excluded, or at risk of being excluded, from school. Some of this provision, for example Pupil Referral Units (PRU), is not funded by GEST. The GEST-funded projects which were inspected included the following main types of provision:

- a discrete unit on the secondary school site, offering a modified curriculum;
- off-site units, often in youth and community education premises, offering informal counselling and a modified, basic curriculum;
- 'Bridge'-type courses, involving work experience placements and Further Education (FE) College link courses;
- group work projects, involving informal counselling and skills development for pupils and parents.

The main advantages of making separate provision for disaffected pupils are:

- they can receive provision which is carefully tailored to their particular needs, using approaches which have a high degree of direct relevance and include opportunities to succeeded in new activities;
- the staff involved are carefully selected for their ability to establish good relationships with the young people concerned;
- the work of other pupils, following a normal timetable at school, is less prone to disruption.

The main disadvantage is that it is often difficult, unrealistic or impossible for the pupils to return to a normal timetable and they therefore do not receive the full curriculum to which they are entitled.

Case study A

In one LEA, alternative educational provision is made for pupils in Y11 in a large coastal town. The project caters mainly for pupils who, for reasons which include severe emotional and/or behavioural problems, have been unable to continue in a normal school placement; it also admits others who would have difficulty in returning to the mainstream system because of severe attendance problems. Provision is made for single sex groups, with the main aim of helping pupils to achieve success and gain confidence in their own ability within a relaxed, non-threatening environment.

Pupils attend part-time (up to four sessions a week) and are offered a flexible timetable which may include work experience and/or college link courses. They are usually disapplied from part or all of the National Curriculum (NC) and a modified curriculum is offered according to individual needs. Individual tuition is provided so that pupils can develop basic skills in numeracy, literacy, science and information technology. Pupils also follow a life skills course. Accreditation is provided through CoE and GCSE examination courses, or under the modular Northern Partnership for Record of Achievement Unit Scheme (NPRA).

The following outcomes were achieved by pupils in one group, consisting of eleven girls:

- average attendance of 80 per cent;

- individual attendance levels ranging from 65 per cent to 100 per cent, with seven girls achieving more than 80 per cent and four of these achieving more than 90 per cent attendance;
- eight girls gained CoE passes in English, seven of these at Merit level;
- seven gained Merit passes in CoE mathematics;
- two achieved GCSE passes in English and mathematics at grades ranging from C to E;
- all were awarded NPRA certificates;
- three girls were awarded certificates resulting from their attendance at a 6-week certificated course in parentcraft and childcare at the local FE college;
- several girls arranged their own work experience placements;
- most progressed to employment, further education or training schemes.

Similar outcomes, albeit slightly more modest in terms of attendance and examination success, were achieved by pupils in a parallel group of four boys.

Overall, the project has been valuable and cost-effective in enabling pupils to increase their self-confidence and gain worthwhile qualifications.

Some of the 'Bridge' courses supported by 'Cities in Schools' are also particularly successful in securing good levels of achievement and attendance. Although it was not part of the survey to inspect the provision made on these courses, the information made available provided evidence of successful results. In one LEA, pupils on a 'Bridge' course last year achieved an overall attendance rate of 94 per cent; although final figures were not available at the time of the inspection, this year's attendance rate is said to be comparable. The pupils on last year's course also attained good levels of achievement in certified courses in literacy, numeracy, word-processing and the Youth Award Scheme. Some of the projects successfully incorporate aspects of physical education, such as outdoor activities, which enable pupils to develop self-discipline and a range of social skills.

Case study B

Another school in an industrialised area uses GEST funding to staff an Independent Learning Centre (ILC) which caters for pupils who are 'at risk' because of poor attendance and/or behavioural problems. They are provided with a modified curriculum which is seen as more relevant to their needs and offers opportunities for post-16 progression. The curriculum is adapted to match the needs of individual pupils, but consists mainly of the following elements:

- a day each week attending a vocational 'link course' (e.g. motor vehicle maintenance, bricklaying) at a local tertiary college;
- a work experience placement;
- outdoor education to develop personal confidence and team building;

- teacher support in the ILC, where pupils continue their study of core subject (and sometimes others) and catch up on work missed during their off-site placements.

Unfortunately, the outdoor education elements, which are said to have been successful, have been curtailed because of staff changes. Nevertheless, the ILC has achieved successful results with its eighteen Y11 pupils (of whom seventeen are boys). The outcomes include:

- no permanent exclusions;
- only one temporary exclusion;
- improved attendance rates, with some pupils achieving more than 90 per cent;
- progression to employment with training, or to FE college, for all except one of the pupils.

Features of successful provision

The main features of successful alternative curriculum provision are:

- a broad, strategic framework (within which 'alternative provision' is only one among several options including PRUs, link courses, etc.) enabling pupils to be placed appropriately according to their needs;
- access to a curriculum which continues to develop basic skills, including literacy, numeracy, information technology and life skills, and forms a suitable basis for progression post-16;
- learning activities which offer an appropriate level of challenge, and enable pupils to make clearly visible progress and to experience success;
- opportunities for pupils to benefit from counselling, whether formal or informal, and to raise their self-esteem and confidence as necessary;
- the accreditation of pupils' achievements;
- clearly identified progression routes to employment and training, or to further education;
- provision of feedback to schools on their pupils' experience, with consequent impact in terms of reviewing and revising the school curriculum.

Improving home–school communication

Schools need to inform parents of what is expected of them by using a variety of methods. These may include:

(a) issuing all new pupils in Year 7 with a booklet possibly entitled 'Rights and Responsibilities – Attendance at School';

(b) regularly including information about attendance in the school newsletter;
(c) speaking to parents at parents' evenings about the need for excellent attendance and punctuality;
(d) informing the police, social services, psychological service and the local community of the monitoring on attendance that has been carried out in the school;
(e) listening to parents: communication is a two-way process;
(f) interviewing parents formally to ascertain their views on the real reasons for their children's absences;
(g) being prepared to change or modify school rules/systems/curriculum accordingly;
(h) regular home/school bulletins;
(i) school policy documents on attendance;
(j) publishing an attendance staff bulletin weekly;
(k) providing a 'tips for tutors' pack on attendance regulations and related issues;
(l) spot checks on post-registration truancy;
(m) placing proper emphasis upon pupil and staff punctuality;
(n) using Sims or other technology to its maximum potential.

Use of social workers in schools

There is a growing view that large secondary and some primary schools require full-time social workers to be based in them. The rationale for this view includes:

(a) a history of poor inter-agency communication between social services and education/schools;
(b) the fact that some teachers spend too much time on social work (note: not pastoral care) issues;
(c) the avoidance of duplication which, in cases of truancy, often comes to a head in court cases;
(d) the belief that teachers and social workers operating together in cases of social need and deprivation are likely to achieve more than when working apart;
(e) both sets of professionals will see the wider picture in individual cases. Too often cases involving social workers are blighted by issues about confidentiality.

One danger to this service will be to possibly demean the role presently played by existing education welfare officers/social workers. The alternative view is that it would enable the EWO services to focus specifically upon attendance issues.

Second chance opportunities

There is a growing belief – fuelled by the move towards lifelong learning – that some school dropouts, disaffected pupils and educational failures can flourish given second chance opportunities. Often these opportunities are best provided in FE Colleges rather than schools. Evidence is mounting that some school failures, including truants, perform much better when they are given a second chance.

Use of private schools

Some thinkers believe that disaffected pupils, like truants from the state sector, could be better re-integrated by placing them in independent schools. The thinking behind this suggestion is not too dissimilar from arguments regarding the advantages of national service.

Improved health checks

Data obtained from school-based studies indicate that a small proportion of pupils are inclined to miss school for comparatively minor health, social or psychological reasons. Sometimes, regular health checks with the school nurse can help to identify and overcome problems. Such issues include 'nits', itches, rashes and other embarrassing facial or skin traits.

Figure 8.1 provides a possible model for improved communication between the school nurse, medical service and education welfare service.

The appointment of attendance support teachers

Some schools are now beginning to appoint attendance support teachers (see Chapter 10) who specialise in attendance issues in the school. For example, one grant maintained school advertised for a 'truant adviser' at a salary of £33,000 in 1998.

Case study

As many as 120 pupils – 10 per cent of the total roll – skip lessons at Mellow Lane school in Hillingdon, London, in any one day. On average pupils miss 14 days' schooling a year. Nearly all the absences have been authorised by parents who, according to headteacher, Rod Stafford, feel it is acceptable for their children to miss a few days here and there. But he said: 'The message has to be crystal clear: it is not'.

The attendance adviser, funded jointly by the school and leading businesses, was in post in early 1999. The appointee is backed up by a family literacy teacher and a support member of staff during the 4-year £300,000 project which aims to respond rapidly to truancy.

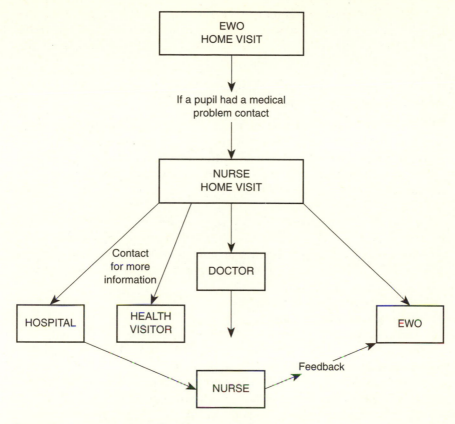

Figure 8.1 Liaison between school nurse and EWOs

The school targets pupils who are absent from 8 to 15 per cent of the academic year. Missing pupils will be identified on the first day and contacted immediately at home. Patterns of absenteeism are studied to see if they reveal underlying problems in the classroom – such as particular subject dislikes. The curriculum is then developed to satisfy pupils' needs. Links are established with the police to reduce anti-social behaviour in the community and home problems. The aim is to challenge a culture where casual absence is condoned.

Hillingdon's educational welfare officers will continue to work with the school on long-term truancy. The Hayes and West Drayton Partnership – which consists of Hillingdon Council training providers, the local community and businesses such as British Airways and Marks and Spencer – is putting up £140,000 for the project. The school is providing £160,000.

Spokesman Angus Johnson said:

'Today's pupils are the workforce of tomorrow and it is imperative that they gain the right qualifications and skills to get the best jobs that will be on the market. Persistent absenteeism, is hardly the kind of habit that will impress a future employer and if this is the cause of poor exam results then these youngsters will be drawn into a spiral of unemployment and, potentially, crime.'

AST: The Mountain Ash model

The duties of the attendance support teacher could be to improve the attendance in the school and to ensure attendance and related issues are given a much higher profile in the school and within the local community.

The specific functions of the post will involve further development of the management systems in the school to:

1　ensure attendance of pupils is correctly monitored;
2　ensure prompt follow-up action to deal with absenteeism and lateness;
3　tackle specific attendance problems and to have strategies in place to address the difficulties, e.g. re-integration programmes, support groups, Governors' Attendance Panel;
4　promote good links with parents;
5　foster good links with other agencies;
6　further develop the links with the communities on Fernhill and Rethcelyn;
7　ensure that the transition from the primary to the comprehensive school is less traumatic for pupils and to acquire knowledge on the pupils who may require additional support before and after this period;
8　provide advice and support for pupils returning to school after long periods of absence;
9　reward good attendance;
10　liaise with the following to ensure that the above strategies are being dealt with efficiently and effectively by:

   (a)　the headteacher and the senior management team;
   (b)　the heads of department;
   (c)　the heads of year;
   (d)　the special education needs co-ordinator;
   (e)　the education welfare officer;
   (f)　other agencies that may be involved with pupils experiencing attendance difficulties;

11　provide in-class support where necessary;
12　provide in-service training where appropriate;
13　be able to communicate effectively and sensitively both orally and in writing to a wide range of audiences;
14　have a sound understanding of why some children do not attend school regularly and have an awareness of how some of these difficulties can be overcome.

Another example of the work of the attendance support teacher in relation to a specific project undertaken in a comprehensive school in South Wales is presented in Chapter 10 from a different perspective.

Appointment of attendance support secretary

In some schools, to download one or more senior manager, appointments are sometimes made of a full-time attendance secretary to provide the administrative support and back up on attendance. This appointment often frees EWOs to spend all of their time on home visits. It also enables staff in schools to deal with re-integration and prevention in the knowledge that the paperwork on attendance and truancy is in good hands.

Extension of primary school practice

Most pupils spend longer in primary than secondary schools. They forge early friendships with peers from the same locations. Too often, secondary schools undervalue these links. Care should be taken at the point of primary–secondary school transfer to ensure that friends have the opportunity to sit and be together in the same forms and, in at least some teaching classes.

Some pupils become very unhappy very quickly in schools when they are sseparated from their friends. Research shows that peer group unhappiness is one of the prime causes of truancy. It should be remembered that in outside school hours, pupils visit and/or play with their friends rather than their class peers. As pupils grow older, especially in adolescence, having close friends becomes increasingly important.

Compensatory programmes

Many truants are educational failures. Therefore, existing National Curriculum and attainment target guidelines are not always suited to their needs. Few truants, for example, are competent modern linguists. Theoretically, protagonists argue that time spent on subjects in classes which are meaningless to lower achieving pupils would be better spent in remedial or compensatory programmes on such issues as literacy and numeracy, work placement schemes and in preparation for adult life classes.

Schools are beginning to become involved in local neighbourhood, community and anti-social exclusion programmes. Often, these are focused on the local school or in deprived locations nearby. These opportunities can provide pupils, their parents and neighbours with specialist second chance or specifically targeted programmes to meet local needs.

Supporting teachers and schools in preventing exclusions

Education Action Zones

The Government already provides support to individual schools through Standards Fund projects and other means. But, as with truancy, the Government plans to make exclusion issues central to the programme of Education Action Zones, with high levels of exclusion one of the priorities for the next round. Bids already include a large number of schools with significant behaviour and exclusion problems.

Targeting funds

The Government also has a commitment from 'Excellence in Schools' to review the funding arrangements for schools. This Government takes specific measures to target funds on schools for preventative work with children at risk of exclusion and schools that receive excluded children: such funds will be conditional on there being joint plans and partnerships locally to engage all the relevant agencies.

Local authorities

Local authorities too, should and do provide staff and financial resources for schools in tackling pupils at risk of exclusion. Local authorities are in future going to be required to provide full-time out-of-school education for all children excluded for more than three weeks. Since out-of-school provision is commonly up to four times more expensive than the average cost of maintaining a child in school, LEAs will acquire strong incentives to support schools better in holding on to children at risk of exclusion: a logical system would be for them to offer 'dowries' to schools as a support package to receive or hold on to children at risk of exclusion.

Groups particularly at risk

African-Caribbean pupils

A number of the measures already covered will bear particularly on African-Caribbean children. Exclusion statistics will be broken down by ethnic group. OFSTED will be targeting special inspections on schools with disproportionate rates of exclusions among high-risk groups. In addition to this:

- the Government will ensure that equal opportunities issues, as well as behaviour management, are adequately incorporated in the requirements for initial teacher training, and in in-service training;

- a DfEE Task Group is considering how to forge a new partnership at national and local levels to tackle the wider problem of raising achievement of ethnic minority pupils. It will also look at what can be done to promote community mentoring in ethnic minority communities. Many such projects are already supported by Government funding.

Children in care

Improving attendance and reducing exclusions among children in care is critical to improving their very poor educational outcomes. The Government announced that it intends to set targets for the educational attainment of children in care. It has in mind that the starting point might be that 50 per cent of all children in care should achieve a qualification by 2001, and 75 per cent by 2003. Specific proposals to underpin this, particularly to promote the better co-ordination of professionals that is necessary, will be announced in 1999. In addition, effective education should be considered a key outcome of relevant social services work involving school-age children.

Better solutions for children who have to be excluded

No one would disagree that solutions for children excluded from school need to be flexible and suitable for their particular problems. But there is no defence for the routine assumption that part-time education, or none at all, will do. The Government has therefore decided that LEAs must be obliged to provide every child who is excluded for more than three weeks with full-time and appropriate education. This can be imposed through changes in guidance. Although some local authorities come close to this now, many do not. This is undoubtedly a new burden on local authorities, and the resource implications are now considered within the Comprehensive Spending Review. Full provision will need to be phased in, but this should take no longer than three years.

It is not easy to say what the real resources will be needed to deliver this recommendation. One effect of the other changes the Government is announcing is that fewer children should be excluded. And it must not simply be a matter of extending existing PRU provision to all excluded children on a full-time basis. Many would argue that some of the provision LEAs currently fund is both ineffective and unduly expensive. Some voluntary organisations believe that they are both more effective and cheaper. The Government is attracted to the idea that LEAs should look at such options and DfEE can also require the LEA to contract the services out if it is failing in its performance.

On the content of 'education otherwise', the Government plans that:

- all children should have a clear individual plan, including a target date for re-integration. Mentoring could be a key component of this;

- for children coming up to the end of compulsory school, further education or training may be a more realistic aim than school;

The LEA's arrangements should all be set out in its Behaviour Support Plan.

Mentoring of truants

The mentoring of truants and other non-attenders is gaining increasing credence in the literature. There are a whole variety of mentoring schemes in practice. These include:

- peer mentoring;
- adult mentoring;
- school mentoring;
- parent mentoring.

Peer mentoring schemes often involve able pupils helping less able pupils with schoolwork and adjustment problems. Sometimes, they involve older pupils working with younger pupils e.g. sixth formers with Year 7, 8, 9, 10 or 11 pupils. These schemes are often conducted as part of the normal, adjusted or alternative curriculum provision. Some peer mentoring schemes are undertaken full time; others are part time or for special times/periods during a school day/week.

Adult mentoring involves a grown up working with a single or group of needy, difficult, disaffected or non-attending pupils on a full or part-time basis. Who this adult is varies considerably. It can be a student, teacher, parent, retired teacher or retired professional. In one sense, who it is does not matter. What matters is that the scheme – notably the liaison between the pupil/s and the adult – works.

Teacher mentoring usually involves a full or part-time member of staff working with an individual or group of pupils. This can be done on a full-time, part-time or special times basis over a short or long-term period. The critical question is how and when to end this relationship and enable the pupil/s to return to class and attend normally.

School mentoring is when the LEA or institution makes special arrangements for an individual or group of pupils to attend a specially constructed curriculum (a form of alternative education) on or off the school premises. The mentor could vary from a specialist off-site tutor to qualified teachers who are currently not working full time. It is essential that schools vet these mentors thoroughly before placements begin.

Parent mentoring takes place when a parent (often a mother or extended family member) takes responsibility for a child or group of children in or out of school to help with short or long-term learning, adjustment or behavioural problems.

The key to successful mentoring lies in developing a positive relationship between mentor and pupil. The aim is to provide the pupil with confidence, trust, a willingness to co-operate and learn and, eventually, a desire to return to a normal full-time timetable on as equal a basis with other pupils in class as possible.

Flexibility of approach

The preceding sections of this chapter, and other parts of this book, provide a wide guide on good practice in work with truants and in tackling truancy in schools. It is important that schools are as flexible in their approaches as possible. Do not try one scheme at the expense of everything else. Try as many schemes as possible and discover what works best for you, the pupils and your school.

Unfortunately, some schools have tended to be too rigid in the past. For example, mentoring may be successful with one pupil or group of pupils but fail completely with another. Either way, it does not mean that mentoring is the only way to tackle truancy in-house or cannot work in your school.

Evidence from research suggests that schools which are the most successful with combating and preventing truancy are those which:

(a) operate as a team;
(b) implement whole-school policies;
(c) have clear guidelines and procedures for dealing with non-attendance;
(d) have good re-integration strategies, and are vigilant and flexible in approach.

Finally, the best schools are pupil and goal-orientated, *and* treat all pupils equally. These are the themes which permeate the next chapter.

9 Whole-school approaches to reducing truancy

This chapter focuses upon the creation of whole-school policy documents on attendance. Clear evidence exists to show that for whole-school approaches to be successful they have to involve the *entire* staff in a constructive and positive manner. No school will be successful when the staff are pulling in different directions. This is particularly true on attendance strategies as unwilling pupils will quickly take advantage of any staff lapses. Whole-school approaches require dedicated teamwork from the leadership of the headteacher and senior management at the top, down throughout the entire school including form tutors, classroom assistants, secretarial staff and, critically, the education welfare officer.

School policy documents

Good attendance is vital to the future success and attainment of every pupil of school age. These days, no school would be without a curriculum policy document; indeed policy documents for every curriculum area. Similarly, no school should be without a policy document on attendance. This document should not be written immediately prior to an OFSTED inspection but be part and parcel of everyday school practice.

School policy documents should be endorsed and formally approved by the whole staff (following a period of consultation) and subsequently, by the governing body. Copies should be given to all parents and pupils attending the school and the guidelines uniformly and rigorously enforced. From time to time, the attendance policy document will need revising in accordance with the experience of the school.

School policy documents are a key weapon in the school's preventative approach to non-attendance. The creation and implementation of a policy document can be used to:

(a) focus attention and create positive attitudes among the staff (pupils and governors) towards regular attendance;

(b) highlight the importance of the school as a caring organisation, its pastoral care policies and links with external agencies;

(c) help create a positive school ethos.

School policy documents need to be both coherent and consistent. Coherence refers to the ways by which policies, plans and procedures are formulated and articulated. It applies to the ideas and discussions engaged in by senior management and, most particularly, the extent to which the whole school staff is involved.

Consistency refers to the means by which the attendance policy is put into practice by everyone involved with the school. The school policy document needs to be *owned* by all staff – not just senior management, heads of year and the education welfare/social worker.

The objective of the school policy document is:

(a) to promote good attendance and a respect for the school;

(b) to implement a sound system for monitoring pupil behaviour and progress.

Four steps in developing a coherent policy on attendance

1   Teachers, ancillary staff and pupils need to be closely involved in the creation and review of the school attendance policy in order to have a clear understanding of their role as well as to gain their commitment, e.g. through discussion of school rules, referral procedures, sanctions and punishments, the role of the pastoral system, the value of praise, rewards and incentives.

2   If the rationale and application of the policy is to be understood it must be articulated to all members. Pupils need to have a clear understanding of what is acceptable and unacceptable behaviour as an essential prerequisite to their evaluation of their own behaviour. For parents it must be clearly stated in school prospectuses and at parents' meetings. The same applies for governors.

3   If a positive school and classroom ethos is to be established, then staff need to present and conduct themselves as good role models in the way in which they put the agreed policy into practice. Therefore, teachers' own behaviour and standards are important, e.g. punctuality, good preparation, prompt return of marked work, etc.

4   Two key issues stand out in this process:

(a)   the organisation and operation of pastoral care in schools;

(b)   a school's policy on rewards and incentives.

Let us now focus on the latter as effective pastoral care is considered in more detail in a later chapter. There are four categories of rewards. These are:

1   material rewards – prizes, trophies and badges;
2   symbolic rewards – title, status or housepoints;
3   assessment – marks, grades, stars and similar devices;
4   teacher reactions – as in praise, encouragement, approval and recognition.

The types of rewards which schools can use include:

- a quiet word or pat on the back;
- an exercise book comment, either in general terms – 'well done' – or in a more detailed way, picking out specific points or ideas that gave pleasure;
- a visit to a more senior member of staff and/or the headteacher for commendation, e.g. a written comment, star, etc.;
- a public word of praise in front of a group, a class, a year or the whole school;
- public, written acknowledgement through a special merit record book of some kind;
- public acknowledgement by presentation at an assembly or by giving some special responsibility;
- some system of merit marks or points, with or without public acknowledgement of that award;
- marks, grades and assessments – for behaviour as well as work – but having some danger of an adverse effect on those excluded;
- school badges or certificates, formally presented or otherwise, for good behaviour, community support or positive attitude;
- prizes which reflect attitudes, not least of service in the community;
- use of school reports to comment favourably, not only on good work and academic achievement, but on behaviour, on involvement and on general attitudes;
- a letter to parents informing them specifically of some action or achievement deserving of praise. (Too often schools write only when something has gone wrong.)

For the remainder of this chapter, the materials presented focus upon ideas which need to be considered for inclusion in a school policy document on attendance. These suggestions emanate from the Bolton guidelines on 'School Attendance Matters' as well as the author's experience of running numerous practical training days with schools to help them to produce their own policy documents often in advance of OFSTED visits.

It is suggested that the *ideal* school policy document could be created from a reading of the Bolton guidelines, put into a practical policy outline, while using some of the ideas for good practice contained in the rest of this book. The use of the enclosed documentation could also be utilised to discuss and update existing school policy documents on attendance as well as for professional development days in school.

School attendance policies

As a matter of good practice, all schools should have in place their own atten-dance policy. All the staff of a school should be fully aware of the policy, its contents and its ethos. They should apply it fairly and consistently to all pupils.

An effective attendance policy should:

- support the aims of the school;
- ensure that legal requirements are met;
- offer clear guidance to parents with regard to their legal responsibilities in relation to school attendance. This should also include information on punctuality;
- outline the ways that the school will encourage attendance by promoting a positive school environment;
- identify clear channels of communication with parents; and
- specify the school's policy and arrangements for authorising absence from school in special circumstances, e.g. religious festivals.

Schools will need to have agreed criteria for the kinds of special circumstances which will be authorised, even if in practice there is some flexibility. These guidelines will need to be based on the needs of the community, the situation, and the sorts of reasons parents may have for wishing their children to take leave of absence.

Consideration should also be given to:

- ways of identifying what is considered as authorised/unauthorised absence;
- clear procedures to identify and follow up all absences;
- a range of strategies to promote good attendance and deal with absenteeism;
- guidelines on sensitive approaches to deal with the needs of individual pupils;
- ways of setting attendance targets for individual pupils, forms, groups, etc.;
- procedures by which parents shall contact school in case of absence;
- the procedures that school will adopt in relation to the follow-up of absence in the short and the long term;
- procedures agreed with the education welfare service and LEA on policies for the external referral of cases;
- the procedures for a child's return to school, including procedures for re-integrating long term absentees;
- the needs of particular groups such as travelling families.

A draft policy document

This section is intended to offer helpful suggestions to schools drafting atten-dance policies. Clearly, any policy – if it is to have meaning and relevance –

must be school specific. There are, however, elements common to most school attendance policies, e.g. a mission statement (in some form), an account of registration procedures, an explanation of authorised/unauthorised absence, and so on. This section gives examples of these and suggests possible formats the policy might take, such as the ways in which the policy might be presented. It also offers schools a possible 'policy draft'. An attendance policy can, of course, only be developed after extensive consultation with the school community. The intention here is to provide schools with a possible policy framework on which to hang their own unique and individual practices. Primary schools may wish to take appropriate elements, suitably amended, for their use.

Policy contents

A school attendance policy should cover and explain the following:

- Mission statement
- Rights and responsibilities
- Registration (including lateness)
- Authorised/unauthorised absence
- Procedures for following up absence/lateness
- Strategies for promoting attendance/punctuality

Other/alternative headings could include:

- Statutory requirements
- Aims
- Key points
- Guidelines for staff
- Communication with parents
- Role of the education social worker

Alternatively, schools may wish to produce a relatively brief policy statement and then to follow it with a number of more detailed appendices.

Every school policy document may begin with a brief introductory statement; for example:

> This school policy document on attendance has been produced to explain to all concerned the rights, responsibilities and rules relating to the attendance of pupils at this school. If children do not arrive in school, they cannot be educated. Furthermore, good attendance promotes the best learning opportunities, punctuality and reliability: all valuable attributes for a successful working life after leaving school.

The mission statement

The policy can usefully begin with a statement of intent. Examples include:

xxx School aims to encourage and assist all pupils to achieve excellent levels of attendance and punctuality.

xxx School aims to ensure the achievement of high levels of attendance and punctuality by all pupils.

With the intention of enabling all students to take full advantage of the educational opportunities available to them, xxx School aims to encourage excellent levels of attendance and punctuality.

Rights and responsibilities

The rights and responsibilities of the school, its pupils and their parents will need to be covered; for example:

School

xxx School expects pupils to attend school regularly and to arrive on time in a fit condition to learn.

xxx School will encourage good attendance and will investigate all absenteeism.

xxx School staff will set a good example in matters of attendance and punctuality and will promptly investigate all absenteeism and lateness.

xxx School will work closely with parents should attendance/punctuality give cause for concern.

Pupils

Pupils will ensure that they attend regularly and on time.
Pupils will attend all lessons punctually.
Pupils will be listened to and respected.
Pupils will have individual records of attendance/punctuality acknowledged by the school.

Parents

Parents are responsible for ensuring their child's regular and punctual attendance.

Parents are responsible for ensuring that their child attends school regularly, punctually, properly dressed and equipped and in a fit condition to learn.

Parents are responsible for informing the school at once of the reason for any absence (by letter, phone call or personal visit).

Parents can expect the school to keep them fully informed of their child's progress.

Registration (including lateness)

This part of the policy may need to be more detailed and prescriptive. It should cover:

- registration procedures;
- times at which the class registers open and close (morning and afternoon);
- use of symbols;
- registration in subject classes.

The policy may also wish to stress the importance of registration – its legal aspect, as part of an orderly start to the school session, etc. for example:

Registers will be taken punctually each day at 9.00 am and at 1.00 pm.

Each pupil should be called by name and should respond in the prescribed formal manner – 'Here', 'Present', etc.

If a pupil arrives after the registers close, they should sign the lateness book.

All staff will take a register in each lesson.

It may be useful to remind parents that if a child arrives in school after the registers have closed and there is not an acceptable explanation, then such lateness has to be recorded as 'unauthorised absence'; for example:

When a pupil misses registration altogether and fails to provide an adequate explanation, then that pupil will be marked as an unauthorised absentee for that session, even though they may arrive later.

Authorised/unauthorised absence

It will be useful to emphasise that it is the school which decides whether an absence is to be authorised or unauthorised. Parents may need to be reminded that a letter does not in itself authorise an absence; only the school's acceptance of the explanation offered by the letter authorises the absence. For example:

All absences must be explained by parental note. The school will then decide whether or not it will authorise the absence.

It is important to be totally clear as to what constitutes authorised/ unauthorised absence. The policy should leave no room for ambiguity on this issue. For example:

Absence from school will be authorised if it is for the following reasons:

- sickness;
- unavoidable medical/dental appointments;
- days of religious observance;
- exceptional family circumstances, such as a bereavement;
- if permission for absence has been granted by a headteacher.

Absence from school will *not* be authorised for:

- shopping;
- haircuts;
- missed bus;
- slept late;
- no uniform;
- looking after brothers, sisters or unwell parents;
- minding the house;
- birthdays.

It will be useful to emphasise to parents that all medical/dental appointments should be made, whenever possible, outside of school hours. A late book is normally kept in which names are entered and a late mark is recorded in the register. Parents should also be urged strongly to avoid booking family holidays during term time. Parents do not have the right to take their child out of school for such holidays and should be advised to apply to the school for permission in advance of any such holiday.

Procedures for following up absence/lateness

This is perhaps the part of the policy which will be most school specific. Accordingly, only a few very general examples are offered in this section:

As soon as a pupil misses school the parents are informed immediately. [This is now the Government's preferred requirement.]

If a pupil is absent for more than 3 consecutive days (without an explanation being forthcoming) the school will write to the parents.

If a pupil is absent at morning registration, the form tutor/teacher will attempt that day to make contact with home unless a message about the absence has been received.

If a pupil is late on more than 2 occasions in a week, a detention may be imposed.

When a pupil is persistently late or absent and the school's efforts to effect improvement have been unsuccessful, it may be necessary to refer the matter to the school's education social worker.

If a pupil is persistently late or absent, the form tutor/year head/ headteacher will write to the parents/invite the parents into school.

Pupils who arrive late – either to school or to a lesson – may be required to make up the time after school that day (subject to parents' consent).

All notes from parents regarding a pupil's absence should be stored on the child's file after they have been initialled by the form tutor and year head/ headteacher.

If a pupil returns to school after an absence without a note then the form teacher will write to the parents.

All absences will be displayed daily on a single chart in the staff room.

Strategies for promoting attendance/punctuality

Here again, the policy will be very school specific; for example:

In the belief that all pupils are more likely to attend regularly if the curriculum is lively and meets their needs, this curriculum will be regularly reviewed.

The curriculum will be monitored and developed to meet the needs of all pupils.

Attendance statistics will be collected and used to inform pastoral and curriculum practices.

Parents, pupils and staff are to be regularly reminded of the types of absence which are recognised as authorised and unauthorised.

The school will award certificates each term to all pupils whose attendance/punctuality is either excellent or much improved.

Pupils whose attendance falls below 90 per cent will be set targets for improvement. These targets will be regularly reviewed by the form tutor/ year head/headteacher.

Good attendance and punctuality will be promoted and rewarded through merit awards made each term by the headteacher.

Regular, structured meetings will be held with the school's education social worker in order to identify and support those pupils whose attendance/punctuality is a source of concern.

Parents will be kept regularly and fully informed of all concerns around attendance and punctuality.

Reports will be made each term by the headteacher to the school's governing body on the issue of attendance/punctuality.

Pupils are to be constantly reminded of the importance and value of good attendance.

Pupils who have been absent for any extended period of time will be integrated back into school through a structured and individually-tailored programme.

All issues which may cause a pupil to experience attendance difficulties are to be promptly investigated by the form tutor/headteacher.

Photographs of pupils who achieve the highest levels of attendance are displayed in the school foyer.

Parents of pupils whose attendance is a cause for concern/congratulation will be written to by the headteacher at the end of every half-term.

Visits to feeder primary schools will be made in order to ensure the fullest support for all pupils during secondary transfer.

Ideas for inclusion in the policy document

Possible strategies for combating absenteeism

The seven areas for consideration for inclusion in a school's policy document are now presented. The text needs to include ideas and school policies on all of the following:

1 Re-integration after long-term absenteeism

- Child needs to feel welcome;
- support needs to be available – appoint a key person to whom the pupil relates well;
- relevant information should be given to appropriate staff to prevent further breakdown;
- reasons for absence are discussed and possibilities of change within school, home or pupil are considered;
- a negotiated and reviewed timetable is individually produced;
- initially a part-time timetable is possible;
- negotiate an agreement with pupil highlighting specific aims and targets;
- consider the possibility of a social mentor.

2 Rewards system (see Box 9.1)

- Intention of reinforcing improved attendance for all, providing a positive link between home and school;
- certificates for 100 per cent termly attendance – excellent;
- certificates for 95+ per cent termly attendance – highly commendable;
- improved attendance letter where termly attendance has increased by at least 10 per cent;
- best overall attendance percentage improvement termly per tutor group – certificate plus use of senior management for praise;
- inter-tutor group competition on: attendance with tutor group trophy (made internally) received termly by winners;
- half-termly attendance screening for those on 'at risk' attendance list – report home by letter any improvements.

3 Additional curriculum approaches – extended work experience

- Intention of increasing/maintaining motivation and providing meaningful involvement, particularly within an area of interest post-16;
- relate experience of the world of work to areas of the National Curriculum;
- prospective employers are contacted and their agreement to take part is obtained;
- negotiated times are agreed with school, pupil and employer;
- signed undertaking – pupil and member of school staff;
- possible subject link with school-based work, e.g. maths, English.

4 Attendance panels

- A school-based panel: possibly pastoral staff/tutor plus pupil, parent and EWO determining pupil's difficulties and considering negotiated changes to facilitate improved attendance +SENCO;

Box 9.1 Rewards and improvement notification

End of term attendance procedures

1 100% Certificate
2 Highly Commended: 95+% Certificate (anyone)
3 Improvement Certificate: Improvement, e.g. +10% at pastoral
                               discretion to further motivation
4 Letter 1   Improvement – some
5 Letter 2   Concern under 90% (unless specific
                               reasons, e.g. long-term illness,
                               problem, etc.)

Additional possible rewards to motivate

1 End of term 'DIPS' (£20 total   e.g. £3 McDonalds voucher
  cost)   £5 Music voucher
                                  £5 WH Smith voucher
                                  £2 Surprise gift
                                  Free school meal
                                  £5 cash or 5 × £1
                                  ½ day off with mark

2 Termly inter-tutor group   e.g. 10 points per 100%
  competitions (trophies)   5 points per 95+%
                                 +% improvement = +1 if below 90%
                                 = +3 if above 90%
                                 −% reduction = −3 points

3 Highest % termly improver   trophy
  per tutor   prize
                                 praise?

- pupil's attendance pattern discussed referring to register data;
- subject teachers' reports available;
- invitation to pupil and parent to express their views;
- feedback from panel to appropriate staff;
- involve outside agencies as appropriate.

5 register checks and spot checks

- Senior management to check tutor group registers and class subject registers at varying times (to check staff are fulfilling their obligation);

- spot checks on class subject registers to identify absences previously marked as present in tutor group registers (post-registration truancy).
- standard 'truancy' letter sent out for any PRT pupils.

6 *Names attendance co-ordinator*

- A focus for liaison with parents and external agencies responsible for co-ordinating issues and strategies related to attendance;
- identify pupils who may need alternative curriculum provision;
- intention to improve communications on all attendance issues with the aim of improving school statistics.

7 *Attendance target groups*

- Identify an 'at-risk' group;
- each morning, group tutors check this group's attendance;
- using standard referral sheet, inform home by telephone or visit (letter if not in) of pupil's absence;
- attempt to see each pupil individually to discuss their attendance and develop strategies for improvement;
- may need to involve 'attendance panel'.

General information on definitions is presented in Box 9.2 as well as in Chapter 2.

XXX Secondary School – The school attendance policy document: a suggested outline

Mission statement

xxx School aims to maximise attendance rates in order to ensure that all students are able to take the fullest advantage of the learning experiences available to them.

Statutory framework

Under Section 444 of the 1996 Education Act, a pupil is required to attend regularly at the school where they are a registered pupil.

The school is obliged by law to differentiate between authorised and unauthorised absence. A letter or telephone message from a parent does not in itself authorise an absence. Only if the school is satisfied as to the validity of the explanation offered by the letter/message will the absence be authorised (see below).

Rights and responsibilities

Improving attendance at xxx School is the responsibility of everyone in the school community – pupils, parents and all staff.

Box 9.2 General information: definitions

Defining absentees

? SCHOOL PHOBIC   Psychological reasons: illness, anxiety, fear of attending school for any reason. Probably needs skilled help and sympathetic care in school.

? TRUANT   Low self confidence, tendency to be shy, pleasant. Generally absent in a group. Parents often not aware of absences from school.

? SCHOOL REFUSER   Selective about days/lessons missed, lively and outgoing, can be un-cooperative. Parents often aware of absences from school.

? POST-REGISTRATION TRUANT   Registers but doesn't attend certain lessons.

Poor attendance can sometimes be caused by a variety of problems, e.g.

- health worries
- uniform problem
- bullying
- coursework difficulties
- career concerns
- family problems
- friendships

Pupils

All pupils are expected to attend school and all of their lessons regularly and punctually. Pupils who do experience attendance difficulties will be offered prompt and sympathetic support, initially from their form tutor, and if the need should arise, from their year head. At the end of each term, pupils whose attendance is either very good or improved will be presented with awards.

Parents

Parents are responsible for ensuring that their child attends school regularly, punctually, properly dressed and equipped and in a fit condition to learn. If a child is prevented for any reason from attending, or is late, parents are requested to notify the school as soon as possible – by phone call or preferably in writing. A pupil's absence from school must be considered as unauthorised until a satisfactory explanation is forthcoming from the parent. Parents will be informed promptly of any concerns which may arise over a child's attendance. Parents whose child's attendance is a cause for congratulation or concern will be written to by the year head at the end of each term. Parents should avoid, if at all possible, making medical/dental appointments for their child during school hours.

Parents whose first language is not English or who have literacy problems will be offered appropriate support from school in matters of communication.

School

Staff will endeavour to encourage good attendance and punctuality through personal example. Attendance is the responsibility of all school staff (not just teaching and pastoral staff). The school will employ a range of strategies (see pp. 191–3) to encourage good attendance and punctuality and will investigate promptly all absenteeism, liaising closely with parents. Staff will respond to all absenteeism firmly and consistently.

Registration

Registers will be called promptly at 8.50 am and at 1.30 pm and will be marked in red or black in accordance with the list of symbols as set out in the register.

Registers will close at 8.55 am and at 1.35 pm. If a pupil fails to arrive before the registers close, they will be marked as 'absent'. Pupils who arrive after the registers have closed should report to the general office and sign the School Late Book. (The form tutor will amend the register entry to read 'absent/late'.) If a pupil is late on two or more occasions in a week, a detention may be imposed. If a pupil is persistently late, the year head will contact the parents.

Parents are reminded that if a child arrives in school after the registers have closed and an acceptable explanation is not forthcoming, the pupil has to be recorded as 'unauthorised absent' for that session. All class teachers will take registers in each of their classes and will notify the year head as soon as possible of any absenteeism. The year head will inspect all registers each half term in order to ensure that correct procedures are being followed, totals are being calculated and entered.

Authorised/unauthorised absence

It is vital that all staff adhere to the same criteria when deciding whether or not to authorise an absence.

xxx School will decide on how an absence is to be recorded in accordance with the latest guidance from the Department for Education and Employment. This currently states that:

Absence can be **authorised** if:

- the pupil was absent with leave (defined as 'leave granted by any person authorised to do so by the governing body or proprietor of the school');
- the pupil was ill 'or prevented from attending by any unavoidable cause';
- 'the absence occurred on a day exclusively set aside for religious observance by the religious body to which the pupil's parent belongs';
- the school at which the child is a registered pupil is not within walking distance of the child's home and no suitable arrangements have been made by the LEA for any of the following:

  1 the child's transport to and from school;
  2 boarding accommodation for the child at or near the school; and
  3 enabling the child to become a registered pupil at a school nearer to his/her home.

- the pupil is the child of traveller parents and the conditions as stated in the Education Act 1996 (Section 444 (6)) are met;
- there is a family bereavement;
- the pupil is attending an interview with either a prospective employer or in connection with an application for a place at an institute of further or higher education or for a place at another school;
- the pupil is attending a Pupil Referral Unit;
- a Year 11 pupil is granted study leave (this should not normally exceed two weeks);
- the pupil is involved in an *exceptional* special occasion (e.g. if a pupil is attending the graduation of an older sibling);
- leave of absence is granted by the school for a family holiday of no more than two weeks (parents should be reminded that they cannot expect that, as of right, the school will agree to a family holiday during term time).

Absence should be **unauthorised** if:

- no explanation is forthcoming;
- the school is dissatisfied with the explanation;
- the pupil stays at home to mind the house or to look after siblings (the guidance suggests that absence in such cases should only be granted in exceptional circumstances);
- the pupil is shopping during school hours;
- the pupil is absent for *unexceptional* special occasions (e.g. a birthday);
- the pupil is away from school on a family holiday for a period of time longer than that negotiated with the school (normally a maximum of two weeks);

Box 9.3 Legal requirements

- Schools are required by law to record attendance every morning and afternoon;
- legal requirements for recording and reporting attendance must be met;
- the Education Regulations 1991 require that attendance registers show whether an absence is authorised or unauthorised.

	Authorised	*Unauthorised*
Condoned	School accepts absences as genuine, so does the parent.	School does not accept absence as genuine, but the parent allows it.
Uncondoned	School accepts absence as genuine but parent has not agreed to it.	School does not accept absence as genuine nor does parent.

Examples of authorised absence include	*Examples of unauthorised absence include*
<ul><li>family bereavement;</li><li>holiday in school time by prior agreement (2 weeks maximum);</li><li>days of religious observance;</li><li>interview, work experience, off-site activities, e.g. educational visit;</li><li>approved sporting fixture, residentials, exchanges, exclusion, sickness.</li></ul>	<ul><li>minding home, looking after brothers/sisters/pets;</li><li>shopping during school hours;</li><li>special occasions, e.g. birthdays;</li><li>no uniform, overslept, haircut;</li><li>missed bus;</li><li>sham illness.</li></ul>

- In some cases, depending on circumstances, school can determine whether an absence is deemed authorised.

- Pupils who miss registration altogether and fail to provide an adequate explanation will be marked as an authorised absence for that session, even though they may arrive later.
- The Children Act 1989 empowers the education authority to apply to the Family Proceedings Court for an education supervision order, bringing under supervision a child who is not being properly educated.
- Legal proceedings can be brought against the parents in the Magistrates Court should a pupil's attendance remain a concern despite extensive measures to improve.

- the pupil is on a family holiday without permission, or the parents have failed to apply for permission in advance of the holiday and instead seek retrospective approval on their return (see Box 9.3).

Holidays

Parents are strongly urged to avoid taking family holidays during term time. Indeed, parents do not have the right to take their child out of school for such a holiday. If, however, parents apply to the school in advance, the school may grant up to two weeks term-time absence in any year to go on a family holiday. Apart from this, leave in term time can only be given in exceptional circumstances.

Occasionally, holidays of more than two weeks to visit family living overseas may be planned. Parents are urged to discuss with school staff, the most appropriate time of year and point in the child's education career for this visit to take place. This will help minimise disruption to the child's progress at school.

Procedures for following up absence (see Figure 9.1)

- If a pupil is absent for more than three consecutive days (without an explanation being forthcoming) the form tutor will write to the parents. If the absentee is a pupil about whom there are already concerns, the form tutor will make every effort to contact the parents immediately.
- If a pupil is persistently (or intermittently) absent, the form tutor will write to the parents and invite them to attend a meeting at school.
- If a pupil returns to school after a period of absence and fails to bring a note, or if the explanation offered by a note is unsatisfactory, the form tutor will write to the parents.
- If a pupil is persistently absent (or late) and the school's efforts to effect an improvement have been unsuccessful, the situation will be referred to the education social worker during their consultation visit.
- Notes from parents will be initialled by the form tutor and kept on the pupil's file. All telephone messages regarding absence/lateness are to be recorded in the telephone message book.
- All absences will be displayed daily on the staff room notice board. This is intended to enable class teachers to cross-check their registers with form registers.

Strategies for promoting attendance

- xxx School will offer an environment in which pupils feel valued and welcomed. The school's ethos must demonstrate that pupils feel that their presence in school is important, that they will be missed when they are absent/late and that follow-up action will be taken.

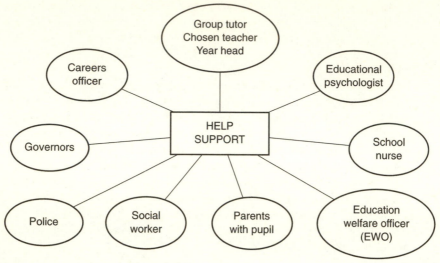

Figure 9.1 Support network for pupils

- A varied and flexible curriculum will be offered to all pupils. Every effort will be made to ensure that learning tasks are matched to pupils' needs.
- Attendance data will be regularly collected and analysed in order to help identify patterns, set targets, correlate attendance with achievement, and support and inform policy/practice.
- Good attendance awards will be presented at the end of each school year.
- Pupils will be reminded regularly (via newsletters, the school brochure, parents' evenings, etc.) of the importance of good attendance.
- Pupils who are absent through sickness for any extended period of time will (when appropriate) have work sent home to them and will be re-integrated back into school upon their return.
- Pupils who have been absent for whatever reason for an extended period of time will (when appropriate) have individually-tailored re-integration programmes prepared for them.
- The headteacher will make an annual report to the school's governing body on attendance matters.
- Year heads will, when appropriate, liaise with other agencies – educational psychology service, social services and other agencies – when this may serve to support and assist pupils who are experiencing attendance difficulties.
- Year heads will have regular meetings with the school's educational social worker in order to identify and support those pupils who are experiencing attendance difficulties.

- Regular visits will be made to feeder primary schools in order to ensure the smoothest possible secondary transfer. Discussions with primary school teachers will seek to identify those pupils who may require extra support during this process.

Once school policy documents have been agreed and implemented, they should be reviewed annually, revised and brought up to date as legislation and DfEE policy on attendance matters is continually being improved and/or amended. Similarly, as schools gain more experience, they are in a better position to change and guide policy, e.g. to set classes, years or the whole school revised attendance targets in line with the Government's strategy.

Some schools prefer to include their policy on attendance as part of a whole-school document on behaviour including, for example, bullying and a list of key school rules (uniform, detention, break-time regulations, etc.). This is acceptable. What matters most is that schools *have* policies and that these policies are sensible and workable. They should always be articulated to every-one involved in the whole-school process – pupils, parents, all staff and the governing body – and reviewed periodically.

10 Improving school attendance: school-based review

This chapter is sub-divided into three parts. Each section provides ideas based on successful good practice to prevent and overcome non-attendance. The first part focuses on improving school attendance through a school-based review process, and the second part on the use of school and/or pupil surveys. While information provided from national data is helpful, research shows that each school is unique. Too often teachers are caught out by failing to understand *why* pupils play truant from *their* school. Research indicates that even schools in homogeneous regions can vary considerably not only in their rates of attendance but also on the reasons why pupils miss school. In one school, for example, it may be bullying which is the major cause; in another it could be poor teacher–pupil relationships. This second section provides a rationale for using questionnaire or survey approaches, then goes on to provide evidence on how this approach has been used successfully within schools. Finally, a sample questionnaire is provided which can be made more or less simple – dependening on its purpose. Alternatively, it can be shortened or lengthened dependent upon need and target group.

The third part of this chapter describes some recent innovative projects to improve school attendance and reduce truancy based on good practice within selected comprehensive schools. The first project started in Year 6 within feeder primary schools and followed this cohort of pupils as they transferred into their secondary schools by year up until Year 11. The project then followed each of the next four cohorts in the same way until attendance in the school had risen significantly and truancy had been much reduced. At the same time, the staff in the school worked with the identified pupils in four colour-coded groups in order to improve their literacy, numeracy and attainment levels as well as their attendance and related behavioural problems.

The next project looks at the efforts of a London comprehensive to overcome its absenteeism and truancy problems. This school concentrated on:

(a) improving home–school communication;
(b) introducing and improving its token economy;

(c) better pastoral care;
(d) the introduction of a corrective reading scheme;
(e) the dissemination of good practice.

The third project provides evidence from a school which was heading for failure following a very poor OFSTED report, and the sudden resignation of the headteacher following a blaze of adverse publicity. This large comprehensive in South Wales set about overcoming its problems through a whole-school approach, gaining external funding for a school attendance project, and by the innovative use of an attendance support teacher to work with and alongside non-attenders and their parents.

In addition to the good practice described in this chapter, there are brief examples of good practice in schools presented at relevant points throughout the rest of this book.

Improving school attendance – school based review

The process

The school-based review process follows distinct stages. These are:

(a) the initial school-based review;
(b) brainstorming to develop strategies to improve attendance;
(c) formulating coherent staff development programmes.

These three stages may subsequently lead to the initial steps that the staff will decide to take which, in turn, will lead to a strategic plan to combat absenteeism. Finally, after a school has developed and introduced its plan and evaluated it, prevention strategies will be needed to ensure that absenteeism is firmly under control.

Planning a whole-school approach to reducing truancy (perhaps to meet the Government's targets for schools to reduce truancy by one third) can be fun and can provide an interesting and varied agenda for one or more professional development day.

Initial school-based review

The purpose of initial school-based review is to:

• analyse what management systems are already in place to manage attendance;
• have a clear understanding of the roles and responsibilities of staff in the school;
• understand the roles of the support agencies;
• formulate an agenda for action.

Developing strategies to improve attendance

This can be carried out by:

- using the SIMS (or other software package) attendance module to record and monitor attendance;
- ensuring that there is quick follow-up action to absenteeism and that the appropriate methods are employed to re-introduce pupils back in to full-time education;
- involving governors, teachers, parents and support agencies in attendance-related issues;
- improving communication links with parents;
- liaising with feeder primary schools to identify potential absentees;
- developing a support system to support pupils with literacy difficulties;
- devising an anti-bullying policy and programme for pupils;
- rewarding good and improved attendance.

Coherent staff development

This is achieved by:

- regularly discussing with the SMT, procedures and processes in relation to any new strategies;
- delivering in-service training on attendance related issues;
- providing the necessary support and staff development for NQTs and students on the initial teachers training course.

Initial steps

The first and most important step is the recognition that there is a problem. The next step is to raise the profile of attendance in the school. This is done by:

1 delivering in-service training on attendance-related issues to all members of staff;
2 introducing or reviewing the use of the SIMS (or other form of computerised package) Attendance Model in the school to record and monitor attendance;
3 ensuring that the form teacher is the key person in monitoring the attendance of all members of their form;
4 involving governors, teachers, parents and support agencies in attendance-related issues within the school and outlining their rights and responsibilities in relation to the role they play with pupils in the school;

5 ensuring that there is quick follow-up action to absenteeism and that the appropriate methods are employed to re-introduce pupils back into full-time education;

6 providing in-class support for pupils who experience difficulties in basic skills; ensuring that pupils who missed school for various reasons – authorised or unauthorised – have the opportunity to make good the work they have missed;

7 encouraging staff to produce work that is differentiated;

8 devising an anti-bullying programme throughout the school;

9 improving communication links with parents and providing transport and child care facilities for parents' evenings;

10 making home visits if necessary;

11 producing a booklet for new staff and supply teachers on the monitoring of attendance in the school;

12 rewarding good and improved attendance;

13 improving links with the feeder primary schools and identifying potential absentees.

Planning stages

The aim of the school is to:

1 improve the recording and monitoring of attendance;

2 identify actual and potential problems early;

3 understand the functions of outside agencies and working together in a partnership;

4 successfully re-integrate pupils after long periods of absence;

5 improve links with parents;

6 create an ethos in the school which encourages success and achievement, a good attendance record being part of this;

7 have awareness and sympathy for problems which some pupils face, while at all times ensuring they have full access to the opportunities that can enhance their lives and raise their self-esteem within the community.

Prevention

To prevent absenteeism schools need to ensure:

1 all pupils have access to the curriculum;

2 support is provided for pupils who may be experiencing difficulties;

3 all pupils are encouraged to succeed and an ethos prevails which is con-ducive to learning;

4 all pupils feel safe and there are strategies in place to minimise bullying and deal with it effectively if an incident arises;

5   all parents are well informed of what is expected of them in relation to their child's attendance at school;
6   all children know:

    (a)   they are part of the school community;
    (b)   they will be missed if they are absent from school;
    (c)   their parents will be contacted to identify the reason for absence;

7   excellent and improved attendance is acknowledged and rewarded.

The use of surveys: understanding your own school

A lot of schools have begun to implement measures to prevent and combat truancy based on their own assumptions. Research constantly shows that truancy is a multi-causal phenomenon. Each truant is unique. While there are similarities between categories of truants, the causes can vary regionally and locally. Schools, too, vary considerably in the extent of their truancy problem. Some schools have major difficulties; others only minor problems. It can be extremely helpful, therefore, when schools are able to obtain precise information on the causes of truancy within their own schools.

One way of achieving this is to obtain direct information from the pupils themselves. This can be achieved through the construction of questionnaires for use with:

(a)   whole-school cohorts;
(b)   whole-year cohorts;
(c)   whole-subject cohorts;
(d)   form groups.

Sometimes, it is sensible to obtain information from the whole of Years 7 to 11 first and subsequently to break down this large cohort into smaller units for more detailed secondary questionnaires. Interviewing a sample of good and bad attenders in addition to, or separate from, the use of whole-school questionnaires is another sound approach.

With today's technology, it is comparatively easy to obtain school data on such variables as:

(a)   specific lesson absence – Is it the same lessons being missed? Is it always the same group of pupils? If so, why? What does this information tell you about the quality of teaching of this subject within the school? If, for example, there are two teachers of chemistry in a school and one always has a high attendance rate and the other does not, what does this imply?
(b)   teacher absence. Evidence is beginning to mount that teachers who miss school frequently tend to lower pupils' confidence, sometimes causing them to either drop out or become specific lesson absentees;

(c) general patterns of absenteeism, daily, weekly, termly, yearly by form, group, year and subject.

These data can be used at staff meetings and reviewed periodically as part of the school policy on attendance. The information can also be fed back to staff and used as part of appraisal processes, and used at parents' evenings and with governors. The details can also be put up, for example, on a special school attendance notice board in the staffroom.

It might make an interesting staff development ice-breaker to discuss the data presented in Tables 10.1 to 10.6. However, the information provided in the tables is only illustrative as the findings for every school will be different. Schools can plan their own questionnaires to ensure they gather the precise information they require. On a technical point, it is wise to:

(a) Keep survey questionnaires simple and limit the number of questions. For young pupils a few questions may be enough. For Years 9 upwards, questionnaires should still be kept to a maximum of 20 questions.
(b) Be careful to ask for information in simple English. Remember less able as well as able pupils will be completing this. Make sure the meaning of the questions is clear. Set out the format of the questionnaire in an easy-to-read, well-spaced style.
(c) Use only a few essential independent variables, e.g. gender, age, form, year, etc.
(d) It is usually better to let the pupils complete the form anonymously. They will give you more meaningful data if you do so.
(e) Decide in advance:
    i   what information you require;
    ii what use you will make of the data;
    iii how you intend to cross-tabulate the independent variables with the dependent variables, e.g. the link between age, gender, subject with pupils' views on their curriculum, teaching or aspects of school life.

The sample questionnaire now presented in Box 10.1 is for use with pupils in Years 7 to 11 to provide general information on attendance from the pupils' perspective. It also provides basic curricular and attitudinal information on the school. This questionnaire could be readily amended for use in any school. Equally, some schools prefer to use supplementary in-depth questionnaires with samples of good and bad attenders and then to compare and contrast the two.

By way of an illustration, the findings obtained from a school in South Wales with approximately 900 pupils in Years 7 to 11 are now presented. No particular significance should be attached to these data as they are school-specific.

The details presented in Tables 10.1 and 10.2 were obtained from the initial questionnaire. Secondary data was obtained from a follow-up questionnaire

Box 10.1 A sample questionnaire on attendance

Please answer as many questions as you can. Your answers are CONFIDENTIAL.

1 What year are you in at school?
   (please tick one box)

   Year 7 ☐   Year 8 ☐   Year 9 ☐   Year 10 ☐   Year 11 ☐

2 Are you male or female?
   (please tick one box)

   Male ☐   Female ☐

3 What form and year group are you in?
   (please write in form, e.g. 9G, 9H in box below)

   Name of form [   ]

4 Do you enjoy coming to school?
   (please tick one box)

   Yes ☐   No ☐

5 Do you try to attend school every day?
   (please tick one box)

   Yes ☐   No ☐

6 Roughly what percentage of attendance did you manage within the last twelve months?
   (please tick one box)

   roughly 100% ☐   between 96–99%
   between 90–95% ☐   between 70 and 89% ☐
   less than 70% ☐   hardly ever ☐

7 Do you ever play truant?
   (please tick one box)

   Yes ☐   No ☐

If you answer yes to this question, please answer questions 8 to 11. If you answer no, please go straight to question 12.

8 If so, why?

(only answer this question, if you have ticked yes in question 7). If you do play truant please give as many reasons as you can for missing school.

_____

_____

_____

_____

9 Do you ever skip off specific lessons in school? (e.g. maths, games, languages)

(please tick one box)

Yes ☐   No ☐

If you have answered yes to question 9, please answer question 10. If not, go straight to question 11.

10 Why do you miss certain lessons in school time?

(please give as many reasons as you can)

_____

_____

_____

_____

11 Please give three reasons why you dislike attending this school on a regular basis.

_____

_____

_____

_____

12 What are your three favourite subjects?

(please list in order) (all pupils to answer this question)

1 _____

2 _____

3 _____

13 Why do you like each of these subjects?

(please give an answer for each subject)

Subject 1 _____

Subject 2 _____

Subject 3 _____

14 Which three subjects do you least like?

(please list in order)

1 _____

2 _____

3 _____

15 Why do you dislike each of these three subjects?

(please give an answer for each subject)

Subject 1 _____

Subject 2 _____

Subject 3 _____

16 Have you ever been bullied in school?

(please tick one box)

Yes ☐   No ☐

17 What are the three things you most enjoy about school?

(please list up to three items e.g. sport, music, school trips, etc).

1 _____

2 _____

3 _____

18 What would you change about this school if you could?

(please write as much as you wish)

_____

_____

_____

_____

Thank you for answering this questionnaire. We remind you that your individual answers will be treated in confidence.

Table 10.1 School performance

	Levels of pupils with 95%+ attendance	Levels below 95% and above 71%	Truants with less than 70% attendance
Year 7	84	16	7
Year 8	79	21	8
Year 9	73	27	9.5
Year 10	72	28	12
Year 11	64	36	14

Table 10.2 School performance by gender

	Levels of pupils with 95%+ attendance		% of truants with less than 70% attendance	
	Boys	Girls	Boys	Girls
Year 7	85	83	4	3
Year 8	77	81	5	3
Year 9	71	75	6	3.5
Year 10	70	74	7	5
Year 11	59	69	9	5

Table 10.3 Pupils' favourite subjects in order

Year 7	Year 8	Year 9
English	English	English
History	History	History
Geography	PE (boys only)	PE (boys only)
RE	Welsh (girls only)	Welsh (girls only)
Science	Technology	Science
	PSE	Technology

Table 10.4 Pupils' least favourite subjects in order

Year 7	Year 8	Year 9
Languages	Languages	Languages
PSE	Science	Maths
Maths	Maths	PE (girls only)
Technology	RE	RE
Welsh	Geography	Geography
		Welsh (boys only)

Table 10.5 Pupils' favourite subjects in order by gender

Year 7		Year 8		Year 9	
Boys	Girls	Boys	Girls	Boys	Girls
English	English	English	English	English	English
History	History	PE	History	PE	History
Science	Science	History	Welsh	History	Welsh
PE	RE	Technology	PSE	Science	Maths
Technology	Technology	Maths	Technology	Technology	Science

Table 10.6 Truants' least favourite subjects in order by gender

Year 7		Year 8		Year 9	
Boys	Girls	Boys	Girls	Boys	Girls
Languages	Languages	Languages	Languages	Languages	Languages
Welsh	Technology	Science*	Science*	Science*	Science*
RE	Geography	RE	Maths	Geography	Maths
Maths	PSE	Geography	PE	Welsh	Technology
Geography	Maths	Welsh	RE	RE	PE

Notes
* Especially chemistry and physics.

used with specific target groups of pupils from within the same school. Examples of this information are shown in Tables 10.3 to 10.6.

Table 10.3 is interesting. It shows the five most preferred subjects for the pupils in Years 7, 8 and 9. Apart from PE and Welsh there were no major gender differences. However, the same gender differences – for whatever reason – are to be found in Year 9 in Table 10.5.

Table 10.4 provides the pupils' least favourite subjects in order. Table 10.6 shows the truants' least favourite subjects, also in order.

Bear in mind these results have been obtained from only one school. However, for this school the results indicate a few clear points. Why is 'English' consistently in first or second place with history in Years 7, 8 and 9? Equally, why are languages and maths and science much less highly regarded? Note that the truants consistently least like languages followed by science (in Years 8 and 9). What does this tell us? These kind of data can lead to healthy discussions during a school's staff development event and can lead to appropriate action being taken which, in turn, can lead to better staff–pupil relationships, improved behaviour and reduced levels of non-attendance.

Projects to improve attendance

A *five-year project to improve attendance*

Background

A large comprehensive was considered by OFSTED to be failing largely due to poor attendance. Pupil disaffection appeared to start as soon as the primary-age pupils transferred to their neighbourhood comprehensive. The attendance and related issues within the school were deemed to be so daunting that it was decided to adopt a longer-term strategy to overcome the problems. The scheme coincided with the appointment of a new head.

The concept

It was decided to focus attention on Year 6 pupils in the local primary feeder schools. They were categorised into the following groups:

- *Green* – No anticipated problems.
- *Red* – Pupils who were already truants at primary school.
- *Blue* – Pupils who were deemed to be 'at risk' of becoming truants based on:

    (a) their current profiles;
    (b) previous family history, e.g. brother or sister who had become a truant.

- *Yellow* – Pupils who were considered to be 'at risk' because they were seriously underachieving at school and whose reading ages, levels of numeracy and literacy were more than two years behind their chronological ages.

Primary/secondary transfer

The comprehensive school devised appropriate strategies to support each colour-coded group of pupils at their point of transfer. The following measures were taken.

Red group

Pupils in the red group were put into a range of different form groups at the start of Year 7. However, all these pupils came together for their PSE classes including specialist sessions on truancy, behaviour and bullying. These pupils were monitored daily and, on every occasion, absences were followed up immediately. These pupils were given specialist help with literacy and numeracy skills on a weekly basis in special sessions arranged by the attendance support teacher within the school. Twice a term the parent(s) or guardian(s) and the pupil were seen together by a governors' attendance panel comprised of the headteacher, a governor (drawn from a list of three), EWO and the attendance support teacher. At the meeting, each pupil's attendance and academic performance was discussed in detail and, when necessary, appropriate action taken. These meetings usually took place between 4 and 6.30 pm to give a chance for everybody to be present at a pre-arranged preferred time.

Each of these pupils and their parent(s) or guardian(s) signed the attendance charter and a home–school contract before starting at the comprehensive school. The interviews with the governors' attendance panel focused on how these contracts were operating, the individual pupil's level of attendance, academic progress and related in-school and external difficulties.

Pupils remained in this red group until their truancy had ceased and their academic performance was not causing concern. By the end of Year 11, 70 per cent of the original cohort of truants were no longer in this group. Their places were taken by new truants either from the blue or yellow groups or from outside those pupils named in the original scheme. Over a 5-year period (form years 6 to 11), the size of the red group decreased overall as the scale of truancy within the school reduced to much more manageable proportions. At the same time, the academic performance of the school rose.

Blue group

Pupils in the blue group followed a similar format to those in the red with the following significant differences:

(a) Their progress and attendance interviews were undertaken by a lower level school attendance panel comprised of the year co-ordinator, the attendance support teacher and an education welfare officer.
(b) As soon as these pupils were deemed to be no longer at risk they moved into either the yellow or green coded groups as appropriate. Given the support within the school, and the experience the staff gained over a comparatively short period, the overall numbers entering the blue group gradually decreased year on year. Moreover, after three years of the scheme, only a handful of pupils progressed from the blue to the red group.

Yellow group

As the yellow group pupils did not have an attendance problem at the point of transfer, their programme focused on overcoming learning and behavioural difficulties. The processes followed were identical to those for the red and blue groups except:

(a) No formal interviews with parents and pupils were conducted by panels established by the school.
(b) The key focus of the school's work was on prevention.

(c) Individual and group timetables were modified to enable time to be found for extra help with reading, writing and numeracy. This time often came from the use of first and second language periods as it was found that these pupils often lacked the aptitude to learn foreign languages.

Over the five years of the project, the average size of the yellow group gradually decreased, but always remained the largest of the three designated at-risk groups.

Outcomes of the project

Primary schools' benefits

Before the project started, there were huge variations between the primary schools in their rates of attendance, levels of literacy and numeracy and behavioural problems despite the fact that the schools all served the same neighbourhood comprehensive within a homogeneous area. Over the five years duration, the rates of truancy between the primary schools levelled out and were much reduced because:

(a) primary school teachers benefited from the focus on truancy and pupils' progression undertaken by the comprehensive school staff;
(b) the schools and pupils benefited from (i) early identification and (ii) early remedial strategies;
(c) the parents of the truants and underachieving pupils became much more supportive of their local comprehensive and primary schools;
(d) reduced levels of sibling-related truancy took place;
(e) confidence grew between the primary schools and the comprehensive school greatly facilitating the primary–secondary transfer;
(f) visits by Year 6 pupils and their parents to the comprehensive for taster classes gradually became the norm.

Benefits for the comprehensive

(a) Levels of absenteeism were reduced by 16 per cent over the 5-year project;
(b) the school inherited fewer truants from primary schools into Year 7 year upon year;
(c) by the end of the fifth year of the project, only twenty pupils in the comprehensive remained in the red group;
(d) overall levels of literacy and numeracy improved;
(e) the school's academic outcomes gradually improved to much more acceptable levels;
(f) the comprehensive school's attendance booklet was refined and improved; a much better student handbook and school guide for parents was produced;

(g) parental confidence in the school was greatly enhanced. For example, by year 4 of the project:

- Some mothers of truants had returned to education themselves. A few mothers were encouraged to start taking GCSE English and maths. One mother and her truant daughter both achieved a grade C pass in English Literature in the same year. The school began naturally, therefore, to participate in lifelong learning schemes.
- Other mothers gave up their free time to become pupil helpers in the school. Some acted as unpaid classroom assistants. Others listened to less able pupils read. A third group helped in PSE classes having the benefit of being able to speak from personal experience.
- The school ethos improved. The malaise and disaffection of the staff disappeared. The school's status in the community was greatly enhanced.
- One member of the staff was seconded to a nearby failing comprehensive to facilitate the school improvement programmes.
- Vandalism of school buildings decreased.
- The overall behaviour of the pupils improved.
- Bullying was a major problem within the school at the start of the project. All four groups in the initial Year 7 – red, blue, yellow and green – undertook a range of special PSE programmes on bullying. This included making a school video on bullying, using drama lessons and assemblies to act out themes on bullying, completing questionnaires on the extent, causes and outcomes of bullying. The school no longer has a significant bullying problem.

School life goes on. The project has ended but the staff have not become complacent. The same processes for new pupils are in place. The school is benefiting from positive rather than negative publicity. In an area of renowned deprivation and socio-economic disadvantage, the community has a school and teaching staff of which it can be proud. Today, the school is in a mid-table position within its authority. Previously, at the start of the scheme, it was bottom of the league tables for examination success within the LEA. It was considered a failing school. It is now regarded as a 'rising' school.

Exemplars of good practice: school-based experiences

Exemplar 1 Overcoming truancy and school absenteeism

School A

A large comprehensive school based in London with serious truancy problems. The aim of this project was to reduce non-attendance through improved communication between home and school, within the school and between the school and support agencies.

1   *Method:*
    regular home/school bulletins;
    school policy documents on attendance;
    attendance on agenda of open/parents' evenings;
    publish an attendance staff bulletin weekly;
    provide a 'tips for tutors' pack on attendance regulations and related issues;
    spot checks on post-registration truancy;
    place proper emphasis upon pupil and staff punctuality;
    use of SIMS to its maximum potential.

2   *Introduce and improve token economy*   To encourage pupils to attend on a
    regular basis, a reward system based upon a token economy was introduced.
    This was linked to the school's merit and credit system. Pupils received, for
    example, merits, credits, certificates, key rings, pens, mugs, etc. for reaching
    attendance targets over specified periods of time. The presentation of these
    tokens took place at a public event, e.g. year assemblies. Pupils with a full
    attendance record were displayed by photograph in the entrance hall of
    the school.

3   *Improved pastoral care*   The school introduced truancy and exclusion as
    topics within part of the Personal Health and Social Education Pro-
    gramme. They also used suggestions from pupils' own self-referrals as
    topics within the programme. This helped to change pupils' social attitudes
    to issues within the school and helped to prevent attendance-related diffi-
    culties becoming too firmly entrenched. (NB Peer pressure is one of the
    foremost reasons for truancy.)

4   *Corrective Reading Scheme*   The learning support department introduced a
    corrective reading scheme aimed at raising basic literacy levels through
    the use of a daily structured group reading programme. (NB More cost
    effective than individual support.) The programme was designed to be posi-
    tive and supportive for pupils. Staff teaching on the scheme including the
    head of learning support department, the headteacher and the attendance
    project co-ordinator. The need to attend on a regular basis each day was
    emphasised. Success in the programme was also linked in with the reward
    system of the school and pupils received merit stickers for regular atten-
    dance and progress. Over 60 pupils were involved in the initial phase of
    the programme. Average gains in reading ages on the New Macmillan
    Reading Analysis were between 18 months and 2 years over a three-
    month period across all four levels of the programme, and there were
    cases of persistent absentees specifically attending for the reading
    programme.

5   *Dissemination of good practice*   The project team produced a regular news-
    letter for schools, and was able to provide INSET to schools. A secondary
    INSET session took place at the project school for other secondary schools
    within the borough and attendance was regularly discussed at primary
    headteachers' meetings. Members of the project management group also
    ran sessions for other boroughs through the Special Educational Needs

Joint Initiative on Training (SENJIT), based at the University of London Institute of Education, and workshops at the University of North London. Most recently, HMI has visited the school in the wake of the positive publicity for the school to examine the current reducing truancy projects. Improved contact with feeder primary schools also took place.

Exemplar 2

School B

A response to an OFSTED inspection. During the visit and subsequent report this 11–18 comprehensive school was criticised for:

(a) its school attendance record;
(b) aspects of its literacy and numeracy policy in Years 7 and 8;
(c) lack of opportunities for Year 7/8 pupils to play a responsible role within the school.

Below is presented an example of how the school staff responded following 'brainstorming' sessions. This section provides a detailed individual school response to specifically identified problems.

Year 7/8 pupils:

1   listen, during two registration periods a week, to the reading of Year 7 pupils who had been identified by the Year 6 teachers from the ten feeder primary schools, prior to transition;
2   are trained to use a handwriting package which is used to correct handwriting defects of some Year 7 pupils, who have been referred by their form tutors;
3   return to their old feeder primary schools to listen to the reading of Year 6 pupils who had been identified as being in need of additional support.

The tutoring scheme in 3 above was acknowledged as being innovative on the grounds that it could contribute to the personal development and general achievement of pupils in Years 6, 7 and 8. The scheme won a Barclays' New Future Award.

Apart from the above, the school was asked to consider the following issues in relation to their attendance strategies.

1   effect of a named person in the school with responsibility for overseeing all attendance-related issues in the school;
2   setting up of an inter-agency panel within the school and the effect it has on improving individual pupil attendance;

3 development of a school policy on attendance, involving staff, governors, parents and pupils;
4 effect of COMPACT on the attendance of pupils in Years 10 and 11;
5 gender differences in relation to achievement at KS3 and 4;
6 direct involvement of parents of pupils with poor attendance;
7 follow up to five pupils with poor attendance compared with five pupils with excellent attendance the year after KS4;
8 effect of home visits on pupils with one day's absence;
9 effect Court has on the pupils whose parents have been prosecuted for their child's non-attendance;
10 effect of an attendance support group in Year 7 on pupils whose attendance is giving cause for concern;
11 effect the activities week has on the attendance of pupils during the last week of the school year;
12 effect a 'family literacy' project has on the attendance of the pupils who are involved in the project.

Exemplar 3

School C: Hurlingham and Chelsea School

This brief exemplar focuses on this school's initiatives which have all played a part in improving attendance in Key Stage 3.

1 Literacy programme – one hour a week for all KS3 pupils (includes use of sound).
2 Termly raffle – best attenders' names are put into a hat and winners get a prize, e.g. books, vouchers for shops, Fulham FC tickets.
3 Improvement of SEN department and Code of Practice to help to better understand pupil needs.
4 Truancy watch – jointly working with ESW and police.
5 Target setting by year and from tutor groups.
6 Employed a truancy/attendance officer.

Exemplar 4

School D: Mountain Ash Comprehensive School – improving attendance project

Several years ago, the school received a highly critical HMI report. One of the major problems identified at that time was school attendance. Since then, the school has worked prodigiously to improve its image, culture, attendance and achievement targets. The school appointed a new headteacher who, in turn, focused staff attention on attendance. He created a post of attendance support teacher which, in the first three years, was filled by an experienced and empathetic member of staff, Elaine Reynolds, who was funded by the Welsh Office out of GEST money. Subsequently, Elaine returned to her original post having worked assiduously to achieve the school's improved targets; something she achieved with great distinction. Elaine also used her 'field' experiences to obtain a research degree at Swansea Institute of Higher Education.

The following pages provide exemplars of how Elaine and the school achieved their goals. The process started with an initial school-based review followed by regular programmes of coherent staff development, intensive data collection on attendance by year, form, and subjects over a 3-year period. This led to a change of referral system, a whole-school policy document and the establishment of an attendance support panel, a governors' attendance panel, improved inter-agency co-operation, continuous staff development and feedback on the project's progress. The job description for the attendance support teacher, her duties and the subsequent role of her successor, the attendance project officer, are provided at the end of this section in case other schools may wish to replicate the ideas (see also pp. 168–9).

Mountain Ash no longer has a serious attendance problem. The staff have worked hard as a team to overcome their original problems. Led by the Head and co-ordinated by Elaine, they have shown tremendous determination to overcome the endemic truancy problems which were typical of this part of South Wales in a socially deprived and disadvantaged geographical environment. The school continues to apply the lessons it has learnt in as diligent a manner as possible and is now finding that as its local reputation has improved, so has its pupils' educational outcomes as measured by examination performance and attendance variables.

Elaine undertook the co-ordinating role on attendance within the school. This is how she did it.

1   By establishing and utilising an *attendance support panel* for less serious non-attenders. Membership of the panel consisted of:

- the educational psychologist;
- the education welfare officer;
- the attendance support teacher.

The group met twice a term. The aims of the group were to improve the attendance of pupils in Year 7 by:

(a) interviewing parents and pupils, to establish reasons for absence; and
(b) monitoring attendance closely over a period of 6 weeks, to maintain good attendance.

Procedure The educational psychologist and the attendance support teacher looked through the registers in order to identify pupils that had erratic attendance. A meeting was then held with the education welfare officers who had knowledge of the social and educational backgrounds of these pupils. A list of pupils was drawn up and letters were sent to their parents inviting them to a meeting.

The meeting The education welfare officers provided the attendance figures and any other relevant information. The group discussed this information and the parent(s) and child were then invited in. If the parent(s) did not attend, the child was interviewed. The group tried to establish the reason(s) for the child's poor attendance. A plan was then devised to support the child and consequently improve their attendance. A letter was then sent home thanking the parents for attending the meeting. In the case of parents who did not attend, the school expressed its regret at their non-attendance at the meeting and explained that it was essential that their child's attendance improved. Subsequently, a letter was sent home explaining the action which had been taken.

2   By establishing a *governors' attendance panel* for serious non-attenders. Membership of the panel consisted of:

- the headteacher;
- three other governors (one to attend each meeting according to availability);
- the education welfare officers;
- attendance support teacher.

The panel met twice a term. The aims of the panel were to interview the parents of pupils whose attendance had fallen below 75 per cent without an acceptable reason.

Procedure A letter was sent to the parents inviting them to attend a meeting to discuss their child's attendance. This letter accompanied the first warning letter from the District Education Officer. The second letter was sent (by Recorded Delivery) within three weeks of the above, confirming the date and time of the meeting.

The meeting The education welfare officers provided the attendance figures and any other information. The panel discussed this information and the parent(s) were then invited into the meeting.

The panel tried to establish the reason(s) for the child's poor attendance. When possible, a plan was designed to help the pupil achieve an acceptable attendance level. The plan might have involved the headteacher speaking to the pupil, or the attendance support teacher may have offered remedial support for the pupil. It was made clear that unless the pupil achieved 80+ per cent attendance, the prosecution procedure would continue. The headteacher wrote to the parents summarising the meeting.

Non-attendance of parents   If parents did not attend and had not contacted the school, the headteacher wrote to them expressing his disappointment and explained that unless 80+ per cent attendance was achieved by their child, prosecution proceedings would continue.

Within the school   The educational psychologist visits the school once a fortnight but has been involved with the attendance support group from the outset. He was instrumental in setting up the group.

The child and family clinic hold meetings once a month. It is a joint psychological service and child and family clinic meeting, with the attendance support teacher invited to attend when the pupils that were to be discussed were those with attendance-related problems.

3   By utilising the help of social workers. If a pupil had a *social worker* and that pupil had an attendance problem, the attendance support teacher attended relevant case conferences or, in some cases, informal discussion meetings took place with the pupil's social worker.

4   By involving the police. The attendance support teacher arranged meetings with the inspector of police at Mountain Ash Police Station. The purpose of the meeting was to establish links between the police and the education welfare officers. The police then took the following steps to support the initiative:

(a) Patrolling officers. When seeing children of school age out of school during school hours, they would request the name of the child and the reason for not being in school. On returning to the Police Station, the name of child, date, time and reason for absence is recorded in a book. The EWOs look at this book at regular intervals and each case is followed up.

(b) Occasionally, an EWO and a police officer patrol the locality, in an attempt to identify absentees and, if necessary, return them to school.

5   By establishing interagency co-operation. This has involved the various agencies working together at two levels:

(a) discussions at interagency meetings;
(b) within the school environment.

Discussion at interagency meetings   The attendance support teacher has been a member of the following groups outside school as a representative of the school:

- Perthcelyn Interagency Group;
- Cynon Valley Juvenile Crime Prevention Panel;
- Cynon Valley Court User Panel;
- Cynon Valley Interagency Group.

The general aim of all of the groups is to improve the quality of life for all people living in the Cynon Valley.

6   Special needs. Elaine, together with a group of non-teaching members of staff, and six Year 12 pupils, undertook the City and Guilds Basic Skills Tutoring Course. Elaine arranged for it to be held in school and consequently the successful participants make up the team that gives the support to the individual pupils on a daily basis.

Three years ago, a grant was obtained from the Basic Skills Agency to develop work with parents. A project was planned and put into action. As part of the evaluation process, a detailed proposal was sent to the LEA indicating ways in which this project could be developed. The proposal was accepted and over the last two years various programmes for parents have been run with their main aim being to enable parents to support their child's learning at home and at school.

Over the years the school has operated 'twilight' classes for GCSE pupils who choose to undertake extra study. Two external organisations that work in the community are involved in this project. Funding and the use of premises has been secured to enable 'Homework Clubs' to be set up on local housing estates.

Elaine's job description as the school's attendance support teacher is now presented. Elaine undertook this work full time, funded by GEST, since when she has returned to a full-time teaching timetable within the school. Subsequently, to continue its drive against non-attendance, the school advertised for an attendance project officer. Both job descriptions are presented in full to provide ideas for schools working to implement similar schemes using funds which may have recently been allocated by the DfEE.

Attendance support teacher: job description

Post
Attendance Support Teacher

Period
Fixed term (3 years)

Purpose of job
To increase the attendance in the school and to ensure that attendance and related matters are given a higher profile in the school and within the local community.

Line management
The post holder will be directly responsible to the headteacher.

Specific duties

The construction of effective management systems in the school to:

- ensure accurate monitoring of attendance;
- ensure prompt follow-up action to deal with lateness and absenteeism;
- to tackle specific attendance problems and to have strategies in place to address the difficulties, for example, re-integration programmes, support groups, governors' attendance panel, and dealing with pupils who are experiencing attendance problems;
- promote good links with parents;
- promote and foster good links with the outside agencies;
- further develop the links with the communities of Fernhill and Perthcelyn, through Save the Children Fund;
- ensure that the transition from primary school to comprehensive school is as untraumatic as possible;
- ensure the early identification of those primary school pupils who may need support at this transitional period;
- provide advice and support for pupils returning to school after long periods of absence;
- reward good and improved attendance;
- provide, where appropriate, in-service training on attendance-related matters;
- enable effective and sensitive communication to take place, orally and in written form, to a wide audience;
- ensure that the above strategies are being carried out through effective and efficient liaison with the following:

  1 headteacher/senior management team;
  2 heads of departments;
  3 heads of year;
  4 SENCO
  5 EWO
  6 other outside agencies dealing with pupils experiencing attendance problems.

Qualifications and experience

Essential

- qualified teacher status;
- at least five years teaching experience;
- experience of relevant attendance-related in-service training.

Desirable

- experience in this specific field of work;

- possession of the inter-personal skills to relate to headteacher, colleagues, pupils, parents and other agencies.

Knowledge required

- an understanding of the current legislation dealing with the attendance of pupils at school;
- an understanding of the current issues related to the attendance of pupils at school;
- a vision of how these current issues could be addressed.

Attendance project officer

Main aim (job purpose)

To improve the attendance of pupils in Years 7 and 8.
There are two key areas which need to be looked at:

- Pupils with an attendance below the given target figure during a half term period.
- Daily absence of pupils in Years 7 and 8.

The project officer shall be responsible for the identification, monitoring, and follow up of those pupils who fall into either of the above categories.

Specific duties
Liaise with:

- feeder primary schools
- heads of Years 7 and 8
- attendance support teacher
- education welfare officer.

Year 7

- Liaise with the feeder primary schools during the half term period prior to transition, to identify those pupils with an attendance below the target figure.
- Visit these pupils and their parents at home to discuss what is expected of them in relation to their child's attendance at school.
- Monitor these pupils on a regular basis during the first half term of Year 7.
- Visit the parents if the child's target figure is not being achieved.
- Write to those parents whose child has achieved their attendance target and to acknowledge the success.

Year 8

- Liaise with head of Year 8 to identify those pupils with an attendance below the target figure during the last half term of Year 7.
- Write to the parents of these pupils during the summer holidays, explaining that their child will be monitored closely and to remind them of their parental responsibilities regarding their child's school attendance.
- Monitor these pupils during the autumn half term.
- Visit the parents of pupils whose attendance falls below the target figure.
- Write to those parents whose child has achieved their attendance target and to acknowledge the success.

Daily monitoring of absences
To contact the parents of pupils who are absent daily but who have not notified the school of the reasons for absence. Contact may be by telephone or in person as appropriate.

Summary

All the schemes presented in this chapter are capable of being adapted to suit the individual needs of particular schools. For those schools which are failing, are in special measures, or have serious non-attendance difficulties, the two schemes presented on pages 205–8 and 211–15 are especially commended. Both these schemes aim at longer-term solutions in order to change the image and culture of the school. The colour-coded scheme is especially useful for those schools who accept pupils from the same primary schools every year. Otherwise, the Mountain Ash Project may be better. Both of these schemes will work best if a thorough review of a school's attendance policies and needs is conducted first, as outlined in the two sections on school-based review (pp. 195–8) and using pupil surveys (pp. 198–204), with appropriate action being taken.

11 Teachers, teaching and truancy

Research shows that good relationships between teachers and pupils are essential in combating truancy and re-integrating truants back into the classroom. This chapter, therefore, provides guidance on:

- successful teacher behaviour;
- classroom management skills;
- findings from research into school effectiveness from both primary and secondary schools;
- effective pastoral care;
- OFSTED evaluation criteria on the quality of good teaching;
- a checklist on the outcomes of research into effectiveness and truancy.

Box 11.1 presents evidence on the main reasons (in order of importance) for the causes of truancy at six very different secondary schools in the Midlands in the estimation of the staff teaching in the schools. This box is interesting for the following reasons:

(a) it shows the range of diversity among the six schools;
(b) it suggests that teaching and teacher-related problems are key in most of the schools;
(c) it indicates the importance of curriculum issues;
(d) it suggests that the staff now appreciate that most truants miss school for educational reasons.

Clearly, the reasons given in Box 11.1 would change school by school, region by region, in any other similar analysis.

Excellent teaching

Teacher behaviour – findings from research in the USA:

For the highest quality of teaching, the following characteristics of teacher behaviour are important:

Box 11.1 Reasons for truancy at 6 secondary schools

School 1
Perceived as a failing school
Teachers' expectations too low
Teaching styles not appropriate

School 2
National Curriculum issues
Parenting problems
Expectations among staff too low

School 3
Parental-condoned absence too
high
School avoidance of internal
problems, e.g. misbehaviour
Homework

School 4
Disaffection among Year 11
Parental-condoned absence too high
School phobia → undetected

School 5
Adolescent problems/adult
relationships – girls especially
Home problems
Poor teacher–pupil relationships

School 6
Teachers' lack of understanding/
own backgrounds unsuitable for the
type of school
Parenting problems
National Curriculum inappropriate
for less able pupils

- Management of the classroom in order to create a situation where learning can take place. This implies an orderly and quiet atmosphere in the classroom; although learning itself requires more than a well-organised class. Moreover, effective teaching itself contributes to management of the class.
- Provision of homework. If properly organised, homework contributes to effectiveness. This implies a clear structure of assignments, and supervision and evaluation of homework.
- Expectations teachers (and schools) have of their possibilities to influence student outcomes probably influence what teachers do. These expectations become apparent in actual teacher behaviour.
- Clear goal setting. This includes a restricted set of goals, emphasis on basic skills and emphasis on cognitive learning and transfer. The content should be chosen in line with these goals.
- Structuring the content. This includes the ordering of the content according to the hierarchically ordered goals. The use of advance organisers can only structure the content for students. The use of prior knowledge can increase students' own contributions and responsiveness for learning.
- Clarity of presentation, which implies the above mentioned elements, but also refers to the transfer process itself (avoiding vagueness and incomplete sentences).

- Questioning by means of low and higher order questions keeps students at work and can be used to check their understanding.
- Immediate work exercise after presentation. Like questioning it provides a check for understanding and can be used to clarify problems.
- Evaluating whether the goals are obtained by testing, providing feedback, and corrective instruction.

Classroom management

Combating school indiscipline

The following measures can be successfully used to overcome indiscipline in schools:

1 Changing existing timetabling structures so as to reduce the 'slack' time when vandalism and conflicts between children, or between children and teachers, tend to occur. Effective measures include the use of staggered lunch-breaks and reducing the number of pupils out of class at any one time; making for easier control and less pressure on open space.

2 Agreement between staff on united and coherent policies to reduce opportunities for deviant behaviour and teacher–pupil confrontations to take place: enforce a minimum (rather than maximum) number of indispensable school rules; provide an adequate system of remedial education; ensure good lesson plans and viable classroom management policies. Staff should be consistent in their interpretation of rules in the classroom and endeavour to overcome erratic, unfair or idiosyncratic sanctions.

3 Paying particular attention to organisation at the beginning and end of lessons and avoiding confusing commands. It helps to specify seating arrangements to keep mutually-provocative pupils apart and prevent unseemly scrambles for seats. Teachers should ensure the work they set is suitable to all levels of ability in the group, and make certain that less able children experience success as well as the able. Shouting or 'gunning' for pupils should be avoided; sometimes misdemeanours can be more successfully dealt with privately after the lesson rather than immediately – giving time for the situation to calm down and for rational processes to reassert themselves.

4 When confrontation occurs, defusing the process by taking firm immediate action. It is important not to overreact. Sometimes cracking a joke can help. On other occasions, removing a pupil from the classroom may be a last resort.

5 Starting lessons promptly and finishing on time.

6 Making use of effective rewards. Regular praise for the recognition of good behaviour, work and achievement is strongly associated with high achievement in schools.

7 Promoting pleasant working conditions in schools and encouraging pupils to take an active part in the daily life of the institution. Schools should ensure physical conditions are as pleasant as possible. It is important to give pupils opportunities to assume responsibility through monitor and prefect schemes, and for looking after resources and equipment, as well as encouraging their participation in meetings and assemblies.

8 Openness and honesty from teachers about their problems with individual pupils, groups of pupils and difficult forms. Colleagues should not regard such frankness as a sign of professional incompetence or weakness. Even the most experienced teachers make mistakes in their handling of classroom crises.

9 Considering pupils' perceptions. Pupils seem to prefer teachers who are strict but fair, have a sense of humour, are approachable and are empathetic in manner. They dislike teachers who are soft, ineffective, rigid, harsh, uncaring and whose demeanour provokes classroom confrontations. Pupils particularly dislike staff who fail to learn their names.

10 Taking account of group dynamics in class. Teachers should look for leaders or troublemakers and, if necessary, find ways of changing the group layout. A useful strategy is for the teacher to stand in different places.

11 Avoiding a tendency to accuse groups of troublemaking when only one or two pupils are involved. Similarly, teachers should not punish whole classes for offences committed by individuals.

12 Giving pupils the benefit of the doubt if they make excuses which cannot be checked – such as a stomach-ache.

13 Trying not to become too personally involved in confrontation. Irrespective of 'cause', keep your true feelings to yourself. A teacher who is in a bad mood can overreact and this is often the worst possible response. If you do decide to have a confrontation, have it on your own ground and on your own terms. Never be led into events. Know exactly what you are going to say in advance and choose your words carefully.

14 Using punishments wisely and sparingly. Do not over punish for minor misdemeanours.

Primary schools: effectiveness issues

Findings from research into primary school effectiveness suggest that the following twelve variables are of paramount importance:

1 *Purposeful leadership of the staff by the headteacher* Important aspects of headteacher's leadership were seen to centre around active involvement in the work of the school, in discussing curriculum policy and guidelines with teachers, and guiding staff on to suitable in-service courses. The head emphasised record-keeping as part of a systematic monitoring policy.

2 *The involvement of the deputy head*   The deputy headteacher's role in the primary school may be somewhat problematic, sometimes leading to role-conflict. For example, is the role one of class teacher or administrator? The effective school headteachers delegated to deputies and involved them in a 'sharing of responsibilities'.

3 *The involvement of teachers in the running of the school*   In the effective school, teachers were involved in curriculum decision-making. Consultation was important too, so that teachers felt they have a part in school policy.

4 *Consistency among teachers about behaviour and their aims and objectives* Continuity of staff was found to have 'positive effects'. However, note the importance of continuity and consistency within teaching approaches, emphasising the need for clearly agreed school policies and guidelines.

5 *Structured sessions*   Pupils benefited from a positively structured and organised framework to their activities, where they 'were not given unlimited responsibility for planning their own programme of work'.

6 *Intellectually challenging teaching*   Children's progress appeared to be promoted best when teachers were interesting and stimulating, asking 'open-ended' questions which encouraged a creative response from their pupils. Frequent direction of work had a negative impact: 'What was crucial was the level of the communication between teacher and pupils'. Progress was also linked to high teacher expectations of pupils. This led to teachers allowing pupils some measure of independence over their work.

7 *A work-centred environment*   Progress was assisted in schools where teachers spent a shorter time discussing routine matters with their pupils and 'more of their time discussing content'.

8 *Limited focus within sessions*   This is an important factor for new entrants to teaching. It is suggested that learning activities centred in one curriculum area during a session promote better pupil progress. When attempts to organise sessions to include two or three distinct curriculum areas predominated, learning was not so successful. This is not to suggest that all children ought to be doing identical work at the same time. Indeed, appropriate 'match' of level of work to pupils is another important factor in promoting progress. Work may be undertaken in the one area in a variety of ways.

9 *Maximum communication between teachers and pupils*   Pupils benefited from a greater degree of teacher communication. Therefore, the teacher who attempted 'individual' contact clearly limited him or herself to a minimum time with each child. 'Whole-class' contact increased the 'overall number of contacts with pupils'.

Therefore, a balance between individual and class contact is suggested. Referring to point 8 above, the findings suggest that where children worked in a single curriculum area within sessions (even if they were engaged on individual or group tasks) it was easier for teachers to raise an intellectually challenging point with all pupils.

10 *Accurate and maintained record-keeping* Where teachers reported that they kept written records of pupils' work progress . . . the effect on the pupils was positive.

   Though it is sometimes seemingly a laborious task, the benefit to the teacher of a record of children's work is highlighted. It is easier to plan with purpose, to match work and to diagnose areas of difficulty if suitable records are kept. It is important to emphasise the professional nature of teaching and regard record keeping as a part of good professional practice.

11 *Parental involvement* In keeping with much recent work, parental involvement is seen to aid pupil progress. This takes many forms, such as helping in classrooms, meetings to discuss children's progress, and assisting with reading at home. The presence of a formal PTA did not seem to be related to pupil progress. It could be that a formally constituted PTA which may see its brief in terms of fund raising or as a social focus for parents, is not necessarily linked to the specifically 'educational' work of the school; a province perhaps traditionally regarded as the exclusive domain of headteacher and staff. Many parents in primary schools may indeed have little to do with a formal PTA.

12 *Positive climate or school ethos* An effective school has a positive school ethos or climate. This ethos is evidenced in the amount of emphasis on praise and reward rather than on punishment, and on firm and fair discipline. Teachers' enthusiasm and interest communicated itself to pupils. There is also positive evidence of extra-curricula activities; trips and visits as well as 'the use of the local environment as a learning resource'.

   When teachers had non-teaching time allocated, this helped progress. So the leadership of the head in creating a positive and helpful working atmosphere for teachers in turn communicated itself to pupils.

Effective secondary schools

Summary of what is known

What emerges from the mass of evidence of research into school effectiveness is:

1 The leadership role of the headteacher and the senior management team is vital (head and deputy head in primary schools).
2 It is crucial for schools to be well-managed organisations. In this context, a 'happy', efficient staff is of key importance. So is the part played by inservice training. Staff operating on agreed, united policies appear to be the most effective.
3 A favourable school ethos or school climate is necessary for positive outcomes to accrue – how to achieve such an atmosphere is less well documented.

4 Effective schools are orderly at all times, both inside and outside class-rooms.

5 The quality of teaching staff is perhaps the *single* most important factor. Schools with weak staff will never be as effective as those with strong staff.

6 Schools need to concentrate much of their endeavour upon teaching *per se* while at the same time promoting empathetic pupil care and learning-centred approaches in the classroom.

7 The curriculum should be as important for low-achieving as for high-achieving pupils.

8 Regular feedback on performance needs to be given to all pupils.

9 The academic demands of courses, allied to a commitment to traditional academic and behaviour values, is extremely important.

10 Pupils should expect and receive high professional standards from teachers at all times. When this happens, it seems that pupils will reciprocate.

11 Proper use must be made of classroom teaching as part of standard practice within schools.

12 Traditional 'core' subjects should be emphasised by schools, particularly reading, writing and maths. It seems that reading standards are vitally important. Once pupils fall behind in the basics, student disaffection may replace a desire to learn.

13 Pupils should be encouraged to participate in the running and organisation of their school. When pupils identify with their school and its staff, they will be more respectful and show more positive behavioural and learning features.

14 Pupils are more likely to feel part of a school unit in buildings which are clean and well cared for, and in schools whose organisational structure does not make them feel 'lost'.

Characteristics of effective schools as organisations

Research suggests that the following characteristics of effective schools as organisations are important:

1 The balance of intellectually able and less able children in the school. When a preponderance of pupils in a school are likely to be unable to meet the expectations of scholastic success, peer group cultures and an anti-academic or anti-authority emphasis tend to form.

2 The system of rewards and punishments – ample use of rewards, praise and appreciation being associated with favourable outcomes.

3 School environment – good working conditions, responsiveness to pupil needs and good care and decoration of buildings were associated with better outcomes.

4   Ample opportunities for children to take responsibility and to participate in the running of their school lives appeared conducive to favourable outcomes.

5   Successful schools tended to make good use of homework, to set clear academic goals and to have an atmosphere of confidence as to their pupils' capacities.

6   Outcomes are better where teachers provided good models of behaviour by means of good time-keeping and willingness to deal with pupil problems.

7   Findings on group management in the classroom suggest the importance of preparing lessons in advance, of keeping the attention of the whole class, of unobtrusive discipline, of a focus on rewarding good behaviour and of swift action to deal with disruption.

8   Outcomes are more favourable when there is a combination of firm leadership together with a decision-making process in which all teachers felt that their views were represented.

9   Schools have well-integrated gender, equal opportunities and anti-racist policies in place. There is little or no bullying or victimisation of any kind.

Effective schools: lessons from the USA

America's best-run schools: evidence from research

Evidence from research with effective schools in the United States indicates that the following factors are important:

1   *Commitment*   Good schools project a *raison d'être*. The school's mission that is asserted by individual staff members may seem imprecise, but collectively the staff has arrived at and agreed upon sets of behaviours and outcomes that are sufficiently specific to acculturate new organisational members and control the behaviour of veteran members. They are organisations with a sense of themselves.

2   *Expectations*   Good schools and school systems are populated by confident people who expect others to perform to their highest levels of quality. The attitude of success crosses categories and feeds on itself. Teachers expect students to achieve. Students know they are expected to achieve and they expect, in turn, to have involved, competent teachers. Principals are surprised by teachers who fail. Teachers are surprised by administrators who ask little of themselves and others.

3   *Action*   People in good schools *do* things. They have a bias for action, proclivity for success, and a sense of opportunism. They plan for now, seize decision options when they arise, try new ideas, drop bad trials, and play within their strengths.

4   *Leadership*   Peters and Waterman pressed the point that 'innovative companies foster many leaders and many innovators throughout the

organisation'. People with high levels of efficacy and expectancy who are trying and experimenting cannot be restricted to designated leadership positions. Effective educational organisations spawn primary work groups and individual 'champions' in unusual numbers. The designated leaders create an environment for trial and a tolerance for failure so that leaders can emerge and be sustained at all levels of the school system.

5   *Focus*   Good schools pay attention to the task in hand. Student achievement in the classroom commands the attention of teachers and administrators. More classroom time is allotted to academic learning; more of the allotted time is engaged academic learning time for students. Staff development programmes concentrate on classroom-orientated skills and understandings. Good schools know what their core tasks are and focus on those jobs.

6   *Climate*   At a minimum, good schools maintain an orderly and safe environment for students and teachers. But they are much more than orderly. Successful schools work for all people in the building. They are not schools for students; nor are they schools for teachers and administrators. They work for adults and children and adolescents. Good schools are good places to live in and work, for everybody.

7   *Slack*   Good schools have a reasonable level of human resources and slack time. Time is necessary for teachers to participate in staff development activity and to incorporate new practices into their already crowded professional lives. Good practice is facilitated by a reasonable level of organisational redundancy and slack at the classroom level. Tolerance for failure, encouragement of experimentation, and the capacity to invent and adapt innovations are not achievable in organisational settings where effectiveness is regularly traded off for efficiency.

Effective pastoral care

Constraints

The inherent role factors which impinge upon the practice of effective pastoral care in many schools include:

(a)   external constraints (societal change, the effects of the media, malaise and LEA policies as well as matters relating to educational research);
(b)   the way pastoral staff are selected and appointed;
(c)   the lack of initial and in-service training on guidance-related issues for postholders;
(d)   the pastoral–academic dichotomy in many schools;
(e)   the pressure of workloads;
(f)   the absence of certain professional support, especially from outside agencies;
(g)   the demise of counsellors and counselling *per se* in schools;

(h) personality and territorial imperatives;
(i) managerial aspects such as imprecise job descriptions and inadequate role definitions.

Pupil and pastoral care

Pupil-related factors which impose constraints upon effective pastoral care include:

(a) the extent and diversity of 'problems' in schools;
(b) the degree and amount of underachievement, alienation, disaffection, absenteeism and disruptive conduct;
(c) the number of remedial pupils and those with special educational needs;
(d) the tenor of the school 'ethos' and its effects upon pupils' perspectives and their participation in school life;
(e) the institutional variables which are important in research into school effectiveness include aspects relating to:

  • school administration;
  • teacher expectations;
  • teacher stress;
  • teacher–pupil relationships;
  • classroom management and organisation;
  • the curriculum;
  • school rules;
  • pupil profiles and record-keeping systems;
  • resources and buildings;
  • the ability of form tutors;
  • home–school links.

Evidence from research

The evidence from research into school differences and school effectiveness seems to suggest that effective pastoral care is related to some or all of the characteristics below.

(a) Effective pastoral care is probably related to the disciplinary orientation of schools. Institutions which attempt to control pupils by offering rewards rather than punishments seem to be most effective, as do those which avoid the heavy use of physical punishment.
(b) Effective pastoral care is almost certainly related to the degree of pupil participation in school life. Encouraging children to participate in the running of schools appears to be conducive to good attainment, attendance and behaviour as well as to their enjoyment and favourable perception of school life.

(c) The views of teachers and teachers' expectations of pupils seems vital. Studies consistently show that teachers' views and positive expectations of pupils affect outcomes. For instance, when teachers hold negative views of their pupils' home backgrounds, they are likely to get negative conduct in return.

(d) The size of schools, classes and the teacher–pupil ratio may be important, but possibly only under certain conditions. To date, however, there is too little evidence to be certain. Pupils achieve better in schools with more favourable pupil–teacher ratios. Data from successive assessment of performance studies have all indicated that school and class size are not crucial factors. In one sense this is surprising; most teachers will freely admit that it is easier to give pupils individual attention in classes of 20 than of 30.

(e) Effective pastoral care may be related to the form of institutional control which is practised within schools. Once again, the evidence so far on this measure is somewhat contradictory. Some suggest that organisationally 'tight' regimes which attempt high expressive control of pupils within their school lives are most effective. Others argue the opposite – schools with high institutional control are most ineffective. Some have reported that harsh, authoritarian, 'custodial' regimes have an adverse effect upon pupils' perceptions. So too, it seems, do disorganised or 'anomic' institutions, by generating a weakly-controlled environment which caused pupils to lose respect for staff. Research to date seems to suggest that effective schools may be characterised by a form of balanced control. The implications for middle managers are obvious.

(f) The psychological environment of the classroom is very important in effective schools. The evidence from small, large and multi-national studies all show that positive learning outcomes are highly associated with cohesiveness, satisfaction, degree of task difficulty, formality, goal direction and democracy. Negative associations are found in atmospheres conducive to friction, cliqueness, apathy, disorganisation, inequality and favouritism. There are clear indications here, too, for form tutors to be positive.

(g) The academic environment of the school is crucial in effective schools. Research shows that pupils like to be kept busy on worthwhile activities, including homework. Important factors in effecting positive achievements are: the academic demands of course; the students' concern for and commitment to academic values; the amount of time spent on study and on homework; and, in general, a climate of high expectations on the part of students and their teachers. It may be that one of the most crucial jobs of pastoral staff, therefore, is to support academic staff and learning in the school whenever possible, and not pull in the opposite direction.

(h) The professional outlook of staff in a school is another aspect related to effective guidance. There are hints that expenditure on teachers' salaries may have some effect on outcome, particularly in areas of disaffection, strife and malaise. Despite this, successive studies on resource levels, expenditure per pupil, and the quality and quantity of buildings suggest that these are relatively unimportant features, even in split-site schools or in schools with a lot of old buildings.

Some of these findings may appear surprising to many teachers, particularly as OFSTED has linked quality to the state of buildings. There is evidence to suggest, however, that it is the day-to-day upkeep of buildings, rather than their age or appearance, which may be associated with positive school outcomes.

(i) Studies on pupils' perceptions and pastoral care in action suggest that a school's atmosphere is very important to effective pastoral care. The concept of school ethos or school climate is gaining in momentum. Many of the reported differences between schools are in terms of both their overall effectiveness and the atmosphere, policies and several of the non-cognitive aspects of schooling. For the moment, these non-cognitive aspects remain very difficult to measure precisely. Certainly, studies undertaken in the United States repeatedly stress the importance of a school's social climate to promote effective educational outcomes.

OFSTED guidelines on teaching

The penultimate section in this chapter focuses upon the OFSTED guidelines on good teaching and the quality of education. These state:

> Where teaching is *good* pupils acquire knowledge, skills and understanding progressively and at a good pace. Teachers have a secure knowledge and understanding of what they teach and make effective use of them. The lessons have clear aims and purposes. They cater appropriately for the learning of pupils of differing abilities and interests, and ensure the full participation of all. The teaching methods suit the topic or subject as well as the pupils; the conduct of lessons signals high expectations of all pupils and sets high but attainable challenges. The teaching makes clear the importance of applications, accuracy and good presentation, and the need to use critical thinking, creativity and imagination. There is regular feedback which helps pupils to make progress, both through thoughtful marking and discussion of work with pupils. Relationships are positive and promote pupils' motivation. The teaching provides opportunities for pupils to take increasing responsibility for their own work. Teachers appreciate how factors such as ethnicity, bilingualism, gender, social circumstances and giftedness may affect learning. National Curriculum attainment targets and programmes of study are taken fully into account. Where appropriate, homework which extends or complements the work done in lessons, is set regularly and followed up effectively.

Teaching is *unsatisfactory:*

- where pupils fail to achieve standards commensurate with their potential or where the teaching is ill-prepared or unclear;
- the pupils are unable to see the point of what they are asked to do;
- they are not appropriately challenged; nor are they helped to form a useful assessment of their level of attainment and of what areas need to be improved;
- pupils do not have adequate resources or time to undertake the task effectively;
- individual pupils' learning needs are not recognised sufficiently;
- relationships are insecure and inhibit learning.

Evaluation criteria

Teaching quality is to be judged by the extent to which teachers:

- have a secure understanding of the subject or areas they teach;
- plan effectively for continuity and progression;
- set appropriate expectations and convey to pupils clear objectives for each lesson;
- manage classes effectively;
- ensure that lessons have suitable content and purposeful activity, enabling pupils to make progress at an appropriate pace;
- employ methods, organisational strategies and materials that match curricular objectives and the needs of all pupils, motivate pupils whatever their ability, ethnicity or gender and enable pupils to develop their skills for learning;
- ensure work is rigorously assessed and followed up;
- use homework effectively to reinforce and/or extend what is learned in school.

Evidence should include:

- day-to-day planning of work: forecasts, lesson plans and notes on individual pupils;
- lesson observation: all relevant aspects mentioned in the above criteria;
- discussion with teachers and pupils;
- samples of pupils' work, including any work done off site and homework;
- marking, comments and follow-up;
- teachers' records of work done by pupils;
- role(s) of special support assistants employed to work with pupils with special educational needs and other assistants such as nursery nurses and technicians;
- input from specialist teachers.

If everyone managed all these points well, schools would have many fewer truants.

A checklist on outcomes of research into school effectiveness and truancy

Finally, in this chapter, a checklist on the outcomes of research into school effectiveness and truancy is presented. These summarise the findings obtained from reducing truancy projects. They also help to provide a profile on an 'effective' school in relation to attendance. An analysis of relevant projects suggest that good schools are those which achieve the following:

1 Legal requirements are met with particular reference to the identification of unauthorised absence.
2 High priority on the regular attendance and punctuality of all students.
3 Up-to-date figures on attendance patterns within the school.
4 Procedures within the school to identify and follow up unauthorised absences, patterns of absence and post-registration truancy at the earliest opportunity with effective monitoring of interventions.
5 School is alert to critical points of transfer for pupils.
6 A range of effective strategies to follow up intermittent/long-term absenteeism and to promote good attendance.
7 Targets set for individuals and form-groups, short and long term.
8 Mechanisms for rewarding good attendance and punctuality linking with the school merit system, homework diaries and records of achievement.
9 Procedures for re-integrating long-term absentees.
10 Provision to cater for difficult pupils and specific incidents.
11 Differentiation and flexibility in the curriculum and in teaching styles in order to accommodate SEN pupils and ensure maximum access to the curriculum.
12 Regular meetings between the school and education welfare officer on a professional basis.
13 Clear lines of communication with outside agencies (education welfare service, education psychology service, education support service, health service, social services) over attendance issues.
14 All staff are consistent in dealing with authorised/unauthorised absence.
15 Good primary liaison and effective primary–secondary transfer programme.
16 Governors and parents are informed about attendance issues.
17 School is able and willing to share good practice.

The bottom line is that all pupils look forward to attending well taught and interesting classes led by an enthusiastic and competent teacher. They do not look forward to (and often do not attend) those which are the precise opposite.

12 An internal and an external solution

Records of achievement and work placement schemes

This chapter focuses upon two key activities within school. The first is the appropriate use of records of achievement and their role with disaffected pupils like truants. The second is the use of work placement schemes. Work placement/experience schemes are organised differently by schools up and down the country. Therefore, later in this chapter we concentrate upon an innovative scheme which originated in Humberside and developed as part of an education business partnership. This scheme is particularly helpful in encouraging pupils to maintain high rates of attendance, regular punctuality and appropriate behaviour as well as keeping up to date with school work.

Records of achievement

The best possible use of records of achievement (ROA) schemes can be turned to advantage by schools. First, they can help pupils to adjust and understand their feelings and progress in school. Second, analysed collectively, they can help schools understand pupils' attitudes towards their subjects, teaching and school life. Third, they can alert schools to potential problems. Fourth, they can be used constructively to combat bullying, truancy and anti-social behaviour.

The next few pages present an outline of a possible record of achievement scheme designed to give schools and pupils all the relevant information which they need. This scheme gives a selective outline of the main features of an ROA scheme between Years 7 and 11 and is based on Goodacre School: a fictional institution.

Box 12.1 Goodacre School: ROAs

Throughout the year, pupils will be asked to update the ROAs. Pupils must also update the admission form found in the BLUE SECTION as necessary.

Weeks	*Year 7*
1	Introduce the pupils to the filing system as explained in this booklet, as many pupils have not had access to the ROA before. Complete Review Sheet Achievements in Primary School – file in WHITE SECTION.
9 and 10	Complete Review Sheet – the information from this can be transferred to the Christmas Reports.
13 and 14	Filing – photocopy of school report – GREEN SECTION, Review Sheet – YELLOW SECTION, update WHITE SECTION sheets re: Records of Personal Interests and Achievements for term.
26	Complete Results Review Sheet – this looks back at the previous term to compare their expectations with their results, File – YELLOW SECTION. Rest as weeks 13 and 14.
33 and 34	Complete Summer Review Sheet, file – YELLOW SECTION.
36	The final filing of the photocopied report, updating of the WHITE SECTION – filing of certificates.

Weeks	*Year 8*
1	Check previous year's work, update any achievements during the Summer Holiday and complete Annual Review Sheet – File YELLOW SECTION.
9 and 10	Complete Review Sheet for use with Christmas Reports. The rest as Year 7.

Weeks	*Years 9, 10 and 11*
	As Year 8 except that in weeks 33–34, Year 9 have a different Summer Review Sheet. In Year 11, the Annual Review Sheet completed in week 1 is different from the other Annual Review Sheets. Year 10 has a different Annual Review Sheet to complete in week 1.

Box 12.2 Record of achievement

Filing order			
	(1) RED –	SENSITIVE –	Personal details, medical reports, ROPA 1 form psychological report, attendance reports, disciplinary incidents.
	(2) BLUE –	FACTUAL –	Admission forms for schools attended. (This is all that is possible in this section as the children have access to it.)
Files kept in Guidance and children file these sections themselves	(3) YELLOW –	PERSONAL SKILLS AND QUALITIES –	Views about themselves and their methods of working. School review sheets. Junior school pieces of work.
	(4) WHITE –	ACHIEVE-MENT	In school and out of school experiences and achievements, e.g. photos, certificates, newspaper articles, etc.
	(5) GREEN –	REPORTS –	School reports, National Curriculum reports, SATs results, etc.

Note
The colour coding sheets are excluded from this chapter but can easily be adopted by following the instructions given in Box 12.2.

Box 12.3 Review sheet Year 7: achievements in primary school

Comment on your involvement in any of the following in your primary school:

SCHOOL VISITS

ASSEMBLIES

EISTEDDFOD

CONCERTS

SCHOOL PLAY

MEMBER OF A CLUB

MEMBER OF A TEAM

PUBLIC SPEAKING

OUTDOOR PURSUITS

FORM CAPTAIN

LIBRARY MONITOR

ANY OTHERS
Please name them

Box 12.4 Primary/secondary transfer sheet Year 7

NAME ....   FORM ....

1   I went to.. Junior School.

2a   Which lessons did you enjoy most?

2b   Why did you enjoy these lessons?

3a   Which was your best subject at Junior School?

3b   Which was your poorest subject?

4   What activities did you take part in, in Junior School?

5   What were you interested in outside Junior School?

What have you enjoyed about Goodacre Comprehensive School so far?
(please fill in space below)

Box 12.5 Subject progress

Look at the list of subjects on the table below. Alongside each subject tick the word that you feel best describes your progress in that subject at the moment.

Subject	Very good	Good	Satis- factory	Could do better
ENGLISH				
MATHEMATICS				
HISTORY				
GEOGRAPHY				
RELIGIOUS STUDIES				
FRENCH				
WELSH				
SCIENCE				
MUSIC				
ART				
DRAMA				
DESIGN TECHNOLOGY				

Box 12.6 Personal qualities

Look at the table below, then complete it by deciding whether you are Very good (tick), Good (G), Satisfactory (S) or Cause for concern (X) in relation to each of the personal qualities named.

Personal qualities	*Assessment*
ATTENDANCE	
PUNCTUALITY	
BEHAVIOUR	
CONFIDENCE	
ABILITY TO WORK IN A GROUP	
ABILITY TO WORK ON OWN INITIATIVE	
CAPACITY FOR RESPONSIBILITY	
ATTITUDE TO WORK	
ORGANISATION	

What activities have you been involved in inside school?

What activities have you been involved in outside school?

In the weeks ahead, try to think of some specific '*targets*' you could set yourself (no more than 3).

(1)

(2)

(3)

Box 12.7 Goodacre Comprehensive School record of personal interests and achievements out of school

---

It is important that you keep a record of your achievements. Enter each achievement with a date.

NAME ....

DATE OF BIRTH ....

Date   **Interest/achievements (out of school)**

Box 12.8 Goodacre Comprehensive School record of personal interests and achievements in school

---

It is important that you keep a record of your achievements. Enter each achievement with a date.

NAME ....

DATE OF BIRTH ....

Date   **Interest/achievements (in school)**

Box 12.9 Goodacre School diary (insert year) (NB Pupils complete their answers on a blank piece of paper, in keeping with the rubric below)

These sheets are for you to include events, photographs, newspaper cuttings, important dates – showing your achievements in and out of school (could include details of important people in school, e.g. Head of Year, Form Tutor, etc.).

Box 12.10 Goodacre School results review sheet 2

YEAR.................................   TERM ....

NAME.. FORM ....

To complete this sheet, you should refer to your last review sheet and your last report.

1 Give a general comment about your report, e.g. pleased, disappointed, etc. and give a reason why.

2 Comment on your punctuality, behaviour and attendance.

3 Write a short comment about your effort this term in class and for assessments.

4 Which were your best subjects and why?

5 Which were your weaker subjects and why?

6 Comment on how good you consider your homework record and use of your school diary to be, this term.

7 Look back at your targets from the last review sheet. How well have you achieved these targets. Be honest!

Box 12.11 Goodacre School review sheet 3

YEAR ....   TERM ....

NAME..   FORM ....

1   What have you enjoyed about Goodacre Comprehensive this school year?

2   How do you feel you have adjusted to the demands of this school year at Goodacre?

3   Look at the list of subjects in the table below. Alongside each subject tick the word in the column that you feel best describes your progress in that subject at the moment.

Subject	Very good	Good	Satis-factory	Could do better
ENGLISH				
MATHEMATICS				
HISTORY				
GEOGRAPHY				
RELIGIOUS STUDIES				
FRENCH				
WELSH				
GERMAN				
SCIENCE				
MUSIC				
ART				
DRAMA				
DESIGN TECHNOLOGY				

4   Look at the table below, then complete it by deciding whether you are Very good (tick), Good (G), Satisfactory (S) or Cause for concern (X), in relation to each of the personal qualities named.

Personal qualities	Assessment
ATTENDANCE	
PUNCTUALITY	
BEHAVIOUR	
CONFIDENCE	
ABILITY TO WORK IN A GROUP	
ABILITY TO WORK ON OWN INITIATIVE	
CAPACITY FOR RESPONSIBILITY	
ATTITUDE TO WORK	
ORGANISATION	

5a   What activities have you been involved in inside school?

5b   What activities have you been involved in outside school?

6   In the weeks ahead, try to think of some specific 'targets' you could set yourself (no more than 3).

(1)

(2)

(3)

Box 12.12 Goodacre School annual review sheet

PUPIL'S NAME .... FORM .... YEAR ....

You have just entered your next year at Goodacre Comprehensive School. The purpose of this sheet is to look back at your last year in this school and decide what you want to do to maintain or improve your performance.

Look at last year's termly review sheets and reports to answer these questions; above all be honest with yourself.

About school

1   Tick some of the subjects you think you did well in.

ENGLISH	DRAMA
MATHS	SCIENCE
HISTORY	PE
FRENCH	RE
WELSH	TECHNOLOGY
GEOGRAPHY	ART
GERMAN	MUSIC

2   Why do you think you did so well? (e.g. good at subject, enjoy subject).

3   Tick any subject you need to work harder in.

ENGLISH	DRAMA
MATHS	SCIENCE
HISTORY	PE
FRENCH	RE
WELSH	TECHNOLOGY
GEOGRAPHY	ART
GERMAN	MUSIC

4   How could you improve in these subjects? (e.g. work harder, ask for help, sit away from friends, etc.).

5 Were your attendance and punctuality good last year?

ATTENDANCE   YES   NO
PUNCTUALITY   YES   NO

6 If both answers to the above were YES, go on to question 7. If you answered **NO** to either of them, then how are you going to improve this year?

7 Tick the response that best describes your:

Behaviour	Very good	Good	Satisfactory	Cause for concern
Reliability	Very good	Good	Satisfactory	Cause for concern
Confidence	Very good	Good	Satisfactory	Cause for concern
Capacity for responsibility	Very good	Good	Satisfactory	Cause for concern
Attitude to work	Very good	Good	Satisfactory	Cause for concern
Organisation	Very good	Good	Satisfactory	Cause for concern
Ability to work on own initiative	Very good	Good	Satisfactory	Cause for concern
Ability to work in a group	Very good	Good	Satisfactory	Cause for concern

If you have ticked 'cause for concern' for any of these characteristics, then how do you think you could improve this year?

Interests

8 What do you do in your spare time? List any interests you have and what you enjoy about them.

9 List any clubs/societies or teams you belong to inside or outside school.

10   Would you like to try any new activities this year? (Inside or outside school?)

About you

Think about last year in school.

11   What did you enjoy?

12   What worried or concerned you?

13   Can you think of 3 specific ways you can improve in school this year?

(a)

(b)

(c)

Box 12.13 Goodacre School review sheet Year 9

YEAR .... SUMMER TERM ....

NAME... FORM ....

1   What have you enjoyed about Goodacre Comprehensive?

2   How do you feel you have adjusted to the demands of this school year at Goodacre?

3   Look at the list of subjects in the table below. Alongside each subject tick the word in the column that you feel best describes your progress in that subject at the moment.

Subject	Very good	Good	Satis-factory	Could do better
ENGLISH				
MATHEMATICS				
HISTORY				
GEOGRAPHY				
RELIGIOUS STUDIES				
FRENCH				
WELSH				
SCIENCE				
GERMAN				
MUSIC				
ART				
DRAMA				
DESIGN TECHNOLOGY				

4   Look at the table below, then complete it by deciding whether you are Very good (tick), Good (G), Satisfactory (S) or Cause for concern (X), in relation to each of the personal qualities named.

Personal qualities	Assessment
ATTENDANCE	
PUNCTUALITY	
BEHAVIOUR	
CONFIDENCE	
ABILITY TO WORK IN A GROUP	
ABILITY TO WORK ON OWN INITIATIVE	
CAPACITY FOR RESPONSIBILITY	
ATTITUDE TO WORK	
ORGANISATION	

5a   What activities have you been involved in inside school?

5b   What activities have you been involved in outside school?

6   In the weeks ahead, try to think of some specific '*targets*' you could set yourself (no more than 3).

(1)

(2)

(3)

7   Next year as well as starting your option choices, you will participate in a careers programme called JIIG CAL and undertake work experience for two weeks.
    It is important to start thinking about the type of job/career you are interested in well in advance.

(a)   List all the subjects you intend to take in Year 10

(b)   What career/job are you considering after you leave school?

Box 12.14 Goodacre School annual review sheet Year 10

PUPIL'S NAME .... FORM .... YEAR ....

You have just entered your next year at Goodacre Comprehensive School. The purpose of this sheet is to look back at your last year in this school and decide what you want to do to maintain or improve your performance.

Look at last year's termly review sheets and reports to answer these questions, above all be honest with yourself.

About school

1   Tick some of the subjects you think you did well in.

ENGLISH	DRAMA
MATHS	SCIENCE
HISTORY	PE
FRENCH	RE
WELSH	TECHNOLOGY
GEOGRAPHY	ART
GERMAN	MUSIC

2   Why do you think you did so well? (e.g. good at subject, enjoy subject).

3   Tick any subject you need to work harder in.

ENGLISH	DRAMA
MATHS	SCIENCE
HISTORY	PE
FRENCH	RE
WELSH	TECHNOLOGY
GEOGRAPHY	ART
GERMAN	MUSIC

4   How could you improve in these subjects? (e.g. work harder, ask for help, sit away from friends, etc.).

5 Were your attendance and punctuality good last year?

ATTENDANCE	YES	NO
PUNCTUALITY	YES	NO

6 If both answers to the above were YES, go on to question 7. If you answered **NO** to either of them, then how are you going to improve this year?

7 Tick the response that best describes your:

Behaviour	Very good	Good	Satisfactory	Cause for concern
Reliability	Very good	Good	Satisfactory	Cause for concern
Confidence	Very good	Good	Satisfactory	Cause for concern
Capacity for responsibility	Very good	Good	Satisfactory	Cause for concern
Attitude to work	Very good	Good	Satisfactory	Cause for concern
Organisation	Very good	Good	Satisfactory	Cause for concern
Ability to work on own initiative	Very good	Good	Satisfactory	Cause for concern
Ability to work in a group	Very good	Good	Satisfactory	Cause for concern

If you have ticked 'cause for concern' for any of these characteristics, then how do you think you could improve this year?

Interests

8 What do you do in your spare time? List any interests you have and what you enjoy about them.

9 List any clubs/societies or teams you belong to inside or outside school.

10 Would you like to try any new activities this year? (Inside or outside school?)

About you

Think about last year in school.

11 What did you enjoy?

12 What worried or concerned you?

13 Can you think of 3 specific ways you can improve in school this year?

   (a)

   (b)

   (c)

14 What subject areas particularly interest you?

15 What careers do you think might interest you?

16 Where would you consider fulfilling a work experience placement that you feel will benefit you?

Box 12.15 Goodacre School annual review sheet Year 11

PUPIL'S NAME .... FORM .... YEAR ....

You have just entered your next year at Goodacre Comprehensive School. The purpose of this sheet is to look back at your last year in this school and decide what you want to do to maintain or improve your performance.

Look at last year's termly review sheets and reports to answer these questions, above all be honest with yourself.

About school

1   Tick some of the subjects you think you did well in.

ENGLISH	DRAMA
MATHS	SCIENCE
HISTORY	PE
FRENCH	RE
WELSH	TECHNOLOGY
GEOGRAPHY	ART
GERMAN	MUSIC

2   Why do you think you did so well? (e.g. good at subject, enjoy subject).

3   Tick any subject you need to work harder in.

ENGLISH	DRAMA
MATHS	SCIENCE
HISTORY	PE
FRENCH	RE
WELSH	TECHNOLOGY
GEOGRAPHY	ART
GERMAN	MUSIC

4   How could you improve in these subjects? (e.g. work harder, ask for help, sit away from friends, etc.).

5   Were your attendance and punctuality good last year?

ATTENDANCE   YES   NO
PUNCTUALITY   YES   NO

6   If both answers to the above were YES, go on to question 7. If you answered **NO** to either of them, then how are you going to improve this year?

7   Tick the response that best describes your:

Behaviour	Very good	Good	Satisfactory	Cause for concern
Reliability	Very good	Good	Satisfactory	Cause for concern
Confidence	Very good	Good	Satisfactory	Cause for concern
Capacity for responsibility	Very good	Good	Satisfactory	Cause for concern
Attitude to work	Very good	Good	Satisfactory	Cause for concern
Organisation	Very good	Good	Satisfactory	Cause for concern
Ability to work on own initiative	Very good	Good	Satisfactory	Cause for concern
Ability to work in a group	Very good	Good	Satisfactory	Cause for concern

If you have ticked 'cause for concern' for any of these characteristics, then how do you think you could improve this year?

Interests

8   What do you do in your spare time? List any interests you have and what you enjoy about them.

9   List any clubs/societies or teams you belong to inside or outside school.

10 Would you like to try any new activities this year? (Inside or outside school?)

About you

Think about last year in school.

11 What did you enjoy?

12 What worried or concerned you?

13 Can you think of 3 specific ways you can improve in school this year?

(a)

(b)

(c)

Career/job plan

14 Complete the table below by listing your subjects, your level of entry in these subjects and a realistic grade you think you will achieve.

Subject	Entry level	Staff estimated grade	Pupil estimated grade	Actual grade

15   By now, you have completed work experience and Jiig Cal and are anticipating a careers interview.

   (a)   What job/career are you interested in?

   (b)   How are you going to realise this job/career plan after leaving school? (e.g. college, university, training credits traineeship or a different option?)

If you have any queries about your job/career training, remember you can contact the Careers Advisor in the lunchtime '*Careers Club*' or make an appointment to obtain advice.

Work placement schemes

Work placement schemes are regularly used by schools to provide pupils with opportunities to gain experience of the world of work. Most schools use these work placement schemes for many or all of their pupils in Years 9, 10 and 11. Evidence shows that the use of specific or extended periods of work placement can often be particularly beneficial for less able and/or disaffected pupils. One scheme in the North East of England, for example, found that disaffected pupils (including truants) turned up early for work, attended normally and made extremely good progress when placed within the Built Environment department of local FE colleges acting as, for instance, apprentice bricklayers. Similar schemes have reported success throughout the UK with both boys and girls.

   The scheme represented here is the 'Aiming Higher Scheme' developed by an education business partnership in Humberside and sponsored by the Midland Bank. The scheme has many merits; not least its emphasis on attendance, punctuality, progression, structure, and certification. It uses a very constructive form of positive reinforcement.

The Aiming Higher certificate – the Humberside scheme

Introduction

A guide for students, parents, schools and employers

Work experience as part of a planned learning programme aims to give young people a chance to find out about working life for themselves. While they are still at school, young people are encouraged to show employers how reliable they can be. They do this by attending school regularly, being punctual, and completing their school work on time. They can prove this to an employer by gaining an Aiming Higher Certificate.

Working towards achieving this certificate helps them develop skills that they will need in later life and helps them to develop as people. Schools are involved in a range of activities which are designed to prepare the student for the responsibilities of working and adult life and work experience and the other Aiming Higher goals provide the direct link to the needs of the work-place through Years 10 and 11.

The Aiming Higher goals are:

- Attendance of at least 90 per cent;
- Punctuality 90 per cent;
- Completion of work on time;
- Completion of work experience;
- Co-operation in the completion of a Record of Achievement.

The achievement of quality work experience provision involves a partnership between schools, employers, students, parents and the Humberside Careers and Guidance Services.

Information for employers

This scheme is intended to help employers understand the work experience process more fully. The details covering schools, parents and students provide additional useful information.

You can help to provide a good experience of work for students who come to your workplace by:

- Planning a programme of work activities including an induction to your organisation;
- Providing a safe working environment for the student;
- Being prepared to give the student the experience of an interview prior to or during the placement;
- Giving the student a named 'supervisor' while on placement;
- Encouraging the student to write up their work experience diary on a daily basis;
- Allowing the student to collect evidence of the work they have done which they will need to obtain their Aiming Higher Certificate;
- Talking to the student at the end of the placement and helping them to evaluate their performance;

(Continued on page 266)

Box 12.16 Getting started

Schools wishing to develop the Aiming Higher Programme should take the following steps:

In school	**Work with employers**
• Establish senior management support	• Find a partner company to validate
• Identify resource implications:	
– Staffing for link meetings and validation	
– Time for co-ordination of information	• Identify link personnel
– Money certificates, booklets, diaries, checklists	
– Training of work experience co-ordinators	
• Agree co-ordination of information:	
– records, attendance and punctuality	
– monitoring 'deadlines'	• Talk through implications of:
– storage of student evidence	– time and financial support
• Identify other members of your group:	– need to attend regular review meetings
– key personnel and roles	– support for classroom preparation, assemblies and information sessions
– another school	
– validating company	
• Develop a simple policy statement:	
– set objectives in the school development plan	

Arrange publicity to launch Aiming Higher:

In school

- To students:
  - assemblies
  - open events
  - classroom intervention
  - tutor groups
  - displays

- To parents:
  - literature
  - open events

- To staff:
  - meetings
  - displays

- Links to rewards systems (certificates)

- Progress reports to students/parents

- Annual certificates and/or trophies

Wider community

- Newspaper reports of events and presentations

- Well known local figures – to come into school or support events

- Meetings between partners to discuss progress and forward plan

Box 12.17 Aiming Higher goals

Aiming Higher goals for young people

- Minimum attendance of 90% over a 2 year period;
- All deadlines for students relating to coursework completion are met;
- Minimum punctuality of 90% over a 2 year period;
- Completion of work experience assessment programme;
- Completion of National Record of Achievement.

Students achieving all these goals are awarded a Final Aiming Higher Certificate.

Aiming Higher goals for partners

- *Raising achievement* by setting students REALISTIC and achievable targets as part of a valued reward system.
- *Allowing all students the opportunity to achieve* irrespective of academic ability.
- *Providing a coherent programme of preparation* for work experience.
- *Developing key skills* such as:

− communication	− number application
− information technology	− personal skills
− improving learning performance	− problem solving
− decision making	− team work

- *Making students responsible for their own learning* by setting realistic targets/objectives, collecting evidence for an achievement portfolio and working as part of a team.
- *Raising 'quality' levels of work experience placements*

Box 12.18 Work experience programme

This is seen as a three-stage process but still supports the first three goals of attendance, punctuality and meeting deadlines.

All students must have 100% attendance and punctuality and meet ALL deadlines on work experience.

All students must achieve ALL of the targets set below.

Preparation for work experience	**Completion of a placement**	**Feedback**
• Know what makes a good employee	• Have discussed with an employer the placement objectives	• Have completed a full work experience in a satisfactory manner
• Take part in Health and Safety sessions	• Show an understanding of jobs done by company employees	• Have completed a work experience diary
• Know why work experience is offered	• Recognise employer's selection requirements	• Have participated in debriefing activities to include group discussion and presentations which may involve employer, students and teachers
• Make a realistic choice of placement	• Recognise services provided and/or products made by the company	
• Complete a work experience application form or letter	• Complete a personal assessment of performance	• Have completed a self-evaluation against original objectives
• Make an actual or simulated telephone call to an employer	• Have completed a work experience report	

A carefully designed Work Experience diary can help students meet many of the above targets.

Box 12.19   Timetable

End of Year 9

The work experience co-ordinator delivers training to the teaching or tutor team.

⇓

The programme is launched to students at the end of Year 9, or start of Year 10, ideally with the help of supporting employers, the validating company and parents.

⇓

End of Year 10

Throughout Year 10 students are provided with regular updates on their progress towards the Aiming Higher goals.

⇓

Students begin their preparation for work experience using the Aiming Higher framework.

⇓

Students complete their work experience (in the appropriate year). Successful students are awarded a certificate of completion by their school.

⇓

End of Year 11

Aiming Higher Intermediate Certificate is awarded to successful candidates by the school.

⇓

Aiming Higher Final Certificate is awarded to successful candidates by the Education Business Partnership.

Box 12.20 Validation

1 Schools	Two or more schools discuss the project guidelines and how they have applied them to their individual circumstances.
2 Employers	Two or more employers discuss their expectations for schools following the project.
3 Validating groups	Schools and employers meet to discuss joint guidelines and expectations. Once the process is established, a formal validation meeting takes place annually to verify that standards are being met, view examples of student work and discuss any problems concerning the programme and its targets.

Validation – points for consideration

WHEN?	Year 10 and Year 11.
WHO?	All schools and companies within the validating group.
WHAT IS NEEDED?	A sample of students material to represent, HIGH, MEDIUM AND LOW QUALITY WORK, including:

- Diary
- Student checklist
- NROA statement
- Employer report
- Attendance, punctuality and deadlines information including:

  (a) method of calculation;
  (b) time for punctuality deadline;
  (c) deadline titles.

To be retained until after final validation

The *school*
should provide:
- a quiet area for the meeting
- work samples
- access to students if the employer wishes
- the scheme of work used for the Aiming Higher project
- coffee!

The *employer*
should provide:
- a member of staff who knows the background to Aiming Higher
- an ear to listen to individual cases requiring special consideration.

Box 12.21 Certification

It is possible to award **THREE** certificates for the project

1   One-year intermediate Aiming Higher Certificate

2   Work experience certificate

3   Final Aiming Higher Certificate

- The programme is not designed for EVERY STUDENT to succeed – some students will fail – QUICKLY. The school implement their own systems to reward improvement after such a failure, but cannot use the Aiming Higher certificates.

- A student can obtain the FINAL certificate, if they fail the INTER-MEDIATE certificate, *by* achieving 90 per cent attendance and punctuality over the 2-year period.

- A student can obtain a WORK EXPERIENCE certificate but fail the INTERMEDIATE and FINAL certificate.

Intermediate	**Work experience**	**Final**
Student must have:	Student must have:	Student must have:
• minimum 90% attendance	• 100% attendance	• 90% attendance over two years
• minimum 90% punctuality	• 100% punctuality	• 90% punctuality over two years
• met *all* deadlines	• completed a successful work experience	• completed all parts of the work experience preparation programme
• no unauthorised absence		• completed a successful work experience
		• no unauthorised absence
		• met all agreed deadlines

Box 12.22 Aiming Higher Intermediate Certificate

AIMING HIGHER

INTERMEDIATE CERTIFICATE

.... SCHOOL

Awarded in recognition

that ....

Has achieved the following goals during the academic year

and is working towards an Aiming Higher Final Award:

A high level of punctuality

A high level of attendance

Completed course work on time

Signed ....

Headteacher ....

Validated ....

Box 12.23 Aiming Higher Final Certificate

AIMING HIGHER

FINAL CERTIFICATE

Awarded in recognition

that ....

of ....

Has achieved the following goals:

Successfully completed an approved work experience programme

Maintained a high level of punctuality

Maintained a high level of attendance

Completed coursework on time

Produced a work experience report for the
National Record of Achievement

Signed ....

Chair of the North East Lincolsnire Area Support Group
Education Business Partnership

Date ....

- Spending some time talking to the teachers who visit students on work experience, discussing the qualities and skills required for satisfactory performance in your organisation;
- Completing the work experience report form, preferably with the student, and giving it to them or posting it to the school. This then goes into the student's Record of Achievement;
- Evaluating the work experience process and documentation.

Role of the school

Quality work experience placements are part of a carefully planned programme and should include:

- Preparing students for work experience in school, involving employers for support where possible.
- Helping the student to choose an appropriate placement.
- Providing information for parents and encouraging them to become involved with the process.
- Obtaining written permission from parents for student placements.
- Providing the student with details of their chosen placement.
- Providing students with a diary/log to complete.
- Nominating a teacher as contact to deal with any problems which might arise.
- Where students have any special needs, ensuring that employers are fully briefed.
- Visiting all students while they are on placement.
- Involving as many different staff in the visiting process as possible to encourage them to make closer links with employers.
- Organising follow-up and debrief activities involving employers, including the opportunity for students to learn from each other's experience.
- Developing curriculum links to reinforce the learning.
- Writing to placement providers thanking them for taking the students and including appropriate comments from the debriefing.
- Ensuring Records of Achievement are updated to include information about the work experience.
- Encouraging students to review their individual action plan following their experience.
- Evaluating the work experience process and documentation.

Role of the student

Students should know why they are going on work experience and they should understand their responsibilities, before, during and after the placement, to the employer and the school. Students should know what they hope to achieve through the work experience programme and be aware of the goals against which they will be assessed during the programme.

Students will benefit fully from the work experience process by observing the following points.

Before the placement

- Taking a full part in lessons and activities that are a preparation for work experience.
- Reading all relevant literature and understanding what other people will be doing.
- Understanding the placement selection process and talking to parents about it.
- Being prepared to consider alternatives to their first choice of placement. There may not be enough placements of a particular type for everyone who is interested.
- Ensuring they have all the details they might need. Which should include:

  - the name of the employer
  - the hours of work
  - the location of work
  - the contact name and telephone number
  - the clothing requirements
  - the lunch arrangements
  - the employer's telephone number
  - the need for a letter/telephone contact and/or visit/interview.

- Completing an application form or letter of application and handing it in on time.
- Telling the school as soon as possible if anything happens that might affect the placement.
- Contacting or visiting the employer if requested to do so.

For a visit or interview, they should dress appropriately and arrive before the appointed time. Employers are impressed by students who take the trouble to find out something about their company. Students should use the opportunity of the interview to gain more knowledge about the company and to ask questions about the placement. The following may be helpful:

- Who should I ask for when I start?
- Who will be my supervisor?
- What sort of things will I be doing?
- What should I wear?

If an interview or visit does not take place, they should ensure they have made appropriate transport arrangements and know they can get to work on time.

While on placement

- Arriving in good time every day and being appropriately dressed.
- Notifying the school and the placement provider immediately if they are unable to attend for any reason.
- Using the diary/log to record their work on a daily basis and asking their supervisor if they wish to add anything.
- Collecting evidence of the work they have done. They will need this to obtain their certificate.
- Being polite and interested in what happens and trying to make a good impression.
- Trying to find out as much as possible about different types of work in the organisation as well as their own work.
- Talking to their parents about their day when they get home and talking to any teachers or careers officers who visit them.
- Being prepared to talk to their supervisor at the end of the placement about their work and what they have learned.

After the placement

- Returning to school with all the documentation completed.
- Writing a letter of thanks to the placement provider reporting on what they have learned.
- Talking about their work experience to teachers and other students. Learning about other placements and how they compared with their own.
- Using their experiences to further develop their action plan.
- Using the report from their placement provider to learn about how they could do better in the future.
- Being prepared to talk about their experiences when they go for any interviews for college courses, training courses or employment.
- Updating their National Record of Achievement documentation and adding their work experience report to it.
- Being prepared to write about their work experience in lessons.
- Continuing to work towards their other Aiming Higher goals.

If students have any questions about the above they should contact their school work experience co-ordinator.

Role of the parent

All young people need help as they experience the work place for possibly the first time. *Parents play an important role* in helping their son or daughter to get the most out of work experience. They can give much needed support by:

- Reading the information that is provided about work experience and the other Aiming Higher goals.
- Discussing the selection of a placement with their son/daughter and encouraging them to consider all options and to be flexible in their choice of placement.
- Completing and returning on time all forms and reply slips as requested by the school.
- Asking their child to tell them the name, address and telephone number of the placement provider and the same of the person supervising them.
- Discussing with them how they will get to and from their placement, finding out about any costs involved, and ensuring they leave home appropriately dressed and in good time.
- Making sure they know what the arrangements are for meals and breaks. They may need to take a packed lunch with them.
- Ensuring the placement provider and the school are both notified immediately if their son/daughter is unable to attend and unable to make contact themselves.
- When they return home, asking their son/daughter about their working day and the diary or log they have kept. discussing the day with them, for example:

  – What is the workplace like?
  – Who works there, what do people do and how have they been trained?
  – What does their son/daughter have to do?
  – What is the product/service?

- Ensuring their son/daughter has received a completed work experience report that will form part of their Record of Achievement.

Benefits to schools

Working with business benefits schools by:

- Developing quality links between schools and local employers.
- Reinforcing messages about the importance of attendance and punctuality and meeting deadlines.
- Enriching the vocational curriculum.
- Raising the profile of the school within the local community.
- Giving equal opportunity for all students irrespective of their academic ability to achieve a certificate validated by local employers.
- Increasing knowledge of local business.
- Providing a framework for the school's preparation for work experience programme.
- Increasing the involvement of parents within the programme.
- Contributing towards raising attainment initiatives.
- Underpinning in-school initiatives aimed at raising achievement.

Benefits to employers

Working with schools benefits employers by:

- Promoting a positive image of their organisation.
- Providing opportunities for staff development, e.g. through giving talks to or interviewing students.
- Updating their knowledge of education.
- Ensuring that their work experience programme gives maximum opportunity to the student.
- Ensuring that the work experience programme addresses the needs of their business.
- Providing the opportunity to develop closer links with local schools.
- Providing an opportunity to contribute to the vocational curriculum.
- Investing in the local community and a better motivated and trained workforce.

The award of the Aiming Higher final certificate demonstrates that prospective young employees have attained the standards required by future employers.

Benefits to students

Benefits students by:

- Improving their key skills.
- Highlighting their achievements.
- Raising their awareness of the basic standards of behaviour and performance required by employers.
- Developing their self-confidence.
- Helping them recognise the value of personal action planning.
- Making them personally responsible for meeting the Aiming Higher goals.
- Raising their self-esteem.
- Providing them with opportunities for continuous assessment.

Students need (help) to understand the importance of achieving specific personal targets whilst still at school and how these achievements will help them in adult life.

There is considerable evidence that less able pupils like absentees and truants enjoy relevant work experience programmes and make better progress than in some traditional subjects in school.

13 OFSTED: guidelines on attendance and behaviour

Preparation for OFSTED inspections, the inspection process *per se*, and follow-up action plans are part and parcel of school life, more especially internal management processes. Since the first round of OFSTED inspections, HMI have been increasingly asked to report on issues of attendance and behaviour within primary and secondary schools. Interestingly, in cases of school failure, most reports have highlighted attendance and behavioural difficulties within these schools often as much as, or more than, curricular aspects.

The DfEE have now set schools the target of reducing their own truancy rates by one third by the year 2002 from their 1998 figures. These targets will be monitored in future OFSTED inspections.

This chapter presents a summary of OFSTED guidelines on behaviour, attendance, and the overall quality of education and teaching within schools. These guidelines indicate the precise issues which OFSTED will take into consideration when evaluating their own findings on schools' attendance and behavioural patterns. In particular, they show the evaluation criteria on attendance and behaviour, as well as the evidence which schools need to present to OFSTED at the time of their inspection. Headteachers, deputies, heads of year, form tutors and education welfare officers should note that inspectors are given the authority 'to investigate the causes and the school's actions to improve attendance' in individual cases, classes and school years where the levels of attendance fall below 90 per cent. The final sections focus upon two HMI projects on truancy and on improving school behaviour which took place in schools in Wales in 1997.

Attendance

OFSTED guidelines on attendance use the following norms.

A Amplification of evaluation criteria

Attendance is *good* where overall rates compare favourably with the norms for schools of a similar character and where there is little truancy or unauthorised absence. Priority is placed on attendance, and the legal requirements for recording and reporting attendance are met. Pupils are punctual and keen to attend. The school has an active monitoring system and effective strategies for encouraging good attendance.

Attendance is *unsatisfactory* where levels of persistent and intermittent absenteeism significantly affect pupils' achievements and disrupt progress. There are undue differences in levels of attendance between class groups and year groups. Lack of punctuality on the part of the pupils impedes the pace of lessons and other activities. The schools' monitoring and follow-up arrangements fail to take in many of the pupils whose attendance is unsatisfactory.

B Issues for consideration when reviewing evidence

A judgement on attendance will be informed by pre-inspection information provided by the school on School Form 2. Attendance rates should be compared with national and other data as available.

Inspection of documentation should provide evidence of the school's policy and guidance for teachers on:

- the promotion and maintenance of high attendance rates;
- the management of pupils whose attendance is a cause for concern;
- the support for pupils returning to school after periods of absence;
- procedures for noting that pupils are absent and for appropriate follow-up.

Registers should be sampled and, where attendance is poor, analysed in detail. This will enable inspectors to identify trends such as the persistent non-attendance of particular pupils or falls in attendance rates at particular times of year. Examination of registers should also reveal the extent to which they comply with current legislation. Observation of registration periods will help inspectors to evaluate the accuracy of the records.

Observation of learning activities should include comparison of the number on roll with the number present and follow-up of the reasons for significant absences. The prevalence of unaccountable or unauthorised absence from lessons will become apparent and, in such circumstances, can be reviewed with the staff.

Discussion with staff will establish the extent to which the causes of poor attendance are known to them. These discussions and inspection of learning activities and pupils' work will provide some evidence of the degree to which poor attendance is associated with low standards of achievement.

Scrutiny of a sample of pupils' record files, including any correspondence they may contain with parents and other agencies, will show the school's thoroughness in monitoring and, where appropriate, improving attendance. Discussions with staff, pupils, parents and governors will, together with documentary evidence, enable inspectors to judge the efficiency of these procedures.

Discussion with the education welfare officer (or in some cases, the education social worker) where possible, will clarify his or her involvement with teachers, and pupils' records; and any relevant attendance issues at contributory schools may throw light on current attendance patterns.

C *Particular features*

Attendance by students over 16 is not required by law, but a school with a sixth form should have a policy on attendance for students who are registered. Attendance for pupils under five is not a statutory requirement.

Attendance: evaluation criteria

- Attendance is to be judged by the levels of pupils' attendance overall, the extent of intermittent attendance and levels of persistent non-attendance;
- for individuals, classes and years where levels of attendance fall below 90 per cent, inspectors should investigate the causes and the school's actions to improve attendance;
- attendance data should be accurate and valid, complying with the requirements set out in recent DfEE and Welsh Office circulars;
- pupils' punctuality should be judged by the degrees to which the school day and individual lessons achieve a prompt and effective start.

Evidence should include:

- scrutiny of school registers of attendance and overall class and year group attendance figures;
- data on authorised and unauthorised absence and exclusions;
- scrutiny of policy and any other documentation on attendance, including 'Compact' schemes, targets set for individual classes, year groups and the school as a whole; reward systems, prosecutions, information to parents and pupils on expectations and follow-up of absences;
- pupils' records, including correspondence with home and the education welfare service;
- discussion with pupils and staff;
- parental views as expressed at the pre-inspection meeting with parents;
- pupils' punctuality in arriving at school and in class.

The report should include an evaluation of:

- pupils' attendance and punctuality, analysing reasons for absence where attendance falls below 90 per cent or where patterns of absence affect particular groups of pupils;
- progress made in meeting targets.

OFSTED on behaviour

A *Amplification of evaluation criteria*

Where behaviour is good, most pupils show through their actions that they know what constitutes appropriate behaviour, that they understand what is expected of them and that they respond accordingly. They are considerate, courteous and relate well to each other and to adults. Pupils take responsibility for their own actions, appropriate to their age and maturity. They develop self-esteem and self-discipline and adhere to high standards of behaviour which contribute to effective learning.

B *Issues for consideration when reviewing evidence*

Some evidence will be obtained from the pre-inspection analysis of the school's documents, the first visit to the school, and discussion with the head, governors and parents. The meeting with parents should be used to explore their perceptions of behaviour, the information they receive about rewards and sanctions, and the extent to which their children are content and unafraid at school.

Much of the evidence from which to judge the standard of pupils' behaviour and discipline will be derived from direct observation during the inspection. Observation of pupils will show:

- the extent to which they demonstrate good habits of work and behaviour;
- the degrees of self-discipline and mutual support they practise;
- their self-confidence, for example when they show visitors around or help younger pupils;
- the standards of courtesy displayed to one another, to staff and to visitors;
- their behaviour to non-teaching staff;
- any tension between linguistic, ethnic or other groups;
- aggressive behaviour or bullying;
- effects of behaviour on the quality of learning and the overall work of the school as a community.

This will be supplemented by other evidence: discussions with pupils and teachers, and an examination of the school's policy and practice for dealing with pupils whose behaviour is a cause for concern and for recognising the achievements of those who have behaved well. Evidence should also include an evaluation of the number of, and reasons for permanent and fixed-term exclusions from the school.

C *Factors to be taken into account when reaching a judgement*

The presence of a visitor in the classroom or the playground can influence the reactions of pupils, and judgements should be made with caution.

The effects of standards of behaviour on the overall work of the school need to be investigated. This requires the co-ordination of evidence and judgements from different aspects of the inspection, including the quality of teaching and learning, and from the full inspection team.

D Particular features

Inspectors should be aware of the provisions of the Education Act (No 2) 1986 and the Children Act 1989 in relation to behaviour and discipline.

Pupils in *PRUs* have usually experienced significant difficulties in behaviour and motivation before entering the unit. Inspectors should look for the development, from a low baseline, of positive attitudes to learning, good behaviour and personal responsibility. The same is applied to the inspection of special schools for pupils with emotional and behavioural difficulties.

A high priority in *special schools* is the personal development of pupils towards attaining independence and autonomy, personal fulfilment and achievement, and the development of social skills and the formation of effective relationships. Responses will be expected to be observable across the whole curriculum.

Behaviour: evaluation criteria

Behaviour is to be judged by the extent to which the attitudes and actions of pupils contribute to:

- standards of achievement;
- effective learning in the classroom;
- the quality of life in school;
- the functioning of the school as an orderly community;
- the development of self-discipline.

Evidence should include:

- observation of standards of behaviour and the quality of relationships in classrooms, in the playground and about the school;
- pupils' records;
- discussion with pupils and staff;
- parental views as expressed at the pre-inspection meeting with parents;
- data on exclusions and referrals including information on the criteria applied and general monitoring, the school's files and information on the role and involvement of the governing body;
- the views of pupils, parents, teachers and governors on the incidence of bullying and the school's response;

- the school's arrangements for promoting good behaviour including aims, objectives, policies, code of conduct, rewards and sanctions for dealing with unsatisfactory behaviour.

The report should include an evaluation of:

- overall quality of pupils' behaviour in the school;
- the extent to which behaviour has an effect on standards of achievement, the quality of teaching and learning and the quality of life in the school; the functioning of the school as an orderly community;
- how pupils react to school rules and conventions;
- pupils' and parents' responses to the application of any system of rewards and sanctions;
- the measures taken by the school to prevent and eliminate any bullying. Where bullying is considered by parents and/or pupils to be a significant problem, the report should indicate this;
- the effectiveness of the school's arrangements for promoting good behaviour.

Quality of education: amplification of evaluation criteria

Where teaching is *good* pupils acquire knowledge, skills and understanding progressively and at a good pace. Teachers have a secure knowledge and understanding of what they teach and make effective use of them. The lessons have clear aims and purposes. They cater appropriately for the learning of pupils of differing abilities and interests, and ensure the full participation of all. The teaching methods suit the topic or subject as well as the pupils; the conduct of lessons signals high expectations of all pupils and sets high but attainable challenges. The teaching makes clear the importance of application, accuracy and good presentation, and the need to use critical thinking, creativity and imagination. There is regular feedback which helps pupils to make progress, both through thoughtful marking and discussion of work with pupils. Relationships are positive and promote pupils' motivation. The teaching provides opportunities for pupils to take increasing responsibility for their own work. Teachers appreciate how factors such as ethnicity, bilingualism, gender, social circumstances and giftedness may affect learning. National Curriculum attainment targets and programmes of study are taken fully into account. Where appropriate, homework which extends or complements the work done in lessons, is set regularly and followed up effectively.

Teaching is *unsatisfactory*:

- where pupils fail to achieve standards commensurate with their potential or where the teaching is ill-prepared or unclear;
- the pupils are unable to see the point of what they are asked to do;

- they are not appropriately challenged; nor are they helped to form a useful assessment of their level of attainment and of what areas need to be improved;
- pupils do not have adequate resources or time to undertake the task effectively;
- individual pupils' learning needs are not recognised sufficiently;
- relationships are insecure and inhibit learning.

Quality of teaching: evaluation criteria

Teaching quality is to be judged by the extent to which teachers:

- have a secure understanding of the subject or areas they teach;
- plan effectively for continuity and progression;
- set appropriate expectations and convey to pupils clear objectives for each lesson;
- manage classes effectively;
- ensure that lessons have suitable content and purposeful activity, enabling pupils to make progress at an appropriate pace;
- employ methods, organisational strategies and materials that match curricular objectives and the needs of all pupils, motivate pupils whatever their ability, ethnicity or gender and enable pupils to develop their skills for learning;
- ensure work is rigorously assessed and followed up;
- use homework effectively to reinforce and/or extend what is learned in school.

Evidence should include:

- day-to-day planning of work: forecasts, lesson plans and notes on individual pupils;
- lesson observation: all relevant aspects mentioned in the above criteria;
- discussion with teachers and pupils;
- samples of pupils' work, including any work done off site and homework;
- marking, comments and follow-up;
- teachers' records of work done by pupils;
- role(s) of special support assistants employed to work with pupils with special educational needs and other assistants such as nursery nurses and technicians;
- input from specialist teachers.

Improving school attendance

This section reports on the findings of a project undertaken by Her Majesty's Inspectors in Wales during the summer term of 1997 on truancy and on improving school behaviour. Inspection visits were made to GEST-funded projects in a selection of schools and centres in nine LEAs. Aspects of this provision were then reported and discussed with the LEA officers and other staff involved.

The methodology utilised for this project was fairly generic. A wide variety of approaches were used in order to identify a variety of issues among the target groups of pupils and their schools. Nevertheless, the ensuing pages present a number of the key features which, according to OFSTED, are to be commonly found in the more successful school improvement projects on attendance.

The aims of the projects

The main objective identified for bids under Category 5D (Truancy and Discipline) was set out in GEST Circular 41/95:

> To promote better classroom practice; and to raise pupils' achievement by effective management of attendance and to set targets for reducing truancy wherever appropriate.

In addition, bids were expected to:

- identify clearly the scale of needs at the schools designated;
- demonstrate an innovative and well thought out strategy for dealing with potential as well as habitual truants;
- provide a clear statement of objectives, together with performance measures against which the effectiveness of provision could be measured;
- show that appropriate use would be made of the experience and expertise of the education welfare service (EWS);
- show that they were based on, and would further, good practice.

Among a small minority of pupils, usually in KS3 and KS4, there is often a high correlation between poor attendance, disaffection and poor behaviour at school. Many of the projects sought to address all of these inter-linked elements within a comprehensive, coherent approach – often providing discrete, alternative curriculum arrangements for small numbers of severely disaffected pupils.

In the LEAs inspected, staff involved in the GEST projects have identified a number of key factors associated with poor levels of attendance. These include:

- absences condoned by parents who do not value school attendance highly;
- poor resistance to, and recovery from, illness, especially among low-income families;
- disaffection with the curriculum offered at school, particularly in KS4;

- difficulty in coping with school work (e.g. because of under-developed literacy skills);
- poor relationships with school staff;
- poor relationships with fellow pupils, especially in KS2 and KS3;
- difficult home circumstances, including lack of parental discipline and control.

In several LEAs projects focused on pupils in Y6–7, the transition stage between primary and secondary education. It is hoped that early intervention at this stage will prevent a habit of occasional non-attendance developing among pupils who would otherwise be at risk of becoming persistent truants later in their school careers. It is these projects, in particular, which are achieving significant success in improving attendance rates. Other projects target particular pupils, or groups of pupils, at crucial stages of their secondary school careers, such as those in KS4 who are preparing for public examinations. These projects have also achieved measurable success in many cases, though it is usually less pronounced and more variable overall than that of the projects aimed at younger target groups.

Case study 1

In one LEA, which covers an area of high deprivation in the former mining valleys of South Wales, a number of school attendance projects have focused on pupils at the primary–secondary transition stage. One of these projects has centred on a comprehensive school and its three main feeder primary schools. GEST funding has supported the appointment of a project officer who complements the work of education welfare officers (EWO) in the area and maintains close liaison with key members of school staff. All of these staff co-operated effectively to identify pupils in the final term of T5 and Y6 whose poor attendance was causing concern. Pupils targeted for particular attention within the project were selected according to criteria such as family receipt of income support and entitlement to free school meals. This process involved liaison between the project officer and other agencies, including social services, the schools psychological service, and the health service.

The approach involves:

- a prompt response when the pupils causing concern do not attend school;
- visits to pupils' homes by the project officer to discuss with their parents the reasons for the pupil's absence from school and to explore ways of improving matters;
- concentration on a small number of families, providing support for the local EWO and bringing a productive change of approach to the families concerned, many of whom had hitherto developed fairly effective avoidance techniques;

- informal but effective liaison with social services staff based in the local community.

When the Y6 pupils transferred to the secondary school they continued to be monitored by the project officer, who offered support and guidance when needed. A senior member of staff at the secondary school (operating without the support of GEST funding) has full-time responsibility for improving pupils' attendance. The school has also invested in a system of rewarding full attendance with gifts such as a free pen, or a £5 voucher.

Out of 15 pupils formerly in Y5 and now in Y6 in the three primary schools, all except two have improved attendance since the beginning of the project and nine now have attendance levels above 80 per cent. All except three of the 13 pupils in Y7 at the secondary school have improved attendance significantly (illness being a major cause of absence among two of the exceptions); seven pupils now have attendance levels above 80 per cent.

Throughout the LEA as a whole, 114 pupils with attendance of 80 per cent or below were targeted at the beginning of the project, of whom 107 continue to attend schools in the area. Forty-nine of the 53 pupils now in Y6, and 43 of the 54 pupils now in Y7, had improved attendance by the end of the year. Among the first group, average attendance increased from 71 per cent to 84 per cent; among the second, it rose from 72 per cent to 80 per cent. Although attendance rates of around 80 per cent are far from acceptable for the great majority of pupils, for many of those targeted by the project they represent a significant improvement.

One of the main features contributing to the success of the project is the schools' first-day response to absence by the targeted pupils. Overall, however, the effectiveness of the strategy is attributed mainly to stubborn persistence in what can be described as a battle of attrition, together with a planned variety in the tactics deployed in the community in order to eliminate complacency and counteract avoidance strategies. The project benefited from the schools' acknowledgement that they have an important role to play in ensuring that good attendance is seen as a desirable and worthwhile goal.

In another LEA, project work has focused not only on improving the attendance of pupils in Y7, but also on providing additional literacy support.

Case study 2

The GEST project manager is convinced that the difficulties which certain pupils experience in reading and writing contribute to their poor attendance and behaviour. The project therefore aims to provide pupils with literacy support as well as improving their attendance. In one of the two schools involved in the project, both of which are located in the same large industrial town, twenty Y7 pupils benefit from this support.

The following strategies are employed:

- the pupils (who are not included in SEN teaching groups) are withdrawn in small groups from two lessons a week (in rotation) to receive tuition from a visiting literacy support teacher;
- the pupils also attend paired reading sessions after school with Y10 pupils who have received guidance from an advisory teacher;
- as part of the school's first day response to absence, office staff are informed by form tutors of the names of that day's absentees;
- if there is no response to a telephone call to the pupil's home by mid-morning, arrangements are made for the EWO to make an immediate visit.

Partly, if not wholly, as a result of the project, overall attendance in Y7 has risen by several points to just over 90 per cent for the spring term. The work of the targeted pupils shows clear evidence of improvement: they have made significant advances in the presentation, content and accuracy of their writing, and their oral skills have also developed well.

In a separate initiative, the director of the last-named project interviewed a group of fifteen pupils in Y11 to ascertain the most common reasons for absence in KS4. The pupils identified these as:

- inadequate feedback from teachers on pupils' work and prospects;
- inconsistency in the support given to pupils returning to school after a period of absence;
- unhelpful careers lessons and/or guidance;
- dissatisfaction with the curriculum provided by the school.

Features of successful practice in improving practice

HMC reported that the main features associated with *success in improving attendance* are:

- an overall strategy for dealing with absence which is clearly understood, agreed and implemented by all concerned, including school and education welfare service (EWS) staff;
- persistence in implementing the strategy – 'consistent attrition';
- close liaison between school staff, EWS personnel and other agencies;
- an early, 'first-day' response to all absences;
- the careful maintenance of cumulative records of the reasons given for each pupil's absence, as a basis for subsequent analysis and appropriate action where necessary;
- varying the approaches made in the case of the more persistent absentees, including changing the personnel involved in visits to pupils' homes (e.g. school staff and/or project worker instead of EWO);
- use of information technology to provide up-to-date, accurate information swiftly;

- support for the development of pupils' literacy skills where necessary;
- an effective policy to counter bullying, including a positive and supportive response to pupils affected;
- curriculum provision which meets pupils' needs, engages their interest and enables them to achieve good standards of work;
- rewards for good attendance.

Improving behaviour

LEA staff involved in the GEST projects have identified a number of factors associated with poor behaviour, some of which also affect attendance:

- disaffection with the curriculum offered at school;
- difficulty in coping with school work;
- low self-esteem;
- poor relationships with school staff;
- poor relationships with fellow pupils, which may include bullying;
- difficult home circumstances, including lack of parental discipline and control.

For this reason, projects dealing with some of the more acute cases of poor behaviour, involving pupils who are either excluded from school or at risk of being excluded, address problems of attendance and behaviour simultaneously through various forms of alternative curriculum provision.

A number of schools involved in the projects have introduced whole-school strategies for maintaining and improving standards of behaviour in general. The schools achieving greatest success in this respect not only have effective systems of rewards and sanctions, but also take great care to ensure that the curriculum, and the way in which it is taught, are well matched to pupils' needs.

In one of the projects, selected pupils with behavioural and other problems meet for an hour each week as a small group. Under the skilful direction of the group (work) leader, they are encouraged to come to terms with their difficulties through a variety of activities, including discussion and role play. Occasionally the group work identifies specific problems, such as inadequate differentiation for less able pupils, and the school is thereby alerted to the need to improve its provision.

Schools tend to achieve greater consistency in, and place more emphasis on, the application of sanctions than on rewarding good behaviour. In an attempt to remedy this, some schools have introduced rewards systems which involve tangible prizes, such as vouchers which can be exchanged for consumer goods.

This project has sought to improve attendance as well as behaviour through its rewards scheme. Attendance and behaviour are also linked in another project, where the emphasis is on improving behaviour overall by providing a

Case study A

In September 1996, a comprehensive school, which serves a disadvantaged urban catchment area, introduced a system of rewards as its main strategy for maintaining and improving discipline. All pupils have been given cards on which staff record credits in recognition of good attendance, academic achievement, effort, positive attitudes and examples of good behaviour. Ten credits count as a token which can be redeemed against a range of goods from a published catalogue. The list includes stationery and sports equipment which the school purchases in bulk from local suppliers at discounts of up to 20 per cent. A small selection of items from the catalogue is displayed in the school foyer. The range of goods and vouchers awarded (e.g. for free use of a local bowling alley, or for popular clothing shops in the city centre) is reviewed as necessary in response to demand among the pupils.

Pupils clearly value the system, which has had a positive impact on behaviour and effort. They obviously value the rewards and many are prepared to modify their own behaviour in school in order to collect the credits. The school has evaluated the scheme by means of a questionnaire issued to staff and pupils. Returns suggest overwhelming support and a positive impact on pupils' attitudes, especially in KS3 (between 97 per cent and 100 per cent support) and in Y10 (91 per cent support). Even in Y11, where pupils were more cynical at first, they now show more positive attitudes, both to and because of the scheme. Overall, there is ample evidence to show that the scheme has succeeded in improving the attitudes and behaviour of large numbers of pupils.

The scheme represents good value for money. Although final costs for the school year are not yet known (as many pupils are accumulating their credits for larger purchases), it is unlikely that these will exceed £2,000 and they could amount to little more than £1,200. There is little or no demand for some of the sanctions, such as detention, formerly applied to pupils who misbehaved. The time expended on the rewards scheme by year tutors and other staff of the school, including the deputy head who administers it, is less than that formerly spent dealing with instances of bad behaviour.

Case study B

A comprehensive school in a large industrial area serves the most socially deprived catchment in the LEA. It has pioneered the concept of the Individual Teaching Centre (ITC), which aims to improve attendance rates and behaviour, and to reduce the likelihood of exclusions.

Pupils arriving at the ITC do so after extensive consultation between a panel of staff which includes the head and the GEST-funded, part-time educational social worker (ESW). Parental support is sought by letter. Individual teachers do not have the option of sending pupils to the ITC for instances of bad behaviour. A few pupils occasionally self-refer when, for various reasons, they foresee the potential of clashes arising in lessons. On arrival at the ITC, pupils negotiate and agree an action plan; they review their progress and plan for the future at the end of the placement.

A deputy head has overall charge of the centre which is staffed mainly by a team of senior teachers, including the head. It is situated in a small, sparsely furnished room. No more than five pupils can be accommodated at any given time, and on most days only one or two pupils are present.

While they are in the ITC, pupils are expected to work in silence on written tasks related to the subjects of the lessons that they are missing. While some pupils appreciate the respite from their usual timetables, a day in the ITC is not a pleasant experience for pupils; even break and lunch times are spent in the company of senior staff. Some pupils also receive counselling: the ESW is trained for such work, and is able to extract pupils from the ITC to work with them individually.

The school acknowledges that there are no simple solutions to improving behaviour. The extensive records which it keeps on the use of the ITC show that 72 pupils (about 10 per cent of the school population) have attended the ITC for at least a day during the year. More than half of the pupils referred to the ITC have returned after their first placement; about one fifth have had between four and seven placements during the year and a further fifth have spent seven or more days in the centre. However, the school's exclusion rates are low. There were only four permanent exclusions during 1995–96 and only two to date in 1996–97, one of them that of a pupil who had previously been excluded from another school. There have been only five 5-day exclusions this year.

The advantage of this model of ITC is that it minimises the interruption of pupils' normal curriculum. Its aim is to enable pupils to return to their classes at the earliest opportunity. While a significant proportion of pupils require more than one period of readjustment, the ITC is, overall, successful in reducing both the amount and the impact of poor behaviour in lessons. Some pupils facing serious difficulties in their domestic lives have benefited from the opportunity to think and to talk through their problems, and have found a period in the ITC to be an advantage in coping with the additional demands placed on them in school.

GEST funding has helped the school to devote a significant amount of senior staff time to dealing with 'problem pupils'. The additional work of the ESW has provided a valuable extra dimension in terms of home–school liaison and counselling. The ITC has principally provided a framework within which this work has taken place; the educational value of the work which pupils undertake within the ITC is limited, but the time spent there nevertheless enables them to carry on as soon as possible with their usual programme of lessons

short-term 'time-out' facility for pupils on the point of becoming involved in confrontational situations.

In several important respects, this school's ITC differs from some of the alternative forms of provision which are described in the next section:

- the ITC caters for pupils of all ages;
- the great majority of placements are for one or two days only, with pupils then returning to their normal timetables;
- there is no long-term modification or dilution of the mainstream curriculum, within which there is extensive vocational provision in KS4.

Features of successful practice in improving behaviour

The features associated with greatest success in maintaining and improving standards of behaviour are:

- curriculum provision which meets pupils' needs;
- lessons which engage pupils' interest and motivate them to achieve high standards of work;
- a clearly set out system of rewards and sanctions which is understood by all and commands the approval of staff, pupils and parents;
- consistency in the application of rewards and sanctions by all staff;
- suitable provision for pupils whose behaviour in a timetabled lesson becomes unacceptable;
- counselling for pupils who would benefit from it.

14 Parents and truancy

Throughout this book there are sections which are related to parents, pupils' home backgrounds, home–school links, social influences and truancy. However, this chapter specifically brings together the remainder of some of the latest thinking on the importance of parental influences and their relationship to truancy.

For this reason, this chapter is sub-divided into several parts. These are:

- school attendance: information for parents;
- parents and legislation;
- parents and truancy: background aspects;
- parents and sound foundations;
- where parents lay the blame for truancy;
- one-parent families, pupils and schools.

The final section on one-parent families, pupils, schools and truancy is being emphasised because research indicates that a high proportion of truants emanate from single-parent families of one kind or another. Pupils from one-parent families are often monitored closely or placed on 'at-risk' registers by some caring schools. This is especially true for pupils in the early years of schooling, at the primary stage, or at vulnerable points during their secondary years such as at adolescence and puberty.

School attendance: information for parents

If you are a parent of (or are responsible for) a child aged between 5 and 16 who is registered at school, this information explains your responsibilities for making sure your child attends school regularly.

The law

By law, all children of compulsory school age (between 5 and 16) must get a proper full-time education. You are responsible for making sure this happens, either by registering the child at a school or by making other arrangements which provide an effective education. If your child is registered as a pupil at a particular school, that school must give permission for your child to be absent. If your child does not go to the school at which he or she is registered, the relevant education authority can take legal action against you.

Why must my child go to school regularly?

- Having a good education will help to give your child the best possible start in life.
- If your child does not attend school regularly, he or she will not be able to keep up with the work.
- Employers will want to be sure that the people they are thinking of taking on are reliable. So children who have not attended their school regularly have less chance of getting a good job.
- Young people who are off school for no good reason are at risk of becoming victims of crime or abuse. They may also be drawn into anti-social or criminal behaviour.

What can I do to help?

- Make sure that your child goes to school regularly, arrives on time and keeps to the school's rules on going to all lessons. Start these good habits at an early age, while your child is in primary school.
- If your child starts missing school, help the school to put things right. Make sure your child understands that you do not approve of him or her missing school.
- If your child is ill, contact the school on the first day of your child's illness. Staff will be concerned if they do not hear anything.
- If your child is ever off school, you must tell the school why. Do this by following the arrangements made by the school.
- If you want permission for your child to miss school, for example because of a special occasion such as a wedding, you should ask for permission well in advance and give full details.
- Do not expect the school to agree to shopping trips during school hours.
- Take an interest in your child's school work.
- Support the school in its efforts to control bad behaviour.

Family holidays during term time

- Wherever possible, you should take your holidays during school holidays.
- Avoid taking your child on holiday at times when he or she should be taking exams or tests.

- You should not expect your child's school to agree to a family holiday during term time. The school will carefully consider your request and they may take your child's attendance record into account.
- Schools will not agree to your child missing more than a total of ten school days for family holidays in any one school year, unless there is a very good reason.
- If your child is off school for more than ten days, the school may set work for him or her to do while you are away.

The role of the local education authority

- Local education authorities (LEAs) are responsible, by law, for making sure that registered pupils of compulsory school age attend their school regularly.
- Most LEAs employ education welfare officers (also called education social workers) to monitor school attendance and to help parents meet their responsibilities.
- Education welfare officers work closely with schools. Some are actually based in schools.
- If your child is not attending school regularly, an education welfare officer may visit you.
- For your child's sake you should co-operate with the education welfare officer to make sure your child overcomes his or her attendance problems and gets a proper education.
- If you do not do everything you can to co-operate with the education welfare officer and school, the LEA may have no choice but to get an education supervision order. This means that the court appoints a supervisor to help and give advice to you and your child.
- The LEA can also prosecute you in a magistrates court. This could result in you and your partner being fined up to £1000 for each child who is not going to school.

Parents and legislation

The legal framework governing school attendance and the responsibilities of parents, schools and the LEA is set out by a succession of Education and other Acts, Guidance and Regulations. Major legislation and guidance includes:

1   The 1944 Education Act.
2   The Children Act 1989, Section 36.
3   The Education (Pupil Registration) Regulations 1995 (as amended).
4   DfEE Circular 6/95 – The Parents' Charter; Publication of Information About Secondary School Performance.

5 OFSTED Report (1995) – *Access, Achievement and Attendance in Secondary Schools.*
6 The OFSTED Handbook: Guidance on the Inspection of Secondary/Primary/Special Schools.
7 The Education Act 1996, Section 7 and Sections 437–48.
8 DfEE Guidance – *School Attendance and the Role of the Education Welfare Service* (DfEE 1998a).

There is extensive guidance on the law in the 1998 DfEE publication on school attendance. In summary, the essential legal points are as follows:

- parents have a duty to educate their children either by regular attendance at school or otherwise;
- schools have to call the attendance register twice per day – at the start of the morning session and once during the afternoon session; and
- LEAs are required to ensure parents carry out their responsibilities with regard to their children's education.

Responsibilities – parents and carers

All parents who have children of compulsory school age, are responsible in law for ensuring that their children receive an efficient education 'suitable to their age, aptitude, ability and any special educational needs which they may have' (Section 7, Education Act 1996). Most parents fulfil this responsibility by registering their children at a school.

Parents whose children are registered at school are then responsible for ensuring that they attend punctually, regularly and stay at school.

Parents and truancy: background aspects

Parents play a direct role in helping their children to learn especially at an early age. Indeed, 'family' learning is a powerful tool for reaching some of the most disadvantaged in our society and drawing them into the challenge of life-long learning. It has the potential to reinforce the role of the family; change attitudes to education; help build strong local communities; and widen participation in learning. For this reason for example, the Family Literacy Initiative in Wales (promoted by the Basic Skills Agency in co-operation with local authorities) started operating throughout Wales in 1998–99, reaching 2000 parents and 3000 pupils and will be extended in future years.

Parents need help if they are to play a vital role in their children's learning. To be effective partners, parents need accurate information and regular feedback about what is happening in schools. They need to feel a real part of the endeavour to raise standards. No single document or information source can do this. What matters is that the information taken as a whole is user-friendly, and enables parents to make a balanced judgement of a school's achievements.

All schools must publish annual reports and prospectuses, and must give parents a pupil report at least once a year. There are many examples of helpful, informative reporting to parents; but there are cases where some documents, for one reason or another, leave parents feeling none the wiser. Schools should ensure that information is provided in the clearest possible manner. Schools need to consider how this clarity can be best achieved, notably through the dissemination of good practice.

Many schools face great difficulties in getting parents to take an interest in their children's education, and in raising their aspirations and expectations. The Government is considering a process of consultation on the extent to which reports should enable teachers to give parents an indication of what they might be expected to do to help their children achieve more. For example, this could extend to information about mentoring and master classes, as well as homework and vacation support clubs.

Parents should know what homework their children are expected to do and what role they have in supporting them. All schools should regularly review their use of high quality homework as a stimulus to learning and achievement. While some children are set regular homework, too many are not. In 1998, the Government issued guidelines on school homework (see Chapter 7). These guidelines covered the following areas:

- how much homework pupils of different ages should do;
- how much time pupils of different ages should spend on homework;
- what sort of tasks and activities make good homework;
- how schools can develop and implement successful homework policies;
- what is expected of schools and parents.

Effective school–parent partnerships need to be fostered and promoted by teachers, governors and parents alike to raise standards and improve results. Many schools already have home–school agreements. To build stronger partnerships, it will become a legal requirement for all schools to have written home–school agreements. These will explain clearly what is expected of the school, of the parent and of the pupil. Although not legally binding, they will be a powerful statement of intent. The detail will differ from school to school, but all agreements are likely to include expectations about attendance, discipline, homework, the standard of education and the ethos of the school.

Home–school associations can also provide powerful support for partnership with parents. The Government now requires all governing bodies to ensure that their school has an association. It has increased the number of elected parent governors of all kinds of school – and given parents a direct input to LEA education policies by ensuring that there is at least one parent representative on each LEA.

Standards of behaviour in most schools are generally satisfactory, but whenever those standards slip or could be improved, teachers, parents and pupils all have a role to play in raising them. The Government has issued guidance to schools about the provisions of the Education Act 1997 on school discipline. The Act requires every school to have a written policy which sets out the standards of behaviour expected, how good behaviour and discipline will be encouraged and the sanctions which will be applied if expected standards are breached.

Schools sometimes need to be reminded of the importance of dealing effectively with bullying, and of involving the whole school community (including pupils) in the development and application of strategies to this end. The Government is supporting local initiatives to tackle behaviour problems and take active steps to spread information on emerging good practice; for example on the benefits which schools have gained from the careful introduction of 'assertive discipline'.

Where pupils put at risk the learning of others or persist in anti-social behaviour, it is sometimes necessary to exclude them from school. This is generally a sanction of last resort. The 1997 Act provides for fixed period exclusions of up to 45 days per year. The Government is issuing new guidance for schools and local authorities about the circumstances in which exclusion should be used, and on changes to the appeals arrangements introduced in the Act. They are also considering arrangements for the education of pupils excluded from school and the merits of increased financial incentives for schools to admit pupils excluded by others. In the past, far too many schools have excluded pupils for comparatively trivial offences or for truancy, which can be counter-productive.

A number of authorities are already exploring new ways of providing education for children who are in danger of being or have been excluded from school; or are persistent truants. A number of authorities are also undertaking initiatives in partnership with Cities in Schools aimed at keeping young people in mainstream education settings or returning them to those settings as quickly as possible. The approaches include bridge courses for 14–16-year-olds providing a structured full-time programme of education and work experience for groups of pupils; one-to-one programmes for younger pupils; one-to-one programmes for younger pupils involving progressive reintegration into the school setting; and measures in schools for identifying and handling behavioural problems well before exclusion becomes an issue.

Such approaches sit well with the Youth Access initiative whose aim is to help those young people, primarily from the age of 14, who are disillusioned and underachieve, to re-integrate and progress. It aims to help young people:

- under school leaving age, who have dropped out of mainstream education or are in danger of doing so, to be re-integrated into mainstream education or to progress into other forms of education or training which meet their needs;
- above school leaving age, who are not in education, training or jobs, to progress to effective forms of education, training or jobs.

Funding, through GEST and through local initiative funds for TECs, is available to support proposals from local authorities and TECs which set out joint action plans covering a period of three years or more, as from 1998–99. The plans will be prepared in consultation with and with the support of the careers service and a wide range of other local partners, including the youth service, further education institutions and the voluntary sector.

Pupil referral units (PRUs) were included in the OHMCI cycle of inspections from September 1997. The inspection reports will help to inform LEA's work in setting standards which will need to encompass PRUs and the outcomes they achieve for pupils.

The Government introduced one school leaving date from Easter 1998 so that 16-year-olds do not leave school before the end of their GCSE or GNVQ studies and therefore with no qualifications at all. This should also ensure that we meet the following intended results by the year 2002:

- almost all pupils should achieve 5 GCSE passes at A*–G, or the vocational equivalent;
- the number of pupils leaving school without any GCSE or GNVQ qualifications should be reduced by at least 15 per cent as compared with the 1996 level.

Tackling truancy and exclusion effectively will not only serve to raise levels of achievement; the Government considers that it can also help to reduce crime. A survey for the recent Audit Commission study *Misspent Youth* (1996) indicated that 65 per cent of school age offenders sentenced in court had also been excluded from school or were persistent truants. Action to improve attendance and reduce the need for exclusion should therefore contribute significantly to the Government's wider strategy to prevent anti-social and criminal behaviour by young people and to reduce the associated public costs.

Present Government policies on combating truancy and involving parents mean that by 2002 or before there will be:

- family literacy schemes operating in all LEAs;
- better information available to parents;
- a clear recognition by schools, parents and pupils of the importance of good quality homework in raising standards;
- home–school agreements and home–school associations in every school;
- better support for schools in providing for pupils with behaviour problems, less need to exclude pupils from school and better provision for those who are out of school;
- reduced levels of unauthorised absence from school;
- no young people leaving school before the end of their GCSE or GNVQ courses – and as almost all 16-year-olds should be able to achieve 5 GCSE grades A*–G, or the vocational equivalent, the number of pupils leaving school without qualifications should be significantly reduced.

Additional consultation is being undertaken on:

- bringing home to parents their responsibilities for ensuring their children's regular and punctual attendance at school;
- detailed guidance for schools and local authorities on pupil discipline, exclusion, attendance and behaviour support plans.

Parents and sound foundations

It is hard for children to make a success of their lives unless, by the time they leave primary school, they can read and write fluently, handle numbers confidently, and concentrate on their work. Providing pupils with a firm foundation in their early years is best achieved by a meaningful partnership between home and school. Children who achieve well in their early years, and in their primary school years, are much less likely to truant in secondary school than those whose reading and numeracy skills have fallen behind their chronological development.

The Government is presently committed to:

- good quality early years learning opportunities, alongside childcare and support for family learning where appropriate;
- a thorough assessment of children when they start primary school;
- a major programme to raise standards of literacy (with proper regard for oral expression) and numeracy, and to develop positive attitudes to learning;
- smaller infant classes to support more effective teaching and learning.

Assessment when starting school

Assessment of our youngest pupils when they start school is an essential preliminary way to improving basic skills in literacy and numeracy. Taking account of results from research, baseline assessment has been introduced from the autumn of 1998. This involves close partnership between parents and teachers. It will help teachers to check the rate of pupils' progress as they learn and show the value the school is adding. Additional support is being provided through the GEST programme to enable teachers to implement the assessment arrangements.

Raising standards in literacy and numeracy

Targets

Primary education is about more than literacy and numeracy, yet these skills are at the heart of what is done in primary schools: they are fundamental to all future learning. Primary schools know that leaving remedial action to secondary schools inevitably puts pupils' success there at risk; indeed basic skills need to be reinforced constantly, and extended, throughout pupils' formal education. This is why literacy, numeracy and scientific understanding are at the heart of the National Curriculum.

There is wide variation in the performance of primary schools, and thus there are real problems in literacy and numeracy at secondary level. This does not always reflect catchment area. For example, in deprived areas some schools do significantly better than others. Pupils need to be better prepared at ages 7–9; the transition from primary to secondary education should be seamless so as to capitalise on the work done at the end of Key Stage 2, from age 9–11; and pupils should be stretched more at ages 11–13. Standards will rise significantly as and when pupils' ability in language (oracy and literacy) and mathematics is reinforced across the whole curriculum. This is why it is essential that:

- all primary schools (mainstream and special) regularly set and announce their own targets for improvement in the basics;
- all secondary schools (mainstream and special) set and announce their own attainment targets in annual reports to parents and prospectuses – giving particular attention to improvement at GCSE, A level and in vocational qualities;
- every school has a development plan detailing objectives for improved performance in the core subjects of the National Curriculum – and indeed every other subject, including RE.

To help schools achieve all of this, there is a need for a well selected range of targets to steer by. These have to be designed to galvanise more rapid progress to overcome problems of attainment in the core subjects, especially of literacy and numeracy, and to ensure that teachers get the sustained help they need from every quarter to achieve results – fast. There is already an emerging consensus that clear benchmarks should be set against which schools can measure their progress year on year. Thus the Government's expectation is that by the year 2000:

- between six and seven out of every ten children aged 11 should achieve level 4 or better;
- between six and seven out of every ten children aged 14 should achieve level 5 or better.

These benchmarks apply to pupils' results by subject (English and/or Welsh, maths and science), as reported by statutory teacher assessment and statutory tasks or tests.

This is the first step. The second would extend these goals for a further two years. So it is proposed that by 2002:

- between seven and eight of every ten children should achieve level 4 or better;
- between seven and eight out of every ten children aged 14 should achieve level 5 or better – reported on the same basis as the benchmarks for the year 2000.

For purposes of monitoring and accountability, data on performance, and for schools' own target setting, should relate to these national targets.

Information on pupils' attainment in maths, science and English and/or Welsh in combination would feature as at present. This same approach would be carried forward for both primary and secondary schools – so that the emphasis on the basics is sustained over time.

At the same time, local authorities and OHMCI will be invited to focus attention on the performance of schools where results fall in the bottom 25 per cent following statutory assessments at 11 and 14. The aim is to promote better results – and indeed to lift their performance by at least 10–15 per cent by 2002. OHMCI have carried out work on achievement and under-achievement at Key Stage 2. They have work in hand on the steps being taken by low performing schools to improve. They will be publishing short summary reports on standards in English, Welsh and maths in primary and secondary schools (with particular emphasis on literacy and numeracy) in due course.

Excellent teachers

All primary and special school teachers need to know how to teach reading and maths in line with proven best practice. Many teachers find that a success-ful approach includes:

- dedicated time given daily to aspects of literacy and numeracy in which a balance of whole-class, group and individual teaching is used under firm and rigorous teacher direction to enthuse and engage children;
- regular assessment of pupils' progress to enable the teaching to be tailored precisely to their stage of development;
- systematic teaching of phonics in reading as well as sentence and text level skills;
- constructive development of pupils' capacity in mental arithmetic and of applying mathematics in practical and lively ways.

Three years: nine measures

The academic years up to 2000–2001 are crucial to reaching the goals set by the Government in time for 2002. Thus:

- a major element of the GEST programme will be devoted to raising standards of literacy and numeracy. A new component will enable LEAs and schools to deploy innovative approaches to raise standards. LEAs will be invited to prepare and implement local plans to focus intensive training, support and consultancy assistance on improving standards of literacy and numeracy in schools using models already devised at local authority level.
- OHMCI will publish advice to teachers on how to manage time so as to give due weight to literacy and numeracy within the context of the wider National Curriculum. That will be supplemented by guidance on good practice in target setting for primary schools.
- The profession is being asked to give guidance to schools on administering straightforward tests of chronological reading age at 9. Schools will be encouraged to analyse results systematically, setting targets for improvement and reporting results to parents;
- The Government is issuing revised guidance to governors on promoting good practice in raising standards of literacy and numeracy in primary schools. This will include examples of different models for reporting to parents effectively, both at the end of key stage assessments and in the intervening years;
- local authorities will continue their work with the Basic Skills Agency to support family literacy schemes and with TECs to promote educationally worthwhile out of hours activities to lift standards of literacy and numeracy. They will be encouraged to extend their reach to other settings where multi-disciplinary approaches are relevant, such as refuges, foyers, family centres and childcare;
- the DfEE and the Welsh Office will see to it that fuller use is made of voluntary and other support – to focus more support on children with the greatest difficulties especially in the primary sector, and to champion higher standards in co-operation with schools;
- education–business links that have had such a powerful effect in generating positive initiatives and sound mentoring for literacy and numeracy at secondary level will be extended in 1999, to ensure that more primary schools benefit from employer support;
- the out of hours childcare programme had an educational component for the first time during the summer holidays 1997. This brings new support to develop the literacy and numeracy skills of some of the most underprivileged children in our community. The scheme will be rolled forward for future years, subject to evaluation.

Smaller classes

Class sizes will continue to be reduced for 5, 6 and 7-year-olds within the next five years. This will be a key factor in achieving improved results. OHMCI reports confirm the importance of class size for younger children. Smaller classes at this age do not guarantee good results but they can make a significant contribution by enabling teachers to spend more time with each child, to identify individual pupil needs and difficulties early on, and to offer the help children need to master the basics.

Summary

This section sets out how the Government intends to provide a firm foundation for all children's education. Under its latest proposals, by 2002 there will be:

- a high quality education for all 4-year-olds whose parents want it;
- an early years forum in every local authority, contributing to early years development plans;
- excellent examples of integrated services in each local authority to support good educational outcomes in the early years;
- baseline assessment of all children entering primary school;
- a massive improvement in achievements in the core subjects of the curriculum – maths, English and science (plus Welsh in Wales);
- evidence of a sea change in achievement against national benchmarks and targets;
- classes of 30 or under for all 5, 6 and 7-year-olds.

Where parents lay the blame for truancy

Kinder and Wilkin (1998) have reported on their findings of an NFER Project on where parents lay the blame for truancy. They found that:

> Parents believe children misbehave and play truant because they are bored and the national curriculum is failing to address their needs. They also blame their own short-comings as parents, as well as peer pressure and a breakdown in pupil–teacher relationships for truancy and disaffection.

The report found that parents pinpointed the National Curriculum as a culprit in poor classroom behaviour and non-attendance. Parents believed it was not meeting children's needs and interests, particularly those who have special needs and learning difficulties. The report found that complex factors determined the causes of disaffection, and that children needed a combination of support to overcome their difficulties. Schools which employed a variety of approaches to dealing with the problem achieved the best results in improving motivation. Among the most effective were computer registration systems monitoring pupil attendance that enabled teachers to detect patterns of behaviour and absence, and made it more difficult for pupils to truant.

Rewards and sanctions were also effective because they encouraged and reinforced school rules on behaviour and attendance, although some children did not value being seen publicly to receive acclaim. One in eight believed that the giving of prizes and incentives was inappropriate and threw them away.

The authors also found that the prospect of punishment for truancy only worked for those pupils who feared their attendance record could affect their job prospects; others 'beat the system' by intercepting letters home, forging signatures and getting their friends to ring the school. Approaches which provide challenges and offer individual support to pupils were the most effective means of dealing with disaffection. Conversely, those with a strong reprisal element such as withdrawal units, exclusion and suspensions tended not to address the problem.

Parental attitudes towards truancy

In one study of persistent school absenteeism (Reid 1985), 65 per cent of the parents of the non-attenders disapproved of their offspring's absences; 9 per cent 'approved', while 26 per cent of the parents were considered ambivalent. Clearly, there is a great deal of difference between tacit parental approval and outright disapproval, although there was very little overt evidence of parents actively collaborating with the schools in getting their offspring back to school. However, there are undoubtedly major differences between the 'hardened' attitudes of parents of chronic truants and, for example, those of parents of first offenders.

In over half the cases where parental disapproval was acknowledged, the absentees stated that on occasions family quarrels and/or 'rifts' took place within the home because of their non-attendance. These quarrels were especially rife following threats of prosecution, letters from the school and home visits by educational welfare officers. Despite the majority disapproval, only 15 per cent of the parents took any form of 'positive' action against their children in order to discourage their non-attendance. Measures mentioned by the absentees included the stopping of pocket money, returning them to the school gates and detaining them at home in the evenings, 'being grounded'. Many of the absentees specifically mentioned that they disliked being punished by their parents far more than their schools and, according to the absentees, it seems that a large proportion of the parents simply took the easy way out by 'just telling me to return to school and then doing nothing about it', or 'telling me off and then sending the school a false note'.

There is also evidence that more girls than boys are parental-condoned absentees. Research suggests that mothers often keep their daughters at home as company, to help them to undertake specific chores, or, in extreme cases, for protection from violence and/or child abuse. It is also clear that there are occasions when the reasons given by the schools for the absence contradict, or are different from the evidence collected either by the social services or health agencies or both. Illustratively, cases where teenage girls are pregnant and have abortions are often classified as either illness or truancy by schools because they are unaware of the truth.

One-parent families, pupils and schools

Background

Research clearly shows that an extremely high percentage of truants and persistent school absentees emanate from single-parent families. This section is written to provide teachers, education welfare officers, social workers and other caring professionals with the basic factual information they will need in dealing with truants and other kinds of disaffected pupils from one-parent families within schools. Research also shows a clear link between pupils from one-parent families and alienated behaviour within schools. In fact, many aggressive delinquents and disruptive truants (including young offenders) come from single-parent families. This is why an understanding of 'life' for pupils inside single families is so important.

This section provides just a few insights which may help teachers understand their pupils from one-parent families. The cases of Alastair, Annie and Susan show the sort of unique problems which confront these pupils on a daily basis. The cases of Jan, John T, Marion and Frank reflect the position from the real-life standpoints of single parents – whether male or female. Teachers can do a great deal to help and understand their pupils from one-parent families provided they are informed and motivated to do so, and approach their tasks in an appropriate empathetic manner. Research indicates that teachers are the most important professional group for a majority of children. Accordingly, teachers are in a good position to redress some of life's inequalities for pupils from one-parent families. To be fully effective, they need full information from their schools and competent social service/school links to ensure proper procedures and the right kind of help and information is given. Sadly, this is not always the case.

Changing family patterns

The most popular living arrangement in British society is still the traditional marriage. However, it is now just one of a number of options. Fewer people are actually marrying. Another important change is that marriage is more easily broken up today compared with thirty years ago. There are now fewer church weddings and more civil marriages in Britain. The increase in cohabitation reflects fewer constraints now on long or short-term relationships which are not sanctioned by marriage.

Well over one million families in this country are headed by one parent. That is, more than one family in five or six is one-parent, involving some one-and-a-half million children under the age of 16. Almost 80 per cent of one-parent families arise through loss in the form of death, separation or divorce. A significant number of women enter into single parenthood by choice, while some girls become pregnant by accident.

The external system

The following external factors are identified with lifestyles within one-parent families:

1   The extended family lends less support in modern British society because families are more scattered. Intimacy with and support from other family members can no longer be maintained to the same degree as before. Marriage partners therefore put much greater emotional demands on each other for companionship and fulfilment.

2   Divorce is increasingly regarded as an acceptable solution to marital unhappiness and this response is supported in changes in the law governing divorce. For example, divorce in Scotland almost trebled in fifteen years and has continued to increase throughout the whole of the UK.

3   Within conventional marriages and in more casual living patterns, there is considerable blurring of firm roles and obligations which, traditionally, have served as guidelines. There is now more role-sharing and role reversal.

4   There are more 'dual-career' marriages across all occupational levels. Spouses are faced with problems of managing competitive feelings, and of dealing with multiple-role demands, while paradoxically, their material expectations and aspirations remain those characteristic of the traditional mood of marriage. Despite the fact that both partners in most marriages now work, the traditional role model of marriage whereby the husband is expected to be the main provider of economic support and material comforts for the family, and the wife is expected to take care of the emotional needs of husband and children by creating a supportive and comfortable domestic environment, is slow to die.

5   Women have more economic and general independence and therefore, more opportunities to grow apart from their husbands. Wives now have more sources of personal affirmation beyond the house and develop a separate identify which was much less likely in earlier decades. This often contributes, among other factors, to changes in value stances between individuals and spouses.

6   Studies into the characteristics of those who divorce refer to the significance of the place of ritual in the transition from single to a married state. The studies demonstrate a higher incidence of divorce in marriages which had a lack of ritual preparation, in the absence of formal engagements, church weddings and honeymoons. A more ritualised transition, it is claimed, gives the partners a stronger sense of their own new identity, and a more stable family base.

7   It is increasingly acknowledged that the increase in mental illness associated with stress and the general increase in violence in society is mirrored in a growing percentage of marriages.

8   The extended family in Britain has been slowly declining for years.

9   Financial pressures are the single greatest cause of marital stress in marriage
according to RELATE.

Internal system

In looking at the internal, private system of the marital relationship, it is helpful to acknowledge the four phases in marriage which are separated from each
other by crises of transition. Each of the four phases is characterised by a
change in family structure, when some major reorientation is required. When
this is successfully accomplished, marriages normally survive. When this is
not achieved, marriages tend to become unstable.

The first phase of marriage takes place before the birth of children. Each
person makes the shift from perceiving a parent as the most important person
to him/her to perceiving the new spouse in this capacity. Some never make
this shift. Teenage marriages are at particular risk during this phase, and
difficulties in relationships are often exacerbated by economic and housing
problems.

The second phase relates to the period when the children are at home. Each
partner must accept that parental responsibilities will impose restrictions, and
that each must permit the other to have the child or children as additional
love objects.

The third phase is the period of the children's adolescence, and usually
while they are in the process of leaving the family home. The parents will
experience a range of other losses at this stage – the menopause for women,
and for men perhaps a final recognition that career ambitions will remain
unfulfilled. This is a time for enormous mutual support and empathy. The
absence of such support can often be revealed in clear silhouette with the
departure of the children. It is a time when extended family support and
understanding is crucial, but is often unavailable.

The fourth phase is when the final readjustment to a private relationship
between the partners must take place. This is frequently a period of declining
health and fewer outside interests. The ageing period is perhaps the ultimate
testing ground of marital relationships.

Stigma

Although it is always difficult to assess the attitudes of a society to changing
family patterns, there is a tendency to measure such patterns against the
model of conventional marriage. The degree to which new patterns depart
from conventional marriage will determine society's tolerance and approval.
In addition, families which do not conform to this model or stereotype may
be seen as being to blame for their situation. Such stereotyping and negative
discrimination are the experience of members of other minority groups.

Some families and children are keenly aware of discrimination. This discrimination increases their sense of stigma, inequality and social isolation in the community. The following are examples:

1   The family parented by a widow or widower is most likely to be accorded the sympathy and understanding of society.
2   Separated or divorced one-parent families experience considerable disapproval and single mothers endure a low rating of tolerance and approval.
3   Society's attitudes towards the more unusual forms of family patterns (which give rise to new values of equality and self-expression, in contrast to the old values of self-denial, conformity and obligation) are more difficult to assess. There is as yet little awareness of the extent to which such alternative patterns are replacing the conventional.

Stigma as experienced by one-parent families

Many one-parent families are automatically stereotyped as economic risks. For this and other reasons, the one-parent family is often allocated poor housing accommodation in run-down areas. The divorced, separated, unmarried constitute a large number of the hidden homeless in society. They are possibly three times more likely to be homeless than two-parent families. The single mother may never have had her own home. The separated or divorced, even if they gain the matrimonial home, sometimes have to give it up because they cannot afford the mortgage payments.

Lone parents are also at a disadvantage in the job market. Some employers perceive them as unreliable and irregular workers. Lone parents are severely disadvantaged financially. The average income of one-parent families is only half that of two-parent families. National income policies take no account of the hidden extra costs in lone parenting associated with the loss of a handyman/woman in the home; with buying-in day care or child-minding facilities (assuming they are available); with restricted opportunity to take on overtime. Many such families face long-term poverty.

Sometimes professional assessment relating to one-parent families in difficulty is all-too-easily prejudiced by inappropriate labelling. For example, in one case a child's lack of progress at school was attributed to the lack of support at home from the lone parent. It was later discovered that the child was blind in one eye. In another case, one of a group of four involved in a joint offence was taken into care, while the others were recommended supervision. This youngster taken into care came from a one-parent family with quite significant extended family support. In fact, a very high percentage of children in long-term care come from one-parent families.

Some feeling of stigma by lone parents arises from social slights, often unintended, from within the local neighbourhood. Former married friends give up trying to fit one-parent friends into their social circle and may indeed see a single woman (or man) as a threat to their relationship. For a variety of reasons, other social outlets become inaccessible and much stress builds up from growing social isolation. Lack of money and difficulty in obtaining baby-sitters isolate single parents. If the stress results in anti-social behaviour by the children, the family often spirals downwards to become categorised locally as a 'problem' family.

Children in one-parent families feel 'different' to others. This is particularly so in cases of separation and divorce, where the non-custodial parent is still around somewhere in the picture, and relationships remain confused and unresolved for the children in the middle.

Lone parents often feel stigmatised and vulnerable because of dependence on public services such as social work. They guard their privacy wherever possible and so may deny themselves and their children support and understanding when it is needed. Lone parents may feel that if they are seen to be 'not coping' by social workers their child/children may be taken away. For example, if made aware of a family situation, a school teacher could perhaps respond more appropriately to a child's difficulty. However, both teacher and parent may feel sensitive about 'prying'.

One has to conclude from all this that some one-parent families must experience society as not only indifferent but also somewhat hostile.

Children in a single-parent family

There are three ways of becoming a single-parent family: through death of a parent; through the separation of parents; or through being an unmarried mother. About four fifths of single-parent families are headed by mothers. However, these families are not necessarily single-parent *households*; they often live with other relatives. Ten per cent of children under five, and 20 per cent of children under sixteen, do not live with their two natural parents. We do not know how many live with a parent and step-parent figure (i.e. married or cohabiting).

Parental separation, whether or not followed by divorce, brings practical and emotional changes to children. After separation, the children are likely to:

- live in poorer quality housing;
- have a lower standard of living;
- receive less parental care;
- receive more substitute care (especially the under fives);
- be latchkey children (especially schoolchildren);
- take on more domestic responsibilities;
- grow up a little faster.

Possibly:

- siblings will be divided:
- there will be several changes of home;

- there will be changes of principal carer (mother, father, grandparent, foster parent, etc.);
- there will be a step parent (married or cohabiting);
- there will be different surnames within the family;
- children will acquire step-siblings;
- children will acquire half-siblings (sharing one parent).

Many children take all these practical changes in their stride, but they may well lead to emotional problems, which are more upsetting and less tangible. As a result of the emotional effects of parental separation, children are likely to:

- be distressed, confused, angry;
- be concerned for their parent(s);
- lose touch with one parent;
- wish for parental reconciliation, even after parental violence.

Possibly children will:

- regress in behaviour (i.e. cling or bed-wet);
- need psychiatric help;
- lose touch with one set of grandparents;
- become delinquent;
- achieve lower educational standards;
- truant;
- become aggressive;
- be embarrassed, hiding the fact of their parents' separation.

Research also shows that the lower the social class, the higher is the rate of divorce. In some geographical areas, marital breakdown will be almost the norm, but can nevertheless be distressing to the children. In other areas, marital breakdown will be comparatively rare and bring a sense of isolation and stigma to children.

Some, perhaps many, children will experience several parental separations and several step-parental relationships. Some children will become confused about their own identity and about who are their own parents and siblings. Research using case study approaches with truants indicates that a very high proportion experience unhappy home lives with multiple problems within the 'family' home.

Alastair was eight when his mother took him and his older brothers and sister to live in his married sister's house, not far from their family home. He went to the same school as before. His mother always made excuses for him not seeing his father but – week by week – Alastair assumed that they could soon return to live with his father. Not until a year later, when his mother moved the family to a different district, did he realise that his parents had split up for good. Then he felt very angry with his father for not getting in touch with him, and with his mother for breaking up the family. Worse still, he resented the man they'd all gone to live with.

When Annie was 12 her mother left the family and lived alone in a rented room. Annie was thankful that her parents had stopped their endless arguments and she could sleep without fear of violence between them. But her mother came home every Saturday, and did the washing and cleaning and spent the evening chatting to her husband and children. So Annie was shocked to hear that her parents were getting a divorce. She'd always dreamed of the day when her mother would come back to live with the family.

When Susan was ten, she came to school one day and flung her arms round her teacher and sobbed her heart out. Her father had left the family and she didn't know where he'd gone. She thought she'd never see him again. For two months, she couldn't concentrate on any school work. Then one day her father was waiting for her at the school gate; he said Susan's mother had at last agreed that he could take Susan out every Saturday afternoon. Susan was very angry with her mother who had prevented her father from seeing her until then.

Fathers

Before looking at the position of fathers in single-parent families, it is helpful to clarify knowledge and ideas about fathers in general, as this knowledge and these ideas have a bearing on the role of fathers in single-parent families.

Traditionally, fathers have been much less involved than mothers in the upbringing of their children. There have been practical reasons for this. Fathers were, and still are, more likely to be in full-time employment, so they have less time with their children. In former eras there were also cultural pressures which reinforce differences between men and women, mothers and fathers: men don't wash nappies or push prams; dads teach their sons to play football but don't play dolls with their daughters; dads dole out punishments ('Wait till your dad gets home!') but aren't so likely to be sought out when children are hurt or sick or unhappy.

In present-day society things are changing, in particular more mothers are going out to work and families are moving away from relatives who used to help; so, for practical reasons, more men are involved in the housework and with the children. In addition, many men want to take more interest in their children right from the start. For example, more men are asking to be present at the birth, and they are enjoying being closer to their children.

Research shows that fathers are extremely important in the development of their children. For instance, they provide a male example which is especially important to a boy's development. There is also evidence that fathers can be as competent as mothers in nearly every aspect of bringing up children. Research also shows that the role of father varies considerably within society.

In some sections, there is much less overlap between the role of mothers and fathers. In others, fathers may be very involved with their children.

Fathers in single-parent families

Fathers who head single-parent families

- Some facts: approximately 20 per cent of single-parent families are headed by a man. Over 60 per cent of these men are separated or divorced. About one quarter are widowed. How do these men manage? What difficulties and challenges and satisfactions do they encounter?
- *To work or not to work* Approximately two thirds of these fathers work full-time, compared with one quarter of mothers who head single-parent families. As a result they are likely to be better off financially than single-parent mothers. Deciding whether to work or stay at home can be difficult. If they decide to stay at home, they can spend more time with their children, but they lose out financially and in terms of adult company, status and interest, which they gain through employment. Some sections of society disapprove of a man not working. The same people might disapprove of a mother who does work, believing 'a mother's place is in the home'. Men who decide to continue to work may have to change their hours to avoid certain shifts. They may need to make arrangements for the care of the children before and after school, during holidays and when children are sick. It's certainly not easy.
- *Housework* Most single fathers have to get used to doing more household tasks than before – washing, ironing, cooking, mending. Discovering that all your white shirts have turned pink in the wash, because you didn't realise you needed to sort out the coloured clothes, may be funny in some situations, but it can make you despair if you're feeling really down already. It's almost impossible for one parent to attempt to be both father and mother to their children. Fathers who try to do everything run the risk of breaking down.
- *Child care* Many fathers find some aspects of child care more difficult than others, e.g. looking after small babies, shopping for girls, talking personally with teenage daughters.
- *Social life* Single-parent fathers, like single-parent mothers, often feel isolated and find it difficult to get out and meet other adults. It can be especially awkward if they want to start going out with another woman – When do you tell the children? How? . . .

Fathers who no longer live with their children

Research into the effects of divorce on children indicates that many children soon lose contact with their fathers, that children quite often worry about their absent parent and that those children who do remain in good contact often make better progress than those with no contact or occasional, unpredictable contact.

Research into the effects of divorce on men shows that they are often devastated by their marriages breaking up. In losing his wife and children, a man often loses his home and the family friends. His whole sense of purpose and identity may be severely shaken. As a result many men suffer ill health after separation, find it difficult to concentrate at work and may then lose their jobs. Some resort to heavy drinking to drown their sorrows. There may be ways of helping men to come to terms with the new situation which will encourage them to find ways of continuing to be fathers to their children.

Being a part-time father or 'Saturday parent' is very different from living under the same roof as the children, but ways of keeping the relationship alive can be found and some fathers feel they have a better relationship with their children after separation.

Schools and one-parent families

Schools can help single parents and their families in a number of ways:

1 Schools should ensure that information on the child's home circumstances is regularly checked and updated in conjunction with the parents. Where the parents have separated, the school should have details of custody and access arrangements.
2 Where a child's parents have separated or, in the case of a single mother or father, where both parents are involved, schools can help by establishing procedures for keeping both parents informed of the child's progress and of school events. An exception to this might be where violence is involved, when the school should ensure that the mother's safety is protected. If possible make a comfortable room available for meetings with parents to discuss any problems or disagreements.
3 Schools should know their education authority's policy and discuss their own policies for dealing with problem situations, e.g. dealing with possible disputes between parents. It is helpful if children are consulted when disputes arise.
4 Children can be helped if they and their parents feel able to confide in their class teachers, and are assured that any information given will only be passed on with their consent.
5 Staff should be sensitive to significant changes in a child's behaviour or attitudes, e.g. worsening temper, aggression, lack of concentration, depression, loss of appetite, and truancy. Such changes may not relate to a change in home circumstances, but can do so.
6 Schools should, as far as possible, cater for a child's practical needs, e.g. trying to ensure that they eat well and are kept busy without creating pressure.

7   Schools can help to break down the stigma felt by many single parents and their children by ensuring that books portray a variety of family structures and that classroom exercises do not assume a 'clear' family, e.g. making Mother's Day or Father's Day cards may not be appropriate. (A booklist is available from the National Council for One-Parent Families.) It is also important to make sure that problems are not inappropriately related to the family situation.

8   Children from single-parent families should receive the same encouragement as everyone else. Research shows that once social and economic factors are allowed for, the family situation itself has very little effect on school performance. However, some children have found that teachers expect less of them because they come from single-parent families.

9   Schools could make information available on sources of financial assistance for single parents and on relevant organisations in the area who may be able to provide support and help.

10 It is important to be aware of the potential difficulties single parents may have in obtaining after-school care and baby-sitting and, where necessary, provide after-school care and crèches for parents' meetings. Organisations such as the Council for Single Parents can provide information on this. It is also helpful if schools can give adequate warning of early closure to assist working single parents.

11 Parental involvement should be encouraged. If appropriate this might include establishing a regular parents' group for mutual support. It is important that teachers talking to groups of parents do not assume a two-parent family. If at all possible, meetings should be held at times convenient to working parents and teachers.

12 All pupils can benefit from education on the growth and development of children so that they grow up with a realistic idea of what parenting involves.

13 Schools can play an important role in encouraging girls to pursue subjects which are likely to make them more financially independent when they grow up. The majority of single parents are women, many of whom struggle to support their families on the low wages paid in traditional women's occupations.

15 Education welfare service

The education welfare service plays a key role in preventing and combating truancy and school absenteeism. In recent years however, the service has suffered from the 'Cinderella' syndrome for the following reasons:

1 Since the Ralphs Report in 1973, which recommended that EWOs should have social work qualifications, an increasing number of LEAs have regarded them as social workers with specific responsibilities for schools.
2 There are few nationally agreed norms for education welfare officers. Apart from an enhanced professional status, EWOs generally receive better salaries in LEAs which designate them as social workers.
3 The precise roles practised by EWOs and/or education social workers tend to differ by LEA and by the school(s) for whom they are responsible. Fortunately, there is now much more strategic planning, and more written guidance and LEA policy documents than used to be the case only a few years ago.
4 There is no national charter on the role and contractual terms and conditions of service of the education welfare profession.
5 In recent years, with enhanced status and salaries in certain LEAs, the calibre of entrants to the education welfare service has been considerably improved. Similarly, professional development opportunities for staff have been considerably improved by the growth and recognition of training needs. Within the professional associations a wide range of professional advice is available. For example the National Association of Social Workers in Education provides excellent guidance notes on key professional issues. This can range from guidance on children who perform on stage in term time to good practice in intervention by EWOs, a detached analysis of Education Acts (e.g. The Education Act, 1996), understanding and implementing Education Supervision Orders, and prosecuting parents in the Magistrates Courts.
6 Despite these developments, the view persists that the education welfare service has been given too low a status within education *per se*, both by some LEAs and by some schools.

7   There is a growing opinion in some quarters that improving school atten-
     dance would be facilitated by the inclusion of bonus payments for
     improved results to school-based EWOs.
8   The focus of intervention for the education welfare service differs, of
     necessity, from pupil to pupil. The service has four core areas of work –
     school attendance, behaviour (including exclusions), child protection and
     juvenile employment. Another key problem confronting EWOs is their
     potential high caseloads. In an extreme case, for example, in Mid Glamorgan
     in 1986, one EWO was responsible for no fewer than five large compre-
     hensive schools and their feeder primaries, a total of some 7,500 pupils.
     Therefore, resource, personnel and training problems beset this service.

Promoting regular school attendance

In order to consider good practice, three different approaches to the organisation of the education welfare/social work service are now presented. These
are based on the Swansea, Bolton and Bury guidelines.

The Swansea model

The promotion of regular school attendance is a partnership between schools
and the education welfare service (EWS). The EWS aims to ensure that
every pupil within, for example, the City and County of Swansea benefits
from the educational opportunities provided in order to reach their maximum
potential. The service maintains that all pupils irrespective of race, culture,
religion, gender, sexual orientation or social background are of equal value.
It does however, recognise that some young people, e.g. with special educational needs and families who are socially disadvantaged, or looked after
children may, at times, require positive discrimination. The authority expects
schools:

- to develop a whole-school policy for promoting good attendance and
  following up unexplained absences;
- to make early referrals to the EWO when absence remains unexplained,
  providing as much relevant information as possible;
- to maintain registers in accordance with relevant legislation and guidance;
- to consider positive programmes to reward good levels of attendance or
  improvements in attendance;
- to welcome the return of pupils who have been absent, for whatever
  reason, and to provide them with curriculum support to catch up on work;
- to enable relevant staff to meet regularly with the EWO;
- to develop alternative programmes and strategies to meet the needs of
  disaffected pupils.

The education welfare service

- Assists teachers and parents to identify school attendance problems recognising that absenteeism can be for reasons which are complex and may indicate difficulties at home or school;
- investigates all referrals made by the school and provides a written report to the school within the agreed time limits;
- investigates, assesses and plans an intervention to improve attendance;
- involves and consults parents and pupils as much as possible;
- refers to other departments and agencies for advice and passes on a referral to another agency when appropriate;
- advises, supports and assists parents and the school to help the pupil overcome difficulties including offering support and counselling to victims of bullying;
- seeks Education Supervision Orders in appropriate circumstances and, in cases where parents continually condone the absence of a pupil, will prosecute the parent.

The EWS is working with schools that have the highest non-attendance rates to target additional manpower for fixed periods of time to endeavour to improve attendance. This involves working with a comprehensive school and the primary schools in its catchment area to undertake preventative work at an early stage to ensure school procedures are in place and to reinforce the value of good attendance with families and the community. The authority will be setting targets for improved attendance in its schools in line with the legislation.

Support through special initiatives

The City and County of Swansea are developing a number of multi-agency initiatives to promote positive behaviour. At present, the initiatives are tackling issues around exclusion, truancy and bullying. These are in the process of being further developed and the authority is looking closely at developing a multi-agency initiative to promote parental involvement in behavioural issues.

Promoting positive behaviour: primary project

This was originally developed as a GEST funded project as part of the Government's initiatives to reduce truancy and improve discipline. The aim of the project was to establish the facility of time-limited, intensive, in-school intervention initiatives which were directed at target groups of pupils who were presenting behavioural and management difficulties and who collectively were causing significant problems. The main objective was to establish an appropriate interagency team that provided a cohesive and holistic intensive intervention that considered the needs of pupils, teachers, parents and the whole school.

As a result of the evaluation of this project, it has been developed into a more long-term initiative for use in schools to support the collective difficulties of identified groups of pupils. The schools selected for the project will meet one or more of the following criteria:

- headteacher request for group and whole school support;
- multiple stage 3 referrals;
- identification of behavioural needs as a key issue following monitoring or inspection;
- secondary schools identified through the interagency working group on school exclusions and disruptive pupils.

The strategies used to achieve the objective are:

- in-school support of target groups to help them develop their self-management skills;
- specialist teacher support of individual pupils within the target groups, to facilitate the addressing of personal, emotional and behavioural issues;
- training of staff by teacher adviser to raise awareness of issues involved in effective behavioural management.

Use of the education welfare service

The education welfare officer has a very specific role in supporting a school to maintain high levels of attendance. He/she should never be seen as someone who acts instead of the school or when all of the school's efforts have been exhausted. The education welfare officer can only act effectively if he/she acts in partnership with the school supportive of the school's own efforts.

- Meetings with year heads, form tutors and other pastoral staff need to be on a regular basis, with an agreed structure and a set agenda. Full use needs to be made of consultation visits.
- Referral systems need to be jointly agreed.
- Tasks and responsibilities must be clearly defined and agreed upon.
- Feedback, monitoring and review must be regular and systematic.
- Referrals to other agencies where appropriate should be jointly agreed.
- The education welfare officer needs to be known within the school with, if possible, his/her own room and, certainly, his/her own pigeon hole. He/she could also be involved in staff meetings, INSET days, etc. It may be helpful to include the education welfare officer's name and telephone number in the school brochure.

The education social worker

Profile

While being a part of the school pastoral system, the ESW should maintain a separate identity as the representative of the LEA. Pupils and parents as well as the school, must have confidence that in a dispute the ESW can be relied upon to give totally unbiased counsel and advice. The ESW should be known to all members of school staff, pupils and governors who should all be made aware of how to contact the ESW. It must, however, be remembered that individual pupils should not be discussed in governors' meetings, since governors will be drawn from the local community, parents and school ancillary staff. The ESW may also be known in the community which is served by the school.

It is essential that the ESW knows the policy and ethos of the school, as it affects the aims, objectives, curriculum, homework, discipline, etc. in order to explain difficulties and misunderstandings to pupils and parents. The ESW will understand other forms of education like off-site provision, including home tuition and 'education otherwise', and will be able to advise parents about special educational problems, making a referral for assessment if appropriate. A knowledge of, and access to, other agencies both voluntary and statutory, whose specialisms may be required is also necessary to the ESW.

The ESW needs to have a knowledge of the rights, responsibilities and duties of parents, schools and the LEA, and needs to keep up to date with developments in legislation.

There also needs to be a recognised referral procedure which enables staff with designated responsibility for attendance to meet regularly – probably weekly – with the ESW. These referral meetings should be a high priority appointment, and everyone should make every effort to attend.

Referrals to the ESW should be made in a formalised manner, giving as much relevant detail as possible. In turn, the ESW should log all contacts and make notes which can be filed into a case history, this is essential if a matter is brought before the courts, and highly desirable if the case is referred to another professional agency.

There is evidence to suggest that the ESW can make an effective contribution to PSE lessons, and a yearly or termly talk particularly to Year 7 is useful. The importance of attendance and punctuality can be stressed, and the LEA's perspective explained. The ESW can also explain his/her role and attendance issues to student and probationary teachers. Having the ESW present at parents evenings, particularly for those new parents, is helpful.

The courts

Magistrates Court

Parents or carers who fail in their duty to ensure the regular attendance of their children at school should be dealt with by the Court sooner rather than later. The LEA through the education social work Service have a policy and procedures for dealing with prosecutions.

Having identified parents who are not fulfilling their duties in ensuring school attendance the ESWs should write formally, quoting Section 199 of the 1993 Education Act. If there is no improvement the parents should be invited, with the child(ren), to a formal interview with a senior officer of the department. School governors and/or elected members of the education committee could be involved at this point.

The attendance should then be monitored for a finite period, say one half term, and if there is still no improvement, proceedings should be initiated without delay. The decision, concerning which court, being made by a review panel comprising ESW, senior ESW and legal adviser.

Other LEA services

Educational psychologists

Sometimes children will develop attendance problems because of anxiety. This can arise from various sources, the most important of which may not be obvious and may be nothing to do with school at all. If efforts to sort out problems that the child reports (e.g. bullying, not liking games, etc.) have no effect it will be helpful to discuss with parents and ESW the involvement of the psychological service.

This is the best first step that could lead to other services (e.g. home tuition, child and family service) becoming involved.

Attendance is one of the indicators of the success of a school. Everything that goes on in school influences children's motivation to attend and succeed. Seeing attendance in this broader way is very important. Schools may find advice from inspectorate, advisory and support services, psychologists and other officers of the LEA relevant to concerns highlighted by poor attendance.

Good attendance is far more likely if children are motivated to attend. The best motivation comes from feelings of individual success and purpose and from being part of an energetic and successful school.

Operational focus of education welfare service: the Bury model

This section provides a possible outline of operational objectives for the education welfare service within an LEA and is based on the Bury guidelines. The operation focus of education welfare officers and education social workers differs in reality from LEA to LEA.

Pupil attendance

To improve and maintain regular attendance for all pupils the service will:

(a) maintain regular visits to schools to facilitate referrals and the exchange of information regarding individual pupils;
(b) devise and implement strategies aimed at improving attendance and punctuality;
(c) enable pupils to acquire greater self-esteem and self-confidence;
(d) facilitate effective partnerships between parents and schools;
(e) decide on the prosecution of parents under Section 444 of the Education Act 1996 or seeking an Education Supervision Order under section 1 of the Children Act 1989.

Education Supervision Orders

To advise, assist and befriend children and young people who are, or may become, the subject of an Education Supervision Order the service will:

(a) develop and apply skills at supervising young people on voluntary or statutory orders;
(b) encourage young people to take advantage of the educational opportunities available to them.

Special educational needs

To assist the local education authority in carrying out its responsibilities in respect of children who may have special educational needs the service will:

(a) be aware of the requirements of relevant legislation together with the local authorities policy and practice;
(b) contribute to the assessment process;
(c) participate in the SEN stage 3 allocations panel and respond to allocated cases as appropriate;
(d) liaise with and support parents and children throughout the assessment process and beyond, as required.
(e) liaise with out of borough special schools regarding individual ongoing cases where the EWO is the key worker.

Bullying

To ensure adequate advice and support is available to parents and schools on bullying issues the service will:

(a) provide advice and guidance to schools regarding bullying policies and their implementation;
(b) offer counselling support to victims of bullying whenever requested;
(c) give advice to pupils and parents on how to deal with bullying and provide a positive link between school and home;

(d) give advice to pupils who perpetrate bullying in order to reduce the incidence of it, providing group work sessions where required.

Exclusions from school

The service provides a number of functions in relation to exclusions from school, ensuring that advice, guidance and support is available to governors, schools, parents and pupils. The service will:

(a) be responsible for ensuring that statutory legislation regarding exclusions is complied with;
(b) monitor exclusions and prepare an annual report on exclusions for consideration by education committee;
(c) act as a source of advice to both schools and parents regarding exclusion legislation and local procedures;
(d) act on behalf of the Borough Education Officer, as 'clerk to the governors' at governors' disciplinary sub-committees in all county and aided schools that are designated within the scheme;
(e) ensure that wherever possible there is a minimum of disruption to a pupil's education and that they continue to receive appropriate educational provision;
(f) provide advice and guidance to parents of permanently excluded pupils in order to assist them to obtain a place in another school or to ensure alternative, appropriate educational provision.

Pupil learning centre

In order to assist the pupil learning centre (PLC) to meet its objectives the service will:

(a) provide ongoing support to young people who are registered with the PLC;
(b) be responsible for the referral of young people to the alternative provision project for admission;
(c) provide ongoing support to individual young people on the alternative provision project whose attendance and/or behaviour continues to present problems.

Child protection – ACPC

The service will participate in the interagency protection of children from abuse and will:

(a) represent the Education Service on the local Area Child Protection Committee (ACPC);
(b) be aware of the APCP's procedures and the specific responsibilities of the education welfare service;

(c) develop LEA policies in relation to child protection within the education service;

(d) facilitate training and provide support to staff of schools with regard to their role within the ACPC procedures;

(e) identify and monitor individual pupils at risk, within the guidelines of the procedures and the decisions of any multi-disciplinary case conference;

(f) participate in case conferences and/or core groups as required.

Welfare benefits

In order to offer advice and guidance on the range of welfare benefits available to clients the service will:

(a) be familiar with current benefits available to families;

(b) assist in the application of benefits where this would be helpful.

Juvenile employment

To ensure that pupils are protected from the dangers of illegal employment the service will:

(a) be responsible for developing the LEA's policy and good practice in relation to juvenile employment;

(b) give advice to parents, pupils and employers regarding the appropriate legislation governing juvenile employment and entertainment licences;

(c) develop a monitoring system for juvenile employment to ensure that young people within the authority are not exploited and that their employment does not adversely affect their attendance, punctuality or attainment at school;

(d) maintain a register of employers and young people issued with work permits.

Prevention and support services

To promote and/or support multi-disciplinary preventative and support services within the community the service will:

(a) support community projects for families and young people;

(b) support initiatives which encourage families to acquire greater self confidence, reliance and self-esteem, thus improving their quality of life;

(c) be involved in activities which promote educational achievement and social well-being among young people;

(d) promote inter-disciplinary approaches involving other services and agencies for the benefit of children, young people and families;

(e) be aware of, and participate in, initiatives with regard to drug, alcohol and solvent abuse.

Individual support

To ensure that appropriate services are available to pupils who, while having regular attendance at school, have personal, social or relationship problems which are adversely affecting their educational progress, the service will:

(a) offer confidential counselling support to pupils where necessary;
(b) act as advocate for pupils in order to improve their educational opportunities;
(c) enable pupils to benefit from/access other services provided within the community.

Juvenile justice

To be involved in the arrangements for the juvenile justice diversionary panel the service will:

(a) co-ordinate the use of information from the education authority in order that appropriate decisions can be made;
(b) enable young people in the early stages of criminal and anti-social activity to access remedial and preventative services in an endeavour to avoid long-term problems.

Education otherwise

To ensure that pupils educated 'other than at school' are educated appropriately the service will:

(a) monitor children and young people who are educated 'other than at school';
(b) participate in the 'Education Otherwise' co-ordinators' group who ensure access to, and participation in, education for pupils outside mainstream with the exception of those who do so with parental choice;
(c) liaise with the authority's advisory service to ensure that an acceptable curriculum, that meets the needs of the child or young person, is developed and implemented by parents who choose to educate their children 'other than at school'.

Travellers' families

In order to ensure that the educational needs of travellers' children are met the service will:

(a) visit all new encampments and provide advice and support to travellers' families in obtaining appropriate educational provision;

(b) provide advice and support to the designated teacher for traveller children in the Authority;

(c) ensure that travellers' families comply with the attendance requirements laid down within the 1996 Education Act.

Educational welfare service school visits – in Bury

Aim

To provide a framework for education welfare officers and schools to develop working arrangements in order that the needs of service users are met insofar as is practicable within the exigencies of the service.

1 Agreement will be made between the link education welfare officer and individual schools with regard to the frequency of visits to be made to establishments. School visiting arrangements will be made on a needs-led basis. High schools will receive a minimum of a weekly visit from their link education welfare officer. Primary schools will receive weekly, fortnightly or three-weekly visits depending on their individual requirements.

2 Meetings between the school's link education welfare officer and designated members of the school staff should be timetabled.

3 The link education welfare officer and school staff should endeavour to ensure that they meet at the agreed time to avoid unnecessary wastage of time.

4 In order to maximise the effectiveness of the school's pastoral system and education welfare service involvement the meetings should be focused on specific issues and individual pupils.

5 Regular meetings should not include time for normal register checks.

6 Education welfare officers will, insofar as is possible, attend appropriate meetings in schools in addition to their weekly timetabled visit. This may include pastoral meetings, parents' evenings, case reviews, etc.

7 Senior officers in the education welfare service will make arrangements for the inspection of registers to ensure that schools and the education welfare service are responding appropriately to legislation.

Exclusions from school

Aims

- to ensure continuity of educational provision for pupils excluded from school;
- to provide advice and support to parents and pupils in cases of exclusion;
- to monitor exclusions and liaise with other agencies.

1 Schools should consider referral to the EWS or other support services in cases where the pupil is depicting behavioural problems in order to avoid

exclusion. Schools should send a copy of the parental exclusion letter to the principal education welfare officer.

2   The authority's policy and procedure on exclusion should be followed.

3   In cases of permanent exclusion the school link education welfare officer will visit the home within three working days of receiving notification of the exclusion from school. The education welfare officer will provide advice and support to the parent and pupil in relation to the exclusion procedures.

4   Parents should be made aware of their rights to make representations to the governors against both permanent exclusion, and fixed-term exclusion.

5   The link education welfare officer should ensure that the school comply with their legal requirement to provide education for the pupil during the period of exclusion or until the appeals procedures have been exhausted.

6   In cases where a permanent exclusion is upheld by the governing body, the LEA (where it has the power), or an independent appeal (where parents exercise their rights), the link education welfare officer should advise and assist the parent in obtaining an alternative placement.

School attendance rationale

In order to provide a common format for schools and education welfare officers to adopt for dealing with issues relating to school attendance the following good practice should be followed:

1   Schools have the primary responsibility for school issues and for initial efforts to resolve them at an early stage.

2   There is a legal duty on schools to maintain accurate school registers and to decide whether absences are authorised or not.

3   Governing bodies are under a statutory duty to publish statistics annually relating to authorised and unauthorised absences.

4   Schools should consider referral to the education welfare service when a pupil has an unexplained block absence of more than two weeks, where an irregular pattern of attendance has emerged over several weeks, or where attendance after a specified period of time is less than 85 per cent.

5   Where truancy is suspected (i.e. absent without parental knowledge or consent) it may be appropriate to inform the education welfare service as soon as is practicable.

6   Prior to referral, schools should be able to demonstrate their active involvement in attempting to resolve the problem.

7   Once a referral has been made, the education welfare service is responsible for its management of the case, any intervention strategies and decisions relating to it. The service works in partnership with schools, parents and pupils; however any action it takes is independent and on behalf of the local authority.

8 Following referral to the education welfare service, regular discussions between the link education welfare officer and the school will take place in order to update information and plan intervention strategies.

9 There will be an annual meeting between the designated senior education welfare officer, the school's headteacher and the link education welfare officer to discuss relevant issues and to set realistic attendance targets for the following academic year.

The Bolton model: towards good practice

Bolton education social work service

The following services are offered to Bolton schools:

(a) The promotion of regular and punctual school attendance

The school education social worker will make regular and random inspections of class registers. This helps to identify worrying attendance patterns either of an individual pupil or on a class basis such as:

- frequent/regular medical absence;
- odd days absence each week;
- days which correspond with brothers or sisters or other pupils;
- same day absences each week;
- pupils taking 'long weekends' – Fridays/Mondays;
- holidays in term time;
- regular lateness.

(b) Education social work referral meetings

Every school has a named education social worker who will visit the school on a regular basis as outlined in the service–school partnership agreement. The education social worker will meet with nominated pastoral staff or other appropriate person in the school, on a regular, agreed basis. The meeting will cover:

- an examination of school registers;
- the targeting of pupils who are experiencing patterns of irregular attendance;
- an agreed plan of action which will be taken by the school and/or the education social worker;
- the exchange of relevant information in relation to work undertaken by the education social worker and/or the school;
- develop good working practice for the school and the education social worker and
- provide or advise the school on strategies for tackling non-attendance.

(c) Casework

Education social workers will usually work with children whose absences have reached an unacceptable level and where other strategies have failed to bring about an improved level of attendance. Education social workers may also work with children who are experiencing difficulties at home or in school which may result in an escalation or development of non-attendance.

When such a referral has been agreed with the school, the education social worker will undertake a variety of interventions, appropriate to the situation. These may include:

- home visits to assess the situation with the family and to agree a way forward;
- arranging and facilitating meetings between parents, children and teaching staff;
- providing individual support to pupils and parents either in school or elsewhere, and
- mobilising and enabling pupils and parents to access appropriate support from other agencies and services.

(d) Legal proceedings

If parents fail to ensure the regular attendance of their children, the LEA has the power to prosecute them or to seek an Education Supervision Order. Whether to prosecute and the precise point at which that happens, are matters for judgement in the light of each particular case and the best approach to improving the pupil's attendance. In some instances prosecution will be as a last resort, in others it may be instigated much earlier as part of a planned programme of intervention.

As a matter of course, education social workers in Bolton will review, with their team manager, every case within 3 months of initial referral and at 3-monthly intervals thereafter. They will, at each review, consider whether or not legal proceedings are appropriate. The decision to prosecute, or not, rests with the ESW and their team manager. If it is considered inappropriate to prosecute, the reasons for the decision will be recorded in the case file and the relevant school informed.

This does not, however, preclude earlier prosecution if such action is deemed appropriate.

(e) OFSTED

All schools are subject to inspections by OFSTED. Part of the inspection will concentrate on attendance issues. The ESW will:

- offer advice on attendance issues pre and post inspection;

- be available for interview by the inspectors and
- be involved in the 'action plan' where attendance is identified as a cause for concern.

(f) Child protection awareness

Each school should have a designated member of staff who is trained to deal with child protection issues. Further information on whole-school training or training for specific staff can be obtained from the principal education social worker.

(g) Approaches to dealing with bullying

All forms of bullying can have an adverse effect on pupils, which in turn can lead to attendance difficulties. All schools should have a clear policy on tackling bullying which is maintained and updated as necessary.

Schools may therefore, wish to involve their ESW with the victim and/or perpetrator and their respective families. In addition, schools in Bolton may wish to involve outside agencies to assist them to develop and implement anti-bullying policies.

(h) Advice on legal requirements

The key legal requirements are stated as a separate chapter in this document. In particular schools need to implement the Education (Pupil Registration) Regulations 1995 (as amended). Topics covered include:

- marking registers;
- defining absence;
- authorised/unauthorised absence.

(i) The provision of INSET

The education social work service in Bolton will offer or assist with INSET sessions on a range of subjects related to the attendance and welfare of pupils and child protection procedures.

(j) Pupils who cannot be traced

The education social work service in Bolton will follow up all pupils who have been absent from school for more than four weeks and who the school believe may have left the area. The Education (Pupil Registration) Regulations 1995 (as amended) allow for a pupil's name to be removed from a school's roll after 4 weeks' continuous absence provided that the school *and* the LEA have made 'reasonable enquiries' to locate the pupil.

While those enquiries are being carried out the absence must be *unauthorised* and schools must not remove a pupil from their admission register until advised to do so by their ESW. Once such permission has been given, the child's name may be removed with effect from the first Friday of the absence. This will mean that a school will not be 'penalised' for carrying a large amount of unauthorised absence.

(k) Child employment

Bolton Council has passed bye-laws that regulate the employment of school-age children. The education social work service administers their implementation, and provides a licence for children to work during the permitted hours. A copy of the bye-laws may be obtained from the principal education social worker.

(l) Travelling families

Bolton's education social work service provides traveller families with guidance, support and advice when their child's school attendance is adversely affected by the family's mobile way of life. The education social worker's prime responsibilities are to secure the admission of traveller children to school, and to maintain and support their regular attendance.

Responsibilities of the local education authority

Local education authorities have a statutory duty to ensure children who are registered at school attend regularly. In Bolton, the LEA fulfils this requirement through the education social work service, whose primary responsibility is to ensure the regular and punctual attendance of all pupils. Each school in Bolton is allocated a named education social worker who will work in close partnership with them. The education social work service will provide all schools with a service–school partnership agreement.

Service–school partnership agreement

This agreement will:

- outline the level of service that the school can expect to receive from their ESW during the academic year;
- identify the tasks that an ESW can undertake;
- identify agreed targets for raising levels of attendance;
- include a quality assurance statement;
- specify a complaints procedure; and
- be reviewed annually.

There are a range of circumstances which can adversely affect a pupil's continuing school attendance, for example:

- behaviour problems in school;
- exclusions;
- special educational needs;
- child protection;
- drugs and substance misuse; and
- other problems, including domestic violence.

Bolton's education social work service is frequently the first point of contact for a family in crisis. They are ideally placed to support the child and the family by facilitating a return to school or a transfer to a new school, or to undertake an assessment of the wider needs of the family and to act as a channel for reference to other specialist services or agencies.

Governors

Attendance has always been a matter of concern to school governors. The governing body is required by legislation to see that registers are kept accurately. The headteacher may wish to submit reports to the governing body on various aspects of pupil attendance. Governors are also required to publish an annual report for parents which will include a reference to the school's attendance figures.

Governors have an increasingly valuable role to play in establishing the importance of school attendance matters. They could:

(a) look at the statistics and trends;
(b) request information on the progress of children with poor attendance, and
(c) support positive measures taken to improve attendance.

Governing bodies may wish to consider appointing a governor with specific responsibilities for school attendance matters.

Punctuality

Schools need to take active steps to ensure the punctuality of pupils. Lateness should be monitored and followed up swiftly.

To enable this to happen, school policies and brochures should state clearly the time at which each school session begins and finishes, including the time at which registers open and close. Registers may be kept open for a maximum of 30 minutes after the end of the registration period. Schools are free to set a lower time limit if they so wish.

In Bolton schools the following procedures apply:

- if a pupil arrives late and the register is still open they should be marked as 'late' but counted as present for that session;
- if a pupil arrives after the register has closed and provides a satisfactory explanation, they should be marked as 'authorised absent' for that session;
- if a pupil arrives after the register has closed and fails to provide a satisfactory explanation, they should be marked as 'unauthorised absent' for that session;
- if a pupil arrives late having missed registration, their presence on site should be noted in a book in the school office for purposes of emergency evaluation.
- If a pupil arrives late for school on a regular basis, this may be grounds for prosecution of the parents. Such circumstances should be referred to a school's ESW.

Authorising absence

Only the school can authorise an absence. The fact that a parent has provided a note or other explanation (telephone call or personal contact) in relation to a particular absence does not, of itself, oblige the school to accept the explanation offered as a valid reason for absence. If, after further investigation, doubt remains about the explanation offered, or when no explanation is forthcoming at all, the absence should be treated as unauthorised.

Schools should communicate to parents their policies with regard to the notification and categorisation of absence. Some parents, such as those whose first language is not English, may experience difficulty in providing notes. In such cases schools should seek to make alternative arrangements, for example, through a neighbour, brothers or sisters or a community worker.

Schools are encouraged to keep all absence notes for at least a term.

Bolton's procedure

Absence should be *authorised* if:

- the pupil is absent with leave (defined as 'leave granted by any person authorised to do so by the governing body or proprietor of the school');
- the pupil is ill or prevented from attending by an unavoidable cause;
- the absence occurs on a day exclusively set aside for religious observance by the religious body to which the pupil's parent belongs;
- the school at which the pupil is registered is not within walking distance of their home; and no suitable arrangements have been made by the Local Education Authority for any of the following:
  (a)   the pupil's transport to and from school;
  (b)   boarding accommodation for the pupil at or near the school;
  (c)   enabling the pupil to become a registered pupil at a school nearer to their home.

- the pupil is the child of traveller parents who temporarily leave the area giving reasonable indication of their intention to return;
- there is a family bereavement;
- the pupil has a local authority licence to take part in a public performance and the school has given leave of absence;
- the pupil is attending an interview with either a prospective employer or in connection with an application for a place at an institute of further or higher education or for a place at another school;
- the pupil is involved in an exceptional special occasion, e.g. a family wedding. In authorising such absences the individual circumstances of the particular case and the pupil's overall pattern of attendance should be considered;
- leave of absence is granted by the school for a family holiday of no more than 10 school days (or in 'exceptional circumstances' for more than 10 school days). Parents should be reminded that they cannot expect, as of right, that the school will agree to a family holiday during term time.

Absence should be *unauthorised* if:

- no explanation is forthcoming from the parent;
- the school is dissatisfied with the explanation;
- the pupil is staying at home to mind the house or to look after siblings (the DfEE guidance suggests that absence in such cases should only be granted in exceptional circumstances);
- the pupil is absent for unexceptional special occasions, e.g. the pupil's birthday;
- the pupil is away from school on a family holiday for a period of time longer than that negotiated with the school;
- the pupil is on a family holiday without permission or if the parents have failed to apply for permission in advance of the holiday and instead seek retrospective approval on their return.

Further advice on the authorisation of absence can be obtained from a school's ESW or from the DfEE (1988a) publication *School Attendance and the Role of the Education Welfare Service*.

Family holidays and extended trips overseas during term-time

Guidance on family holidays and extended trips overseas during term-time is set out in the section on authorising absence. Where there are difficulties please refer to your school education social worker. Schools should:

- regularly communicate to parents their policies regarding term-time holidays;

- actively discourage parents from arranging term-time holidays;
- remind parents that they cannot expect leave of absence for the purpose of holiday to be granted as of right (schools do have a discretionary power to grant up to 10 school days in any school year);
- grant more than 10 days only in 'exceptional circumstances'.

Responsibilities within schools

Schools need to be alert to changes in attendance pattern. Any absence from school disrupts the continuity of learning and may lead to disaffection. It is important that patterns of regular attendance are established in primary schools. These schools should therefore pay particular attention to those pupils whose attendance is irregular and involve their education social worker at an early stage.

Schools should:

- ensure all registers are completed promptly and accurately in line with Government and LEA guidelines;
- respond promptly to any issues that may lead to irregular school attendance;
- produce whole-school attendance policies; this policy should be communicated clearly to all parents and be applied consistently;
- support parents in promoting the regular and punctual attendance of their children;
- support parents who have difficulty understanding written and in some cases verbal communication;
- have suitable strategies in place for parents who are reluctant to discuss attendance issues;
- not exclude pupils for poor or non-attendance;
- ensure all attendance registers are available for inspection on request of the education social worker; and
- only remove a child's name from the register in accordance with the legal criteria.

Attendance registers

Each year Bolton LEA provides its schools, on request, with attendance registers for use by class/form tutors. The front of each register contains guidance on the marking of the register. The register also contains the symbols suggested by the LEA for the consistent categorisation of absences. These are as follows:

(a) If pupil is present at time of registration   =   AM\   \PM

(b) If pupil is still absent after registration   =   Î
      (NB Absence *unauthorised*)

(c) i If pupil arrives after the register closes   =   —
      ii If pupil arrives after the registration period   =   Ø

(d) If pupil is absent due to sickness (includes time in
      hospital, unless covered by (e) below)   =   TM

(e) If pupil is attending an approved education activity   =   U

(f) If pupil is absent for dental or medical treatment
      (other than in-patient)   =   T

(g) If pupil is granted leave of absence for parental
      annual holiday or religious festival   =   ¤

(h) If pupil is excluded   =   E

(i) If pupil, marked present, is subsequently found to
      have absconded   =   *

(j) If pupil is on educational visit or work experience
      (i.e. curricular activity)   =   C

(k) If pupil is attending interview with prospective
      employer or establishment of further or higher
      education   =   I

(l) If pupil is not in school because the school is closed   =   IA

(m) If none of these symbols apply, a circle of a
      contrasting colour should be made within the
      absence circle (NB This indication of unauthorised
      absence is not required for those who are not of
      compulsory school age)   =   O

1 For the purposes of *statistical* collation, the following may be counted as
   PRESENT:

   \ \   T   C   Ø   I

2 However, for *legal enforcement* purposes, the following should be counted
   as ABSENT:

   —   *

3 The following should be counted as AUTHORISED ABSENCE:

   ¤   E   TM

4 The following should be counted as UNAUTHORISED ABSENCE:

   O

5 The following should be counted as neither present nor absent:

   U   IA

Working with other agencies

Bolton's education social work service and all schools within the borough are an integral part of the wider multi-agency system that operates to protect children from all forms of abuse, harm or exploitation. It is important to understand that this system extends to all 'children in need' and not just to those in need of protection.

In Bolton, education social workers will, as a matter of course, undertake an assessment of the wider needs of children and families, beyond those of basic non-attendance at school. Education social workers cannot, however, replace colleagues from social services and other agencies in all matters concerning families. It is entirely appropriate for ESWs to refer on to colleagues, if their assessment would indicate such a course of action is necessary.

Definition of a 'child in need'

A child is deemed to be in need as defined under The Children Act 1989 if:

- they are unlikely to achieve or maintain, or to have the opportunity of achieving or maintaining a reasonable standard of health or development without the provision of services;
- their health or development is likely to be significantly impaired, or further impaired, without the provision of such services;
- if they are disabled.

All staff that have contact with children and families undertake some assessment of their needs at some time or other. Where there are specific concerns about a child or their family, staff should:

- assess the extent of need;
- assess the level of vulnerability;
- assess which needs must take priority;
- access the most appropriate, least intrusive services to meet those needs.

Improving school attendance

Guidelines on the education welfare/social work service from different LEAs throughout the UK suggest that the most common approaches to combating non-attendance and improving school attendance rates are those listed below. Schools could therefore consider some or all of the following strategies:

- a whole-school approach to the development and implementation of the school attendance policy:
- a reward system for good attendance;
- suggestions about flexibility in teaching styles;

- advice for staff on adopting a consistent approach in dealing with absence and lateness;
- ways of developing clear lines of communication with outside agencies, e.g. social services, police;
- telephone call to parents on first day of absence followed by a letter, after 3 days continuous absence;
- clear guidelines for effective primary–secondary liaison;
- primary schools may wish to adapt Brandwood CP's 'Welcome Booklet';
- methods of ensuring that the whole policy is monitored, updated and evaluated at regular intervals;
- encouragement to staff – including ancillary and administrative staff – to see attendance as part of their responsibilities. It is, however, advisable to have a key, named senior member of staff with overall responsibility;
- clear advice to parents that it is school staff, and not parents, who may authorise an absence;
- clear guidance to staff to discourage parents from taking holidays in term time;
- methods of addressing all issues, such as bullying, which in turn may lead to non-attendance;
- include in each pupil's school report to parents any information relating to attendance and the number of unauthorised and authorised absences accrued during the school year. Schools may wish to comment on levels of authorised absence where this is considered to be a cause for concern;
- information to the governing body's annual report relating to levels of absence, both authorised and unauthorised.

A simple comparison between the policy statements of Swansea, Bury and Bolton reveals the disparity in practice within schools and between LEAs. Another major review of the education welfare service is long overdue. Once the EWO service is fully professionalised and operates within clear national guidelines with similar practice between LEAs and schools, it will start to function more effectively, for the ultimate benefit of those who need it most – pupils at risk.

16 Epilogue

This book has shown the extent of truancy, outlined its causes and provided numerous examples of the recent positive and constructive initiatives that are taking place within schools and LEAs to prevent and combat a phenomenon which harms the progress of the young and blights adult life. In fact, since the election of the Labour Government in 1997, there are currently more initiatives being followed to combat truancy than ever before. However, the fight against truancy has only just started and there is a very long way to go. Like the Government, schools, too, are currently striving hard to reduce their rates of truancy and other forms of non-attendance.

There is plenty of incentive for them to do so. Schools with good OFSTED reports and little absenteeism can be absented from the next round of inspections. A second tier of schools that receive good to moderate reports in the first or second round of inspections may be given 'a lighter touch' in the planning for their next OFSTED: the visiting team focusing solely on areas of concern in a school's previous report and their subsequent action plan on such issues as attendance. However, those schools who are judged to be under-performing, or who have attendance rates below 90 per cent, often with related behavioural difficulties, can now be subject to even greater scrutiny by OFSTED. Moreover, schools with an average daily attendance of less than 90 per cent *have* to be both inspected and evaluated by OFSTED especially on the progress which they are making to improve attendance in the school.

The Government announced in 1999 some modifications to the National Curriculum to enable failing and/or less able pupils, who may be truants, to receive more guidance on their special educational needs. This might include more help with literacy and numeracy, perhaps undertaken during a school's PSE programmes. Alternatively, it might be more help with a limited number of subjects or spending more time on work placement schemes or in vocational educational projects, perhaps in the local FE college.

Schools have started to meet the Government's national targets of reducing truancy by a third by the year 2002. This is not an easy task. For a school with an 80 per cent attendance rate, it means an improvement of approximately 7 per cent within four years. For a school with a 94 per cent attendance rate, it means an improvement of 2 per cent. In certain circumstances, how schools meet these targets could ultimately make or break them.

For schools which are already deemed to be failing, or are in special measures, or sailing close to the wire, all recent evidence suggests that it is attendance, behaviour and exclusions which are often the three key issues from the perspective of OFSTED. Unless ineffective schools can turn themselves round quickly, all the signs are that the Government will turn to others to help them to do so.

It is for all these reasons that this text has been written. Hopefully, it will help schools and teachers to understand the complex issues surrounding truancy and their own truants better. It may help to provide schools with ideas and solutions which can be used by them to combat truancy and other forms of non-attendance.

Until recently, teachers have been fighting an uphill battle against truancy. Truancy is still perceived by the media and general public to be on the increase, but no one really knows whether this is the case. Certainly, more specific lesson absence takes place now than ever before. It also remains true that most teachers have received little or no training in how to combat truancy or how to improve attendance policies within schools. *Truancy and Schools* has endeavoured to redress this balance. At the same time, my companion pack on *Tackling Truancy in Schools*, which is being published simultaneously by Routledge, should also help teachers and schools in this regard. These two texts will be followed shortly by a third volume on *The Challenge of Truancy*. It is to be hoped that from a reading and understanding of these books, teachers and schools will start to fight back. With the Government's support, teachers have a better chance of being successful than ever before.

If we can reduce the present levels of truancy, we will also reduce much human suffering amongst youngsters and adults in their later lives. We will also reduce the dependence of some individuals on the State which, in turn, should reduce costs to the Exchequer. For the sake of our at-risk pupils, their families, teachers and our schools, we need to make sure we are doing everything possible to combat and prevent truancy from becoming even more deeply rooted. It is a fight which our schools and our teachers must win. Hopefully, this book will play a small part in the process.

Bibliography

Audit Commission (1996) *Misspent Youth*, London: The Audit Commission.

Blythe, E. and Milner, J. (eds) (1999) *Improving School Attendance*, London: Routledge.

Bolton Metropolitan (1998) *School Attendance Matters*, Bolton: Education and Arts Department, Bolton, Metro LEA.

Business Education Partnership (1996) *Aiming Higher Booklet*, Humberside: Humberside Careers Service.

Cabinet Office Social Exclusion Unit (1998) *Truancy and School Exclusion Report*, London: Cabinet Office.

Carlen, P., Gleeson, D. and Wardhaugh, J. (1992) *Truancy: The Politics of Compulsory Schooling*, Buckingham: Open University Press.

DfEE (1998a) *School Attendance and the Role of the Education Welfare Service*, London: DfEE.

DfEE (1998b) *Numeracy Matters: Report of the Numeracy Task Force*, London: DfEE.

Kinder, K. and Wilkin, A. (1998) *Where Parents Lay the Blame for Truancy*, Report prepared for NFER, Windsor: NFER News.

Lawrence Report (1999) *Report by the Police Complaints Authority on the Investigation of a Complaint against the Metropolitan Police Service by Mr N. and Mrs D. Lawrence*, Command Paper CM3822, London: HMSO.

Lewis, E. J. (1995) *Truancy – The Partnership Approach*, London: Home Office Police Research Project.

MacGilchrist, B., Myers, K. and Reed, J. (1997) *The Intelligent School*, London: Paul Chapman.

Malcolm, H., Thorpe, G. and Lowden, K. (1995) *Understanding Truancy: Links between Attendance, Truancy and Performance*, Report for SCRE, Edinburgh: Scottish Council for Research in Education.

Mortimore, P., Sammons, P., Stoll, L., Lewis, D. and Ecob, R. (1988) *School Matters: The Junior Years*, London: Paul Chapman.

OFSTED (1995) *Access, Achievement and Attendance in Secondary Schools*, London: OFSTED Publications Centre.

OFSTED (1999) *Raising the Attainment of Minority Ethnic Pupils*, London: OFSTED Publications Centre.

OHMCI (1997) *Truancy and Improving School Behaviour*, Llanishen: Welsh Office.

OHMCI (1999) *A Framework for the Inspection of Local Education Authorities*, London/ Llanishen: OHMCI.

O'Keefe, D. *et al.* (1993) *Truancy in English Secondary Schools*, London: DfEE.

O'Keefe, D. and Stoll, P. (eds) (1995) *Issues in School Attendance and Truancy*, London: Pitman.

Parsons, C. (1999) *Education, Exclusion and Citizenship*, London: Routledge.

Reid, K. (1985) *Truancy and School Absenteeism*, London: Hodder & Stoughton.

Reid, K. (1986) *Disaffection from School*, London: Methuen.

Reid, K. (1987) *Combating School Absenteeism*, London: Hodder & Stoughton.

Reid, K. (1988a) *Staff Development in Secondary Schools*, London: Hodder & Stoughton.

Reid, K (1988b) *Staff Development in Primary Schools*: Oxford: Blackwell.

Reid, K. (1989a) *Helping Troubled Pupils in Secondary Schools, vol. 1: Social and Psychological Issues*, Oxford: Blackwell.

Reid, K (1989b) *Helping Troubled Pupils in Secondary Schools, vol. 2: Academic and Behavioural Issues*, Oxford: Blackwell.

Reid, K. (1989c) One-Parent Families, in K. Reid *Helping Troubled Pupils in Secondary Schools, vol. 2: Academic and Behavioural Issues*, Oxford: Blackwell.

Reid, K., Hopkins, D. and Holly, P. (1987) *Towards the Effective School*, Oxford: Blackwell.

Reynolds, E. (1996) 'An In-depth Analysis of an Initiative to Improve Attendance in a South Wales Comprehensive School', 2 vols, unpublished MPhil thesis, Swansea Institute of Higher Education.

Sherriff, I. (1990) 'A Multi-disciplinary Approach to the Management of Non-school Attendance', unpublished PhD thesis, University of Leicester.

Scottish Education Department (1977) *Truancy and Indiscipline in Schools in Scotland (The Pack Report)*, London: HMSO.

Smith, M., Goodban, L. and Ford, R. (1994) *Attendance Matters: A Guide for Schools*, Herts: Herts LEA.

Tattum, D. P. and Lane, D. A. (1989) *Bullying in Schools*, Stoke-on-Trent: Trentham Books.

Tyerman, M. (1968) *Truancy*, London: ULP.

WISAP (1996) *Improving School Attendance: Some Guidance to Good Practice*, Wolverhampton: Wolverhampton Education Services.

Wragg, E. C. Wragg, C. M., Haynes, G. S. and Chamberlain, R. P. (1998) *Improving Literacy in the Primary Schools*, London: Routledge.

Index